THE STRUCTURE OF INDIAN THOUGHT

RAMAKANT A. SINARI
Professor and Head
Department of Humanities and Social Sciences
Indian Institute of Technology, Bombay

DELHI
OXFORD UNIVERSITY PRESS
BOMBAY CALCUTTA MADRAS

Oxford University Press, Walton Street, Oxford OX2 6DP
LONDON GLASGOW NEW YORK TORONTO
DELHI BOMBAY CALCUTTA MADRAS KARACHI
KUALA LUMPUR SINGAPORE HONG KONG TOKYO
NAIROBI DAR ES SALAAM CAPE TOWN
MELBOURNE AUCKLAND
and associates in
BEIRUT BERLIN IBADAN MEXICO CITY NICOSIA

First published 1970
by Charles C. Thomas, Illinois, U.S.A.
First Indian edition 1984
by arrangement with the author

Printed by Pramodh P. Kapur at Raj Bandhu Industrial Co., New Delhi 110064
and published by R. Dayal, Oxford University Press
2/11 Ansari Road, Daryaganj, New Delhi 110002

PREFACE

Commentators on the philosophical thought in India many a time say that there is an unbridgeable gap between her age-long transcendentalism and her growing interest in the world of praxis today. Although this gap is undoubtedly noticeable when one focuses one's attention on the welfare-oriented activity of modern India as against her salvation-oriented ancient philosophies, it disappears if one observes the perennial attitude of the Indian *cogito* to refuse to remain contented with the given. The unique characteristic of the Indian mind is its concern with the other-worldly and the beyond, the trans-empirical and the absolutely free, or the tranquil and the indescribable. It is this characteristic that has acted both as a challenge to the efforts of the shapers of activity and as a promoter of an all-embracing spiritualistic humanism the world might need when in turmoil.

The Indian consciousness is two-pronged. It has developed with an intense nausea at worldliness and with an aspiration for transcendence; and yet it has belonged to situations here and now. The belief at its core is that to attain a breakthrough to freedom from this two-prongedness is the sole destiny of man. Indian philosophers have always stood for self-knowledge, and ātmalogical preoccupation, an act of self-purification through inwardness.

The emergence of the Age of Awakening in India since the commencement of the influence of Western thought on her must not be looked upon as something that will eventually dislocate modern India from the Vedic-Upaniṣadic *Weltanschauung*. The attitude of the Indian mind towards the building of a socio-politico-economic welfare today indicates its heed to exigencies. There is nothing deeper in this attitude than an obvious willingness to accept the worldly situation. The force of the changing times has posed pragmatism as an antidote for transcendentalism. But underneath this pragmatism lies the Indian's ceaseless quest of the spirit of man.

The history of Indian thought reflects a subtle paradox. I have called it the ātmalogical paradox. It is to be worldly and to be not-worldly at the same time. This paradox is the pivot of the peculiar ambiguity Indians manifest in their ideas, emotions and actions. No materialistically oriented philosophy will sink deep in the Indian mind. Neither positivism nor scientism nor any other outward technique will mitigate its inward search. And if the contribution of the Indian *Weltanschauung* to world ethos, to the culture of the world-mind, is to be of greatest significance, India must maintain the tenor of her spiritual and transcendental path. A commitment to praxis, to a pragmatic way of thinking, must not brake the tenor. At the same time, the transcendental path must not blind the demands of reason, must not rule out the aspirations of the body. With the Age of Awakening in India begins, really speaking, the Indian thinkers' task to resolve the ātmalogical paradox: to wed outwardness to inwardness, objectivity to subjectivity, worldliness to otherworldliness.

My concern with the concepts discussed in this book goes back to a comparative study of existentialism and Indian thought I undertook some years ago. This concern sharpened when I attended seminars in phenomenology and contemporary philosophy taught by Marvin Farber at the State University of New York at Buffalo. Farber's skilful treatment of different aspects of phenomenological philosophy made me see certain areas of agreement between this philosophy and ancient Indian thought.

There have been three preludes to this book. These are my articles "Some Reflections on Philosophy in India," *Philosophy and Phenomenological Research*, XXVI (1966); "The Method of Phenomenological Reduction and Yoga," *Philosophy East and West*, XV (1965); and "The Phenomenological Attitude in the Śaṅkara Vedānta," *Philosophy East and West*, XXII (1970). They set forth, while dwelling on some dominant concepts in Indian metaphysics, my formulation of the perennial vision of ancient Indians.

Several thinkers have, personally or through their writings, drawn my attention to some of the subtleties in the experience of ancient Indian seers. I must specially mention Professor J. N. Mohanty of the University of Burdwan; Professor N. V. Joshi of Ramnarain Ruia College, Bombay; Professor D. Sinha of Presidency College, Calcutta; and Professor J. L. Mehta of Banaras Hindu University. I wish in particular to thank Professor Rollo Handy of the State University of New York at Buffalo, Professor Bernard Baumrin of the University of Michigan and Professor Eliot Deutsch of the University of Hawaii for their encouragement and suggestions.

Finally, to my wife I owe a great debt for her constant fine judgment.

Bombay, India RAMAKANT SINARI

KEY TO PRONUNCIATION OF SANSKRIT WORDS

a	as in but
ā	as in far
bh	as in abhor
ch	as in church
ḍ	as in do (cerebral)
ī	as in eel
kh	as in inkhorn
m	as in mill
ṁ	a nasal sound
ṃ	a nasal sound
n	as in no
ṅ	as in sing (guttural)
ṇ	as in sing (guttural)
ñ	as in sing (palatal)
ph	as in uphill
ṛ	as in rill
ś	as in shut
ṣ	(sibilant)
ṭ	as in Tom (cerebral)
ū	as in foot

CONTENTS

THE STRUCTURE OF INDIAN THOUGHT

Chapter One

INTRODUCTION

THE VEDIC INDIAN

THE manner how a community thinks and builds the principles of its culture is the result of numerous complex forces. Besides the decisions that a society consciously takes, there are many which are like compulsive movements directed by the strokes of its history. It is not always true that a well-calculated plan for the amelioration of a society can dispense with the indeterminate beliefs and myths in its bygone past. At times these beliefs and myths generate as desirable a philosophy of life as the rationally organized activity itself does. However, one cannot fully approve of their general outcome. The exact measure of what Western culture owes to the Greeks is not determinable if we neglect the consideration of their religious and orthodox contributions. And there have been crossroads where Western thinkers now and then antagonized the Greek tradition. For at certain points the makers of a people's mind are bound to feel that the rejection of some of its closely hugged notions is a precondition to progress. Indeed, the facility with which the West has almost totally revised its cultural heritage seems to be singularly due to the utmost concern in the Western mind for exigencies. India, on the other hand, has all along been so passionately dedicated to its Vedic path that even when her changing setting has demanded a new perspective of things, it has hesitated to vindicate adventurous and scientific ways of thinking.

One of the most conspicuous features of the early Greek civilization is the habit of system formation. The zeal with which the Ionian philosophers looked for the single material element capable of explaining the emergence of the universe has no counterpart in the creative age of ancient India. It is perhaps as a result of some inexplicable urge in the European consciousness that its optimistic and naturalistic way of comprehending the world has ever held on as dominant through sporadic outbursts of melancholy and mysticism. Epidemics, depressions, revolutions, wars, or concentration camps have been looked upon as objective phenomena, scientifically explainable and avoidable rather than as human misfortunes that must leave everybody crestfallen. Again, the Greek thinkers possessed so much intellectual arrogance that they would not be cowed down before disagreeable situations and retire into isolation. That the Western mind in its attachment to objects in the universe—be it for the sake of knowledge, acquisition, enjoyment, or improvement—inherits this first intellectual arrogance of the Greeks hardly needs any emphasis. The West has never for long entertained a belief which is not, directly or indirectly, rooted in its confidence in the possibility of at last evolving an intellectual system from which nothing would escape as unexplained.

The temper of the Indian mind since the chanters of the Vedas more than forty centuries ago has invariably subordinated its system-forming endeavor to a metaphysics of transcendence. Whatever might have been the specific socioeconomic conditions in which the creative genius of the Vedic period—approximately between 2000 and 500 B.C.—flourished, its influence on the entire growth of Indian consciousness is never on the wane. Looking at the sheer magnitude of their power of dominance, one finds a parallel between the system-forming intellect of the early Greeks and the ascetic resignation of the Vedic Indian from all types of engagement in the world. In the authors of the Vedic literature, including the Upaniṣads, spontaneity, poetic imagination and a feeling of gravity at the fact of existence surpassed intellectualization. Even the four chambers of writings that go to constitute each of the Vedas [1] maintain not an organizational unity but a continuity of mood or disposition. For instance, the Mantras, the first cham-

[1] They form voluminous literature, consisting of the *Ṛg Veda*, the *Sāma Veda*, the *Yajur Veda* and the *Atharva Veda*. Neither their chronological order nor their authorship can be reliably mentioned. They are admixtures of religious, magical and philosophical impressions, put together by Indians over a period of about 1500 years. The lower limit of the Vedic period is taken as 487 B.C.

ber, are luxurious hymns addressed to gods; the Brāhmaṇas, the second chamber, are prose explanations of religious rituals; the Āraṇyakas, the third chamber, comprise meditations in forests; and the Upaniṣads, the fourth chamber, are secret instructions from *ṛṣis* or seers. Polytheism, pantheism, monism, theology, mysticism and several other tendencies have shrouded the central philosophical thought of the Vedas, filling the Vedic compositions at times with the most knotty linguistic feats world literature has ever offered. However, transcendentalism has remained the single powerful attitude through them all.

One of the reasons why students of Indian philosophy have often been able to confer new senses on the language of the Vedas is that, as it is, it contains illuminations which the Vedic seers were too entranced to articulate with intellectual and linguistic clarity. The Vedic seers might have chosen to communicate with their people with the sole aim of awakening in them a mode of being that needs no alteration according to shifting world situations. They had no desire to cultivate a strictly scientific or logical discipline in their followers. The principal reaction of the Vedic mind to human life, ridden by insecurity and helplessness, is total withdrawal and not a persistence in its study and exploration.

THE WEARY WORLD IN A MAN-CENTERED PHILOSOPHY

For philosophers in the West, the absence of a rational system in philosophy can never be laudable. It is not astonishing, therefore, that even in the earliest theories of the Greeks, an attempt at the organization of experience is distinctly noticeable. Much before they reached any decisive opinions regarding the nature of the primordial source of the universe, the Ionians, the Pythagoreans and the Eleatics might have been, for a long time, careful observers of the empirically given phenomena. As John Burnet has stated, the Greeks produced their doctrines because they were "born observers," or experimenters, who "always tried to give a rational explanation of the appearances they had observed." [2] Their trust in their reasoning powers was complete.

The attitude the Vedic times reflect is of a mind longing for

[2] Burnet, John: *Greek Philosophy*. London, Macmillan, 1961, p. 10.

trans-empirical values: rhythm, melodiousness, meekness, charity, personal triviality, renunciation and freedom (*mokṣa*). The weariness of the world and the fear of alienation from the transcendental, underlying the entire bulk of Vedic literature, represent the temper of a culture four thousand years remote from the despaired generation of the exiles and the existentialists in the West in our own time. What is curious, and of significant contrast when compared to the progressive civilization of the West, is that India, notwithstanding her socio-politico-economic changes, is as if destined to retain its weary mood eternally. Perhaps what the unscrupulous will regard as the rare expression of a kind of mental derangement in European writers, such as St. Augustine, Pascal, Kierkegaard, Unamuno, Kafka and a few others, would figure as *the* chief characteristic of the Vedic mind—a mind running more after the otherworldly and the inane than after the empirical and the concrete.

There is something practically retarding in the forward march of the Indian mind. Its fantastic gifts to human civilization hide underneath a tradition that has not always been a boon to itself. This tradition has entertained a distrust in those indispensable truths without which life in the world would cease to have any importance. From the time of the visionary saints like Gautama, Kanva, Sāṇḍilya, Satyakāma Jābāla, Uddhālaka, Gārgī, Maitreyī, who by the supreme reach of their intuition claimed to have grasped the ultimate explanation of everything, through the universally admired nineteenth and twentieth century reformers like Śri Ramakrishna, Swami Vivekānanda and Śri Aurobindo, Indians have striven to enrich a metaphysical view, mitigated only by the intellectual trends in modern times. Apart from their profoundly man-centered teachings, the Vedas have not seldom been a drag-chain on the outlook of even modern educated Indians.

It would not be a surprise if one heard of, say, an astrophysicist in India taking a holy dip in the sacred waters of the Ganges in order to redeem himself from sins, or of a Fellow of the Royal Society suddenly announcing that all that he has learnt is a *mauvaise foi* affecting his allegiance to the Vedic word, or of a military expert studying the dispositions of stars and planets before making movements against the enemy. For the lacuna between the superstitious and the critical, the naive and the reflective, the mythological and the scientific, is almost nonexistent in Indian consciousness. The most frequently found borders of ennui to all constructive thinking in India, and a kind of perplexity about the final result Indians customarily display whenever they embark upon new schemes are clearly the marks of a people constantly nourished by the Vedic-Upaniṣadic message that the material world being nothing but a long-enduring kaleidoscopic deception, the only thing that is worthy of man's aspirations is transcendence. It is on account of the teaching by the Word of the ancient sages that Indians have found the world to be continually weary, an unwanted hindrance, a spoke in the wheel of their trans-phenomenal ascent, a bondage.

WHAT THE BOOK AIMS AT

Looking back over the years during which the spirit of India's philosophy shaped itself, and partly absorbed and partly repelled religious, cultural, political, militant and intellectual currents alien to it, one is likely to arrive at a certain conclusion. The aim of the present book is to set forth this conclusion. Such a conclusion may ignore the fact that there can occur in the life of a people a totally unforeseeable and inexplicable phenomenon such as the Indians' successful nonviolent struggle for independence against the supremely powerful British or, even if the proposition sounds fictitious now, their emergence sometime in the future as one of the greatest technocracies in the world. The only contiguity phenomena of this type will have with the past is one that critics and historians bestow upon them, surely through a manner of synthesis for which no happening internal to the evolving process of a society should go unaccounted for. By and large, the unfolding of the consciousness of a people hides an idea, or a set of ideas, or a philosophy of life. And it is from the standpoint of this idea that the conduct of that people becomes intelligible.

Histories of the development of Indian thought have paid little attention to the link between the Indian view of the world rooted in the agelong Vedic-Upaniṣadic teachings, and her New Age.[3]

[3] I use this expression to denote the period of the Renaissance in India. This period begins around the first quarter of the nineteenth century and runs through the rise of India in 1947 as the largest democracy on earth. India, in its New Age, is today a self-determining, industrially advancing and technologically equipped peace-loving force, wedded to the principle of action-for-progress.

What is essential, therefore, is to attempt what Talcott Parsons calls "a logically articulated conceptual scheme," [4] and to fit into it some of the most eventful creative periods that have put India on the philosophical map of the world. A complete understanding of Indian consciousness is admittedly handicapped by the peculiar factor that its expression in all fields and at all times is mystical and blurred because of the intercrossing of the native existential feeling and externally governed intellect in it. Often it is charged with spontaneous explosions of intuition, enveloping which there appear acts of ratiocination. Much that India has contributed to the domain of world-thought flows from this extraordinary layering of a sensitive and fleeting life awareness—an awareness tending to be uneasy, self-surpassing, anguished, self-nullifying and transcendent—and sharp succinct reasoning.

The view and ideas incorporated in this book have grown over some years of an academic career, and also from a close observation of the working of the Indian mind in matters of thinking, saying and acting. To point out the single philosophical movement in the West to which the main tenets of Indian thought come very close, I would mention phenomenology, with its offshoot existentialism, as reflecting an attitude similar to that found at the core of Indian thought. I have employed no fixed standard for figuring out the role of intellect in Indian consciousness, or for that matter, in the evolution of Indian philosophy. Nor have I been tempted to make an exhaustive appraisal of all the inspirations, doctrines and practices of Indians. If such an appraisal directly or indirectly occurs, it should be deemed as peripheral to the aim of the book.

In India the control of the metaphysics of transcendence, of the instinct to live *unto* absolute freedom (*mokṣa*), over total human affairs is greater than that of similar metaphysics in the West. And in order to see this, we must bring into focus not so much the behavior pattern of the Indian community but the obscure undercurrent of convictions appearing with great frequency in their *Weltanschauung*. It would not be difficult to find that the pedigree of Indian consciousness lies deep in the ever-unfading Vedic-Upaniṣadic propositions.

[4] See for comments on Parsons's "conceptual scheme," Handy, Rollo: *Methodology of The Behavioral Sciences*. Springfield, Thomas, 1964, pp. 23–24.

Chapter Two

THE BOUND MAN

FOR THE FAVOR OF GODS

PROBABLY there is a causal connection between an intense awareness of insecurity and the feeling of horror at the sensible everyday world, and further between this feeling and the rise of a transcendentally directed philosophy. The Vedic literature that has dominated the mind of India since the beginning of her history contains sufficient evidence of insecurity present in the very atmosphere the Āryans breathed. There was a kind of fear of the unknown forces of Nature. This fear affected the Āryans' way of life and led the most precocious among them to experience a peculiar sense of the worthlessness of human existence. The marvels of thought and poetry these people poured into their compositions have a lining of despair and helplessness, a feeling of being cornered by the cosmos. For centuries together these wanderers, uprooted from their habitation somewhere in Central Asia, must have sustained themselves against all kinds of calamities, and with the advent of less atrocious times, reposed to reflect on their bygone past and uncertain future destiny. And as always in the case of early societies, act preceded thought, and the first form the Āryan response to the world took was religion.

The Vedas call upon *devas* [1] or gods, such as Varuṇa (the sky-god), Sūrya (the sun-god), Agni (the fire-god), Pūṣan (the god of cattle), Rūdra (the militant god), Indra (the atmosphere-god) and Prajāpati or Hiraṇyagarbha (the God of all gods), with utmost meekness and piety and anticipate from them nothing but safety and happiness. Prayers were sung and sacrifices were per-

[1] *Deva* literally means one who gives.

formed with extreme meticulousness. Every rite was looked upon as sure to produce desirable fruits. And the underlying law of all such actions, which aimed at propitiating the spirits in Nature, was believed to be timeless and divine. It was, therefore, necessary for the humans to stick to action (*kriyā*), to follow the rhythm of the cosmic powers, in order to get rid of the constantly haunting danger of disappearance.

It was an a priori truth that anyone who obeyed the cosmic order, addressed his grievances to cosmic forces, and did not succumb to the superficial pride of his authorship in making and remaking things would always stay under the favor of the gods. For all elements of the universe were supposed to conceal a quasi-moral *norma* called *Ṛta,* to whose conduct even gods are subordinate.

Really speaking, the religious belief of the Vedic Āryans that for security and welfare on earth man must completely surrender to the gods of Nature has not considerably diminished in its impression on the Indian mind with the change of time. One can observe that the original view, embodied in the Āryan system of rites, that the only state of affairs worth seeking would be realized when we subjugate ourselves to Nature has acted all along in the history of Indian people as somewhat a fatalistic disposition. And while a similar view in the ancient civilizations of Babylonia and Greece, for example, has not caused any definite retardation of constructive and scientific endeavors of the West, in India it has often discouraged the purposefulness in action, or, perhaps, has taught Indians to misconstrue all activity as something that is to be done because it *is* to be done. Indians derive a strange "metaphysical" satisfaction when priests and pundits repeatedly inform them that the real "victory" over one's circumstances consists in one's total resignation to them, to the divine agencies behind them, to the will of the Creator.

THE UPANIṢADIC *WELTANSCHAUUNG*

All students of Indian thought have consistently recognized that chamber of the Vedas which is called the Upaniṣads as the most important landmark in the evolution of Indian consciousness. While the rest of the portions of the Vedas contain descriptions of the paraphernalia of religious acts, the Upaniṣads (literally meaning sitting before the savants) display abstract and metaphysical speculations of a time more than fifteen hundred years before that of Parmenides, the first metaphysician in the West. Although registered in memory by a hierarchy of teachers called *ṛṣis* or *Brāhmins,* at different periods and in obviously varying social situations, they reflect an admirable unity of experience and goal. Here transcendental musings replace routine religious operations, monism replaces polytheism and monotheism, absolutism replaces a few not too prominent traces of realism, and ātmalogy [2] replaces what can be identified as naturalistic [3] in the earliest parts of the Vedas.

The temper of the Āryan mind which finds its eloquent expression in the Upaniṣads is one of melancholy and distress at the very emergence of man in the world. Of course, the scattered remnants of a type of world-affirming faith of the earliest times are not totally absent here. But these remnants are not worth an emphasis which may give an impression that the Vedic-Upaniṣadic Indian was inclined to promote his sense-experiences in the spatio-temporal world. To his *Weltanschauung,* the empirically known existence is a menace, a cave of boredom, an atrocity on one's essential being, a *saṁsāra* (the circuit of births and deaths). It is this *Weltanschauung* that is justified over and over again in the Upaniṣads, not seldom by means of rational arguments whose range carries one to the extremest point of transcendentalism. The not too celebrated issue of most of the philosophies in Europe, namely, the meaning and purpose of human existence, is the most highlighted issue in all principal Upaniṣads.

The most immediate impression the Upaniṣads and their tail-

[2] The word, coined by the author, may stand for the technique of inner-seeing or self-exploration, by means of which a meditation on and around one's own existence is performed. One of the ever-enduring contributions of the Upaniṣads is the suggestion of this technique. This technique attains its final shape in a quasi-psychological discipline called *yoga.* It will be shown later in this book that ātmalogy as a method of knowledge comes very close to egology in phenomenological and existential schools of philosophy in the West.

[3] For a pointed study of the naturalistic trend in the Vedas and the Upaniṣads. see Riepe, Dale: *The Naturalistic Tradition in Indian Thought.* Delhi, Motilal Banarasidass, 1964, pp. 15–32.

like *sūtra*[4] and *bhāśya*[5] literature leave on any keen reader's mind is that they are the pronouncement of an attitude fraught with utter ennui regarding man's being in the world. For instance, the *Kaṭha Upaniṣad* says that "the Self is not to be sought through the senses," that "the small-minded go after outward pleasures . . . and walk into the snare of widespread death," and that "the wise . . . do not seek the stable among things which are unstable here."[6] For the *Bṛhad-āraṇyaka Upaniṣad,* "when all the desires that dwell in the heart are cast away, then does the mortal become immortal," and "the disembodied, immortal life is . . . light indeed."[7] Further, in his *sūtra* with allusions to the *Māṇḍūkya Upaniṣad,* Gauḍapāda shows that the world and its objects are totally illusory and, therefore, should never be cherished.[8] And again Śaṅkara (6th century A.D.), the author of *bhāśyas* on several Upaniṣads, carries the same argument forward.

Apart from the fact that the Upaniṣads brought under their authority all orthodox and unorthodox schools of thought in India except the Cārvāka school, the literature of profound concern about man's destiny they encouraged over centuries has in a sense moulded the entire culture of the Orient. And not seldom have they been regarded in the West as the most erudite messages on earth. Men such as Schopenhauer, Aldous Huxley, John Yale, E. S. Brightman, Christopher Isherwood, Frederick Manchester, and Allen Watts have clearly come under their influence. Nobody would be able to state what sort of following they may enjoy among intellectuals in the West in the turbulent contemporary times, through the Beatles and the Hippies, who have shown themselves to be most enthusiastic practitioners of the way of "transcendental meditation" from them.

The expression of boredom and of the denial of life's pleasures,

[4] The *sūtra* literature consists of pithy aphorisms, most of which are open to multiple interpretations. Generally, *sūtras* draw on the thoughts in the Upaniṣads.

[5] The *bhāśya* is a treatise on *sūtras*. There are at times several treatises on the same *sūtra*.

[6] Radhakrishnan, S. (Ed.): *The Principal Upaniṣads*. London, George Allen & Unwin, 1953, pp. 630–32.

[7] *Ibid.*, p. 273.

[8] Mahadevan, T. M. P.: *Gauḍapāda: A Study in Early Advaita*. Madras, U. of Madras, 1954, p. 149.

whether it is in the Hindu, the Greek, the Jewish, the Muslim or the Christian mysticism, is the same. However, in ancient India it formed the central characteristic of all religio-metaphysical formulations. A Upaniṣad, a *sūtra,* or a *bhāśya* simply took it for granted that human existence is too formidable a disaster to be only intellectually explained, or to be looked at objectively. It is natural, therefore, that the whole bulk of literature confirming the Upaniṣadic insight directly or indirectly exhibits even today a tendency of going "from darkness to darkness deeper yet" [9] and intuiting the very genesis of life there.

One of the most interesting psychological transitions that must have taken place in Indian consciousness is from the early Āryan belief that the panacea for all evils in the world is prayer, to the metaphysical attitude that one's status in any mundane situation is never authentic. The mind of the Āryan Indian must have been extremely sensitive to the hostile phenomena in Nature. One sees traces of agoraphobia in its utterances in the *Ṛg Veda.* It was a mind which with the passage of time turned within itself, partly owing to the dread of the outward and partly owing to its own dread, and philosophized within its own shell. The extreme form of transcendentalism and pessimism we come across in the Upaniṣads and in their explanations and commentaries is so unlike the usual tenor of philosophy in the West.

Crises in life may be confronted in various ways. But to look upon them as the inevitable accompaniment of man's being in the world is to suggest that if they are to be put an end to then their root-cause, namely life itself, is to be extinguished. The Upaniṣadic savants preached a way of salvation which is not only intolerant of the world of sense-experience but also condemns it outright as a domain where all activity entails hopelessness. And this is a clear case of progression in thought—from the Nature-centered semiutilitarian ritualism of the previous Vedic period to the reflective and transcendence-seeking approach of the Upaniṣads.

In fact, with the coming of the second phase, the first ought to have faced a decline. But what actually happened is that the Nature-centered religion crystallized into a theory of action and

[9] Basham, A. L.: *The Wonder That Was India.* New York, Grove, 1954, p. 245.

subsequently gave rise to the school of Pūrva Mīmāṁsā around the fourth century B.C. It is this phase, again, that is at the basis of the *karma-yoga,* or the method of action, expounded by the *Bhagavad-gītā* about the same time.

The Vedic ritualism—or its reformulation, *karma-yoga,* for that matter—has apparently coexisted perfectly with *jñāna-yoga,* or the method of knowledge, which is a logical development of the reflective and transcendence-seeking Upaniṣadic approach. Even in the conduct of the one and the same individual, the two methods can be seen to coexist as equally effective ways of salvation. This is why, despite the followers of one method sometimes blaming those of the other for their deficiency, it is a routine affair in India that both the mechanical performance of rites and duties and the rational discipline, animism and transcendental meditation, absurd superstitiousness and logic, pervade different social groups without causing any clash.

In India, one does religious duties as automatically or as aesthetically as a devotee in any other conservative country. But underneath an Indian's performance lies a subtle conviction, an unexpressible but firm view, a mystical and yet somewhat ratiocinated proposition, that the universe is a coercion on his essential being. His past repeatedly teaches him to reject worldliness, to surpass it, to be always skeptical about it, and to acknowledge it at every step as a nonentity deserving not even an ordinary sense of commitment.

IN THE FETTERS OF *KARMA*

Some of the important Upaniṣads, such as the *Bṛhad-āraṇyaka Upaniṣad,* the *Iśa Upaniṣad* and the *Chāndogya Upaniṣad,* contain the primordial form of a theory whose domination on the Indian mind has perhaps no equal in the history of mankind elsewhere. This theory, known as the law of *karma,* involves determinism, fatalism and metempsychosis that have shaped the Indians' view of life over centuries. For the law of *karma* is the living faith of all schools of Indian philosophy except the materialist Cārvāka. And because of its remarkable logical consistency it was bound to have a prevalence on the thinking of a people for whom the immediate sensation man's earthly life produced was one of suffering. It can be seen easily that insofar as its religio-ethical implications are concerned, this law is only an extension of the old Vedic concept that human lives are subject to a *norma,* the *Ṛta.* Even the gods of Nature, the Vedas believed, are governed by this *norma.*

The law of *karma* states that every happiness or sorrow in man's life is the predetermined effect of actions committed by him sometime, either in his present life or in one of his numerous past lives. In the same way, no act done by one in one's life hereafter can go without creating a possibility of its results, to be experienced either in this or in some future life. The entire status of an individual, therefore—his pleasures, griefs, successes, failures, strength, weakness, etc.—is *the* necessary event within the system of the fundamentally ethically guided cosmos. Not a single part of this cosmos is independent of or unrelated to the Reason of the whole.

Unlike the law of universal causation that every happening has a cause which is quantitatively equal to it, the law of *karma* is indemonstrable. It is a moral law consistent with the Āryans' anthropomorphism in which *Ṛta,* the cosmic *norma,* was believed to function like a lever or tribunal adjudging man's religious and magical practices. Like the *Ṛta* the law of *karma* determines the righteousness of the total cosmos, gods included, and adjusts fruits to actions in accordance with the quality of the latter.

Like the Logos or Nous of Greek philosophy, the law of *karma* is a universal, eternal, impartial and unchangeable rational principle and is supposed to have pervaded the universe even before the appearance of the world. It is so comprehensive that no phenomenon in the life of an individual, or of a society, could be understood without a reference to its supreme and authoritative nature. Even to the present time one would meet millions of Indians of all ranks whose faith in the supernatural and incontrovertible character of *karma* is unshaken.

It is possible that the Āryan mind imbibed the *karma* notion when it learnt to look at Nature from a somewhat rational point of view. For this point of view, no phenomenon could be regarded as uncaused or unaccountable. Indeed, despite the fact that the explanatory and analytic value of the law of *karma* is discernible from the role it played in the thinking of the Vedic-Upaniṣadic people, its sociological background is still clouded in mystery. Perhaps it is an intelligent configuration of the myth of metempsychosis. And as such, it must have cast a remarkable impact on all credulous as well as rationally awakened minds and made them accept the fact that every creature has got what it sowed for.

It is morally a serious matter to be guided by the belief that every single action we commit works towards determining both our place and our incarnate forms hereafter or in the lives to come. For instance, those who work charitably and do work for the benefit of others would get after death the "World of the Fathers" (*pitṛayāna*), while those who lead a pious and ascetic life would join the "World of Gods" (*devayāna*). In no event, therefore, are souls destroyed with their bodies. The *Chāndogya Upaniṣad* says, "Those whose conduct here has been good will quickly attain a good birth (literally womb), the birth of a *Brāhmin,* the birth of a *Kṣatriya* or the birth of a *Vaiśya.* But those whose conduct here has been evil, will quickly attain an evil birth, the birth of a dog, the birth of a hog or the birth of a *caṇḍāla.*"[10] One's deeds determine one's form. What is kept in store for the souls carrying the aftermath of their acts is fixed and known only to Yama, the death-god.

The entire sequence of births and rebirths is a logical consequence of what mankind has willed through its doing. In this sense, perhaps, mankind has created itself and is responsible for what it is here and now. The circuit of births, deaths and rebirths, the passing from one body to another, the *saṁsāra,* is a permanent feature of human consciousness. "As shade and sunlight are ever closely joined together, so an act and the agent stick close to each other."[11] The only moment when this circuit would be broken in the case of a particular individual is when he realizes the transphenomenal ground, the innermost essence of his own being, and enjoys absolute liberation (*mokṣa*) through this realization.

Pascal wrote that the greatest genius of man lies in his realiza-

[10] Radhakrishnan, S. (Ed.): *The Principal Upaniṣads,* p. 433.

[11] Quoted from the *Panca-tantra* by Monier-Williams: *Indian Wisdom,* 2nd ed. Varanasi, The Chowkhamba Sanskrit Series, 1963, p. 65.

tion that he is miserable.[12] It is the working of the law of *karma* that, Indian thinkers have argued, makes human life miserable. As a matter of fact, *karma* is the intellectual statement of the attitude of a bound man. To this attitude worldliness is a confinement, a restraint on consciousness, a sort of shackle of the spirit. When seen from this attitude, man's very emergence in the plight in which he is becomes a circumstance thrust on his originally free being.

The strangest truth the *karma* theory underlines is that from the point of view of one's consciousness at any given moment, one's birth is a bondage to one; but from the point of view of one's past, it is a willed birth. This is the thing which makes life weary, absurd, awesome. The physical and the mental peculiarities with which we are born, the inmates, the friends, the family and others we get, and the diverse situations we run into while we live are as if prearranged for us without the slightest approval from us. Then there are irritating anomalies we are subjected to. Many humane hearts suffer; those which behave cruelly gain luck. Someone does something with a benevolent intention, but the outcome is disastrous. Millions of poor, diseased, handicapped, frustrated, vanquished, or tearful persons lead short or long lives without knowing why they are as they are. The tensions which corrode human relations, the inequilibrium between expectations and achievements, the loftily built hopes ending in disappointments, make it impossible for man to experience any smooth course of events around him. And yet, all this is entailed by the life or lives in our past, is the creation of our own actions, our naïvely chosen commitment, a kind of self-perpetuation through activity. It is this forced-yet-chosen state of affairs that must have aroused the sense of absurdity in Indian thinkers—an absurdity of being under the *karma*-dominated logic of the world.

Ordinarily, a Western critic would find it hard to unravel the concept of *karma,* or that of bondage, if what he keeps on looking for in his inquiry into human life is a set of empirically determinable causes. Apart from its value as a preeminently rational

[12] See Pascal: *The Pensées.* J. M. Cohen (trans.), Middlesex, Penguin Books, 1961, p. 99.

explanation for the emergence of man in the universe, the theory that human freedom is ever restrained inasmuch as it is subject to *karma* expresses the existential view of life. Generally, situations which breed insecurity and helplessness are responsible for the intensification of this view. But the view itself is germane to the very mind of a people dwelling under an unbearable burden of world's vicissitudes. After describing the fact that it is human consciousness that secretes this view in response to the "absurdity" of the universe, Albert Camus, one of the most perceptive observers of man of all times, writes that our intelligence tells us that this world is absurd. Our faith or "blind reason" may claim that there is nothing which is substantially unclear. But we may wait and wait, and yet the proof will never appear. According to Camus, despite so many "pretentious centuries" and the persuasive assurances of the wise men, we know from the depth of our insight that the universal reason crumbles in the face of the spots of absurdity.[13] These spots are a challenge to all that appear to be explainable through the categories of logic.

Thus for Indian thinkers as for Camus, the weariness of the world, the view that to be in the world is to be in bondage, is awakened in man as soon as he becomes gravely aware of his worldly situation.

No doubt, the frequent ferocious wars that the Āryans and their successors had to fight against all kinds of natural and human forces in order to establish themselves in India, and the state to which they were reduced by the unsurmountable social and political factors prevalent in their times must have invigorated their *karma* attitude. Even today this attitude keeps the minds of Indian masses rather cold and fatalistic with regard to the endeavors needed for the transformation of their conditions. Indeed, this does not mean that the achievements of Indians at home and abroad, the resilience shown by them whenever their independence and honor were endangered by hostile forces, and the zeal displayed by them in constructing and bettering their polity are things that are to be reckoned as accidental in their life. What is curious is that even when these phenomena have occurred as the

[13] Camus, Albert: *The Myth of Sisyphus.* Justin O'Brien (trans.), London, Hamish Hamilton, 1960, pp. 23–24.

results of willfully organized actions, the Indian mind sees them as having been the fruits of people's *karmas.* Most dogmatically guided Indian prophets may even say that the very activity which helps man in improving his material situation on the globe creates temptations for him to continue to be in the world and to do *karmas.*

There is a kind of firmly seated fixation in the minds of Indians that no human agency can liberate energies against the working of the law of *karma.* Since the preordained scheme of things in the universe is fixed, it is not left to man to aspire to produce his own arrangement of *karmas* and their consequences. The pride and confidence borne by the West in its will, resoluteness and power were alien to the Indian spirit, inasmuch as it never discriminated right actions from the wrong ones on any ground other than the ledger of everyone's foregone lives. The general Western attitude towards the universe is one of challenge to the given order of events; it is heavily charged with industriousness, by which it wants to harness everything for the welfare of man. For Indians, on the contrary, until the *karmas* are paid off, the individual has to surrender to whatever he is destined to get and has to stay bound to the world. To free oneself from the state of bondage is to put an end to both the world and the *karma,* both of which are inseparable, and to reduce oneself to an eternally unqualified and inactive existence.

There are perhaps two reasons why the Vedic-Upaniṣadic belief, that the world dominated by *karma* is a bondage or *bandha* of self, was tacitly adhered to by all subsequent trends of philosophy in India. One, by maintaining that it is one's embodied soul (*jīva*) that undergoes metempsychosis while pure consciousness (*ātman*) stays unchangeable and imperishable, it put out the fear that human existence would be extinct with death. And two, the belief itself lay intertwined with the mysterious law of the uniformity of the universe, the *Ṛta,* which was supposed to function at the back of all animate and inanimate happenings.

THE GLUE OF THE SOUL

In Jainism, one of the earliest philosophies in India that was revived by Vardhamāna Mahāvīra in the sixth century B.C., it is stated that every act performed by one mentally, physically or verbally generates peculiar layers of gluey matter called *karma-pudgala* or *karma-śarīra*. This matter surrounds one's soul and then develops into a body. Since the soul is originally pure, it has no reason to be in fetters so long as it does not indulge in activity. But once the soul has begun to act, it gives rise to subtle body-elements, releases the possibility of becoming incarnate, and consequently becomes worldly. According to the Jainas, even the type of awareness we have of the world in this life or may have of worlds in future lives is determined by the *karma-śarīra,* which goes on being amassed as we traverse from one life to another without ceasing to perform some act or other.

In its authentic state, the Jainas hold, the soul (*jīva*) is without any body. It is wholly subsistent and needs not even sensory conditions to acquire knowledge. In fact, the knowledge that it acquires in the phenomenal world is not its real knowledge at all. The real knowledge attributable to the soul is that in which the soul shines by its own light. But as soon as the otherwise immaculate soul acts, the *karma-śarīra* emerges, which inauthenticates the soul again and makes it act further. And until the reverse process is brought about by means of a breakthrough, the soul, with obcure psychic mutations imprinted on it by its own actions, remains glued to some psychophysical state or other. Therefore, death does not annihilate souls, nor has it got the power to cause their cleansing. With death the soul only abandons one particular physical accompaniment and assumes another.

For Buddha too, a contemporary of Vardhamāna Mahāvīra, all suffering or *duḥkha* originates from our state of bondage in the world. Our desires and cravings for objects in the world, Buddha said, are pregnant with sorrow and frustration. Furthermore, the very desire (*tṛṣṇa* or *taṇha*) for being attached to the world springs in us because of certain influences (*saṁskāras*) our past lives and *karmas* in them have left on us.

Buddha's teaching, for which he wholly imbibed the Vedic and Upaniṣadic *Weltanschauung,* is that all men are victims to a world of absurdity. Absurdity is the very essence of worldliness. As long as we cling to our sense organs and to the universe around us, we keep on creating potencies for future births and eventually for more and more desires and increasingly painful ways of existence. Buddha, therefore, consoled his followers by telling them, much after Socrates's style of *Know Thyself,* that they could live a life of eternal security if they forsook their worldly being. It is the psychophysical nature of man that starts all miseries, Buddha said, and consciousness will be in perfect harmony with itself if it is dismantled from such a nature.

> It is the desire for what belongs to the unreal self that generates suffering, for it is impermanent, changeable, perishable, and that, in the object of desire, causes disappointment, disillusionment, and other forms of suffering to him who desires.[14]

To denude consciousness of its unreal status—which is the only thing that man must yearn for as the ultimate value of all—one must practice transcendental concentration (*yoga, samādhi*).

Tradition says that the sudden realization that the whole creation is weary and absurd dawned on Buddha [15] at the age of thirty, when he observed the misery of human life. Born and brought up in a royal family, Buddha's was a "healthy" mind until he ran into the spectacle of an old man, a diseased man and a corpse. The spectacle so deeply penetrated through his conception of life that it was enough to spark off in him an utterly devouring weariness, a sense of grotesqueness of human existence, and plunge him into a serious way of living.

And as in the case of Pascal, Kierkegaard and Camus, the plunge happened to be of mortifying despair to Buddha. He might have felt, like Pascal, that "we long for truth, but find only uncertainty within us." [16] Again, like them, Buddha might have searched for happiness but have found only misery, sorrow and death. It was an intense awareness of not to be able to cease the desire for truth, happiness, certainty and peace, not to be able to contain within himself, that made Buddha tremble before the fact of being in the world.

[14] Holmes's, Edmond: *The Creed of Buddha.* In Humphreys, Christmas: *Buddhism.* Middlesex, Penguin Books, 1952, pp. 91–92.

[15] The term "Buddha" means "the enlightened one." Buddha was an Āryan, of *Kṣatriya* caste, and grew up in the cosy palace of his parents in a territory near Himalayas. He must have lived probably between 563 and 483 B.C.

[16] Pascal: *The Pensées.* J. M. Cohen (trans.), p. 102.

Like Kierkegaard (1813–1855), the greatest religious thinker of the nineteenth century and the originator of existentialism, Buddha underwent an overwhelming experience of "sickness unto death." [17] This is the reason why he is seen to pronounce the immediate ground of his suffering (*duḥkha*) in his advice to his pupils when he says that "decay is inherent in all component things," and that, therefore, the only thing one can do is to work out one's way towards salvation. And what he, like Kierkegaard, discovered through this feeling is the relation of himself with himself, to his past deeds, to the world around him, and to his own destiny. Both were overwhelmed by an emotion of futility at the concrete situation of man in the world. Both felt the agony of dislocation from the eternal and the imperishable—a feeling that is so vividly mirrored in Kierkegaard's pathetic utterances—or, for that matter, a sense of hopelessness at the fact that there is no chance of recovery from despair. For when Kierkegaard confessed that "this sickness in the self, is the sickness unto death," that one who despairs is profoundly ill, that this sickness devours the most fundamental part of man's being and leaves him completely uprooted, "and yet man cannot die, . . . to be delivered from this sickness by death is an impossibility . . . ," [18] he, like Buddha, gave up almost all hopes of the cure of the despaired consciousness.

The feeling of weariness, absurdity, despair, sickness or bondage (*duḥkha, bandha, saṁsāra*) that Buddha, Vardhamāna Mahāvīra and the Vedic-Upaniṣadic thinkers, like their very sparsely seen counterparts in the West, found unbearable has remained the main characteristic of Indian consciousness. The history of Indian thought contains more or less uniform accounts of this

[17] Kierkegaard, S.: *Fear and Trembling and The Sickness unto Death.* Walter Lowrie (trans.), New York, Doubleday Anchor Books, 1954, pp. 147–54. Kierkegaard is one of the most poignant analysts of the melancholic depression of the religious man. The tenor of his sense of alienation has so much in common with that of Buddha's sensation of being miserable in the world. Kierkegaard describes himself as being in "the despair of willing despairingly to be oneself." Buddha had said, "The self is my refuge." The expression "sickness unto death" aptly indicates the Buddhist and the existentialist mood.

[18] Kierkegaard, S.: *Fear and Trembling and The Sickness unto Death.* Walter Lowrie (trans.), p. 154.

feeling and of the ways and means by which Indian philosophers devised a remedy for it. The theory of *karma* has always been the most popular and most cogent attempt not only at defining the feeling of bondage but also at appeasing the severity of it in the Indian mind. But the feeling persists as if something perpetually incurable and irrational lies underneath hope and cure. It is in this sense that Camus said that the feeling of weariness has something "sickening" about it. "From the moment absurdity is recognized," he wrote, "it becomes a passion, the most harrowing of all." [19] The "sickening" sensation and the world stick to the soul, Indians have thought, at the same time.

METEMPSYCHOSIS AND MATERIALISM

For a commonsense man there is hardly any myth more exhilarating than that mortality is not after all the final annihilation of his life. He would be least hesitant to accept a philosophy which proves to him, much to his intellectual satisfaction, that his real being is not governed by the laws of physical creation and destruction but has an unalterable claim to the rewards of his benevolent deeds. Besides, if it is a question of explaining the widely prevalent cases of evil in the world, one leaves nothing unaccounted for when one reasons that each and every situation an individual encounters in his present life could be related to his acts in one of his past lives. As a preeminently self-comforting contrivance, therefore, the theory of *karma* is vastly more effective than any other theory in defense of immortality. Curiously, it silences one who wants to know why members of the same human or animal species should differ from one another as regards their physical and mental endowments.

But the *karma* theory as a philosophical proposition would not be very sound if it does not remain tied to the metempsychotic presuppositions that man is a combination of spirit and body, and that it is the former that successively resides in more than one body. In the state of bodiless existence, man is bound to enjoy freedom from vicissitudes arising out of matter—from poverty, sickness, births, movement, death, etc., which haunt the body

[19] Camus, Albert: *The Myth of Sisyphus.* Justin O'Brien (trans.), pp. 18–24.

rather than the mind. In order to attain this existence, Indian thinkers assert, one must wash off all the *karmas,* pay off the debts recorded in the ledger of Yama, [20] and cause a complete cessation of the process of living. Nowhere is this assertion more forcefully put across than in the *Bhagavad-gītā,* the most revered magnum opus in the ethical literature of India.

In the *Bhagavad-gītā,* a work composed around the third century B.C. and having perhaps the greatest influence on Indian thought and behavior, an allusion is made to the *sūkṣma śarīra* or subtle matter outliving one's physical disappearance. Here Arjuna, who may be taken to symbolize the common man in a given social setup, is told by Kṛṣṇa, the incarnation of God, that there is no one in the world who does not bear the imprints of his past lives. These imprints are in the form of fine, sticking matter, which survives the observable phenomenon of death. It is wrong to suppose therefore, according to Kṛṣṇa, that with death a person's life comes to an end.[21]

The *sūkṣma śarīra* is essentially a psychic composite through which the law of *karma* is supposed to function. Indeed, this composite might have a strange physical extension; otherwise it could not produce the incarnate state that we possess in this world. Once the deeds of a person are judged by Yama, and the fate of his body which his soul should enter in the next life is decided, the *sūkṣma śarīra* develops into this specific body. However, the underlying eternal spirit or *ātman* in man is not affected either by *karma* or by *sūkṣma śarīra.* Kṛṣṇa wants Arjuna to look upon every man as an immutable, imperishable and absolutely free substance, blanketed by the world of mutable, perishable and contingent events. He says to Arjuna: "Know this *ātman* / Unborn, undying, / Never ceasing, / Never beginning / Deathless, birthless, / Unchanging for ever. / How can It die / The death of the body?" [22] He further instructs Arjuna: "Worn-out garments / Are shed by the body; /

[20] According to Indian tradition, Yama is the god of death. He is the personification of mortality. The Vedic Indians believed that Yama judges the worth of human actions, meticulously noted down by him in his "diary," and conducts the souls of their doers to heaven or hell.

[21] Swami Prabhavananda and Isherwood, Christopher (trans.): *Bhagavad-gītā.* London, Phoenix House, 1951, p. 148.

[22] *Ibid.,* p. 41.

Worn-out bodies / Are shed by the dweller / Within the body. / New bodies are donned / By the dweller, like garments." [23]

The entire circuit of births and deaths would be broken through when after a long discipline of transcendental meditation or *yoga,* a realization dawns on one that one's salvation lies in remaining identified with the eternal. And since everybody is assured of this realization in principle, what man has to do as he acts is to regard his own birth, life and death as only passing phases of his worldly being. It is this being that is subjected to the ever-operating law of *karma.* In the ultimate analysis for Kṛṣṇa, man's being in the world is the expression of his imperfection, of the unfinished process of his paying for the past acts, and of laying up, though unintentionally, involvements for the future.

Kṛṣṇa's advice to Arjuna is that since no human body present in the world is able to avoid the consequences of its actions, the births and rebirths entailed by them, and again more actions ahead, Arjuna should concentrate his attention on that permanent principle in relation to which his present body is only an occasion. This permanent principle, called the *ātman,* has been regarded by the entire Indian tradition as the sphere of absolute liberation (*mokṣa*) from the chain of births and rebirths. Hence, what the law of *karma* torments is the bodily state of man—the *sūkṣma śarīra,* the *karma-śarīra* or the *karma-pudgala*—which forms the very basis of his intercourse with the world. For Vyāsa, the author of the *Bhagavad-gītā,* as for the founders of Jainism and Buddhism, the only reality which *karma* and its correlate, metempsychosis, cannot touch is the trans-phenomenal consciousness at the bottom of man's experience of himself and of the universe.

Different schools of philosophy in India have always accepted the *karma* theory and metempsychosis, not so much as a revealed truth, but as a ratiocinated account of human presence in the universe and of a multitude of depressing sensations generated by it. Only the materialistic school of the Cārvākas argues against the theory. The Cārvākas state that all animate and inanimate beings, including men, must be explained as collections of physical ele-

[23] *Ibid.,* p. 42.

ments. Of course some of such collections manifest the property of consciousness. But the property would disappear, they hold, as soon as the collections themselves disintegrate. And since consciousness is always found as an accompaniment of the physical organism, both would appear or disappear simultaneously.

Now human soul, according to this line of thought, is not a nonmaterial or spiritual entity existing independent of the body but is given rise to by an organization of body-elements itself. So, just as with the inception of the physical organism life comes into being, with the decay of the former the latter too ceases to function. It is naive to refer to the past lives, the Cārvākas say, to the survival of the soul after the destruction of the body, to immortality, to reincarnation, to heaven, hell and *mokṣa*. "The only Supreme is the earthly monarch whose existence is proved by all the world's eyesight; and the only liberation is the dissolution of the body." [24]

It appears that the Cārvākas arrived at their materialistic thesis, largely unorthodox and revolutionary in the philosophical tempo of their period, on the assumption like epiphenomenalists today that consciousness is a by-product or hangover of matter. Such a by-product, they thought, is not so independent as to subsist after the death of the body or to pass from one body to another with a blank intermission in between. Moreover, no supernatural force need be presupposed in order to account for the organized behavior of the body. What is ordinarily recognized as intelligence in the body, the Cārvākas said, is reducible to some specific colligation of material components, which, without the assistance of any extraneous spirit, generates spontaneity and order in the organic movements.

As a matter of fact, the *karma* theory looks like a reflective construction of the primitive metempsychosis myth. And what is rather esoteric about this construction is that for it consciousness with its numerous impressions or *saṁskāras* accumulated during its previous incarnate states determines the nature of the embryo into which it will find its entry next. Now to say that the same individual consciousness resides successively in different organisms

[24] Mādhava, Ācārya: *Sarvadarśanasaṅgraha*. E. B. Cowell and A. E. Gough (trans.), London, Kegan Paul, Trench, Trübner & Co., 1904, p. 4.

is to imply that a pig or an elephant might have human ancestry and vice versa. While we may admit, for lack of evidence for or against it, that the postmortem consciousness could be the bearer of the impressions of its previous worldly states, it is difficult to understand on what criterion the correspondence between these impressions and the next bodily endowments is made. The belief that the criterion has its origin in a trans-empirical tribunal, such as one of Yama, the death-god, is only legendary in character. For it is possible to imagine that the disembodied soul rejoices or suffers as the incarnate soul itself does. Again, it need not be supposed that the degree and kind of joy or suffering vary according to the species into which a soul enters.

But all this need not rule out the metaphysical postulate of the *karma* theory that consciousness is independent of and hence can survive the death of the physical organism. What the exact nature of the state of this survival may be is and would remain a riddle in absence of any valuable knowledge we are able to claim of the postmortem region of human life. Perhaps intellect is not the fittest apparatus to ply through this region, so that if anything is stated about it in terms of propositions, it would be a speculation whose truth or falsity cannot be definitely established.

However, it must be said against the Cārvākas that the cases of certain rare persons recollecting experiences from their previous lives, the yogis' and mystics' claim of being able to pierce through various layers of the pure Psyche, and some of the ordinary minds' telepathic communications that have begun to draw the attention of contemporary researches suggest that mental events do possess characteristics which are irreducible to the composites of physical elements. Moreover, the development of man's intellectual activity cannot fully be understood simply in terms of the epiphenomena of bodily components. Even to our day-to-day experience, this activity functions as a nonmaterial drive constantly causing and acting on the conduct of the body.

As mind (*manas*) and inner self (*antarātman*), consciousness not only understands objects perceived by the senses but also displays the ability to connect one bodily event with another, and in not a few cases even to interpret and be affected by these events. The mentalists set themselves on a very strong ground when they argue that minds, unlike bodies, are unique centers of intellection and action. But to take a leap from this to the theory of transmigration, and to reason that every human or animal offspring is the product of *karmas* borne by the *karma-śarīra* or by consciousness in some disembodied state is to sidetrack the main philosophical issue, namely, how the correspondence between the impressions on the soul and the particular kind of the body emerging in a womb is determined.

Although the confidence with which the Cārvāka school criticized the Vedic-Upaniṣadic conceptions of *karma* and metempsychosis proved to be the source of the trends like materialism, naturalism, skepticism and hedonism, which stayed alive here and there in India for some time, it turned out ultimately to be too weak to create any popular feeling against those conceptions.[25] For the Cārvākas could not make people get over the experience of ennui; nor could they convince them of the self-containedness of matter and of the futility of the belief in lives before and hereafter. Even Jayarāśi Bhaṭṭa, the most powerful skeptic of the seventh century A.D., could not stir the Vedic-Upaniṣadic tradition and authority despite his sharply attempted refutation of the role of immaterial categories in knowledge. The real explanation of the antipathy of the Indian mind against the Cārvāka reasoning, and for that matter, against any other reasoning that seeks to demolish the *karma* theory and transmigration is that the Vedic word and the frequently occurring weary situations impressed upon Indians that man's worldly being is not a freak of Nature but an inevitable bondage.

As for the Cārvāka rejection of soul and its successive disembodied states in between the embodied ones, it was at no time in the history of Indian philosophy taken really seriously. Buddha scoffed at the entire manner of the Cārvāka thinking. Śaṅkara did not even consider Cārvākas as philosophers. And Madhva (twelfth century A.D.) condemned them as belonging to the lowest class of thinkers. Being an antiascetic, hedonistic and popular (*lokāyatika*) order, the Cārvāka must have conquered the minds of the people of all ranks who were intent on achieving their immediate

[25] See Sinari, Ramakant: Some Reflections on Philosophy in India, *Philosophy and Phenomenological Research*. Vol. 26, No. 3, pp. 439 ff.

earthly good.[26] But it could not perturb in any remarkable way the fatalistic disposition of Indians—a disposition to which no phenomenon taking place in one's consciousness is without a *karmic* past and a potency for creating a *karmic* future.

IN THE VORTEX OF IGNORANCE

According to India's philosophies any kind of knowledge that is short of the total comprehension of one's innermost and transcendental ego would amount to ignorance or *avidyā*. From ignorance to knowledge or wisdom (*jñāna, prajñā*), the way is very arduous; but it is only by following this way that the bound existence can be snapped and freedom realized. The most irritating thing about ignorance is that a person just happens to be in it in spite of himself. It is not certainly produced by us; nor can it be regarded to occupy any necessary place in the ultimate structure of consciousness. Not to be given to know what the true foundation of the universe is, and yet to have a mortifying sense of weariness at the condition actually prevalent is the situation Indian thinkers have been most gravely aware of.

The state of ignorance is uncalled-for and disastrous in the sense that as long as it deprives us of a wholesome insight into the exact nature of the individual ego, our recovery from the state of bondage is impossible. Ignorance is at the core of our being in the world, is itself the root cause of our subjection to the law of *karma*, is the reason of our view of and attachment to all our experience.

Among all philosophical schools in the world, Indian schools are most acutely aware and most vocal of the fact that ignorance is the basic cause of human bondage. The Upaniṣads have repeatedly pointed out how the individual ego, on account of the lack of an integral perception in it, invites all kinds of wearisome circumstances in which it gets continually entangled. To the Upaniṣadic sages, ignorance is not what we may ordinarily take as the absence of knowledge or the inadequate knowledge of the empirical world. It is not a state that can be remedied with the acquisition of a scientific understanding of the universe.

The worldly man is ignorant, according to the Upaniṣads, in

[26] Chattopadhyaya, Debiprasad: *Lokāyata: A Study in Ancient Indian Materialism*. New Delhi, People's Publishing House, 1959, pp. 2–6.

the sense that the transcendental wisdom or *vidyā* has not as yet dawned on him and caused the most radical change in his outlook. For instance, the *Kaṭha Upaniṣad* speaks of persons living in utter ignorance and going about like "blind men led by one who is himself blind" and yet showing off that they are learned.[27] So long as what is everlasting, pure and infinite, says the *Praśna Upaniṣad,* is seen as the "crooked, false and tricky" world, there is ignorance.[28] And according to Kṛṣṇa in the *Bhagavad-gītā,* it is ignorance that makes us think about objects, remain attached to them, be angry at them, and confuse our minds about them.[29]

Although the Jainas' notion of ignorance is, really speaking, an extension of the Upaniṣadic notion, it has something extreme about it. They hold that the full and transcendental knowledge is implicitly present in every *jīva* or individual consciousness, but that the knowledge which an individual actually has while being in the empirical world is only a limited secretion of it. Sense organs, by means of which the soul obtains the knowledge of the spatiotemporally governed universe, are like blinkers restraining the absolute view of things the soul without sense organs would have realized. What constitutes ignorance, therefore, is the physiological mechanism behind perceptions of objects themselves. The presence of this mechanism prevents the soul from achieving a complete inner seeing, an intuitive and exhaustive wisdom called *kevala-jñāna.*

Buddha's eminent doctrine of Dependent Origination or *pratītyasamutpāda* is perhaps the most ingenious argument to prove that since nothing that takes place in the universe is without antecedent conditions, the whole misery that man experiences in life can be linked through a series of intermediate causes to ignorance. The doctrine, embodied in the Second Noble Truth in Buddha's preachings, mentions twelve causes in a chain in order to show that it is ignorance which has produced man's bound existence. In an attempt to trace back suffering (*duḥkha*) in life to its genesis, Buddha says that suffering is caused by birth, birth is produced

[27] Radhakrishnan, S. (Ed.): *The Principal Upaniṣads,* p. 609.

[28] *Ibid.,* p. 655.

[29] Swami Prabhāvananda and Isherwood, Christopher (trans.): *Bhagavad-gītā,* p. 48.

by the tendency to be born, called *bhāva,* this tendency is the result of mind's clinging to objects, the clinging is due to a thirst (*tṛṣṇa*) for objects, the *tṛṣṇa* is due to sense-experience, the senses have experience because of their past contact with objects, the contact is the result of the working of the organs of knowledge, the organs are further caused by the embryonic organism called *nāma-rūpa,* the *nāma-rūpa* comes from some initial consciousness (*vijñāna*), this consciousness is due to the impressions (*saṁskāras*) left by the previous lives, and these impressions are caused by nothing but ignorance.

Besides the clearly psychophysical links enclosed within the two ethical extremes in this Dependent Origination chain, what is self-explanatory about it is that it starts from the present and runs through the past of a living individual. In other words, the chain is meant to account for man's state of bondage in this world by means of his ignorance of the factors which lead up to it.

In fact, the concept of Dependent Origination takes for granted that the only way to bring about the dissolution of the full chain of twelve causes is to annihilate the instant where the chain has begun, namely, ignorance. It appears that for Buddha ignorance is without any antecedent. That is to say, ignorance and bondage so telescope into each other that they can be observed as two facets of the same phenomenon, namely, man's being in the weary world. When taken in this sense, the beginning and the end of the *pratītyasamutpāda* converge to a point and transform the chain into a circle or wheel, termed in Buddhism as the "Wheel of Dependent Origination" or *pratītyasamutpādachakra.*

To bring about an emancipation (*mokṣa*) from this wheel, one has to shatter the joint link of ignorance and bondage, *avidyā* and *bandha,* or by some other denomination, worldliness and *karma.* What is emphasized by Buddha is not so much the temporal origin of the chain or wheel as its self-determining universal authority. The wheel is beginningless or *anādi,* and the exact reason of its operation is beyond anybody's comprehension. Its ceaseless functioning is maintained by human lives born within it. The tendency to be born, being itself a link on the wheel, is determined by the previous links and determines links to come. Buddha makes it quite clear that the wheel could be snapped only when by means of a breakthrough a sudden flash of wisdom descends on one's consciousness—as it descended on Buddha himself—and tells it that the ultimate source of ignorance is to be found within ignorance itself.

IS THERE AN EXIT?

In spite of a basic consensus of views in different schools of Indian thought regarding the overwhelmingly desperate plight man in the empirical world is condemned to, the possibility of an exit leading up to absolute freedom or salvation (*mokṣa*) is invariably defended by Indian philosophers. Thus here is an apparently irreconcilable opposition between two tendencies: one, to accept with passivity the sovereignty of the law of *karma* and all that it has produced in our lives at present, and two, to repel the weary state of life shrouded in ignorance with a view to causing a permanent impossibility of any future birth and suffering. But it is a historical truth that while the first tendency has prevailed over the second in guiding the approach of the Indian masses to life and the world in general, the second has appeared in the form of the methods of salvation or *mokṣa-mārgas*. The mood of retiring into inaction before the inevitable law of the cosmos is so widespread in India that the oft made remark that Indian thinkers have advocated the theory of purposeful activity does not describe anything beyond the attitude of a few independent and dynamic seekers of pure and transcendental subjectivity.

Indian philosophies have always maintained that every man is capable of steering the course of his life in the direction of final emancipation. The very process of destroying one's own ignorance through the practice of transcendental concentration assumes in the ignorant a will of manipulating his own self towards a definite future. Indeed, a determinist might argue that the working of the law of *karma* is so wide reaching that even this will would arise as a result of an appropriate deed in the past life of an individual. But the scope of the law of *karma* need not be extended so much. For Indian thinkers have often asserted that the most fundamental change in man's outlook towards the world, which is a *sine qua non* for his exit from a bound existence, falls outside the law of *karma* and is not governed by any empirically determinable factors. It emerges suddenly out of one's penetrating vision of oneself. In the *Bṛhad-āraṇyaka Upaniṣad,* Yājñavalkya, a famous savant, explains his wife Maitreyī that for the attainment of the exit "it is the Self that should be seen, heard of, reflected on and meditated upon." [30] And Buddha, it is known, had to spend six long years of awful austerities and total suspension of sensual satisfaction before he could see the truth, the fullest vision of himself. And whatever might be his remote sources of initiation, Śaṅkara happened to feel the coming of the change after the tragic death of his father.

What exact domain an exit from the weary and bound state of life plunges one into is not easy to visualize. One of the aims of the present book is to analyze the nature of this domain. Nevertheless, the fact remains that not a few enlightened ones in India have described the incomparable *sat-cit-ānanda,* or being-intelligence-happiness, of this domain, an ascent to which, they have held, is entirely independent of and uninfluenced by the aftermath of one's past actions. In other words, they have attributed absolute freedom, absolute certainty and complete trans-empirical self-evidence to it.

There has never been any remarkable equilibrium in the Indian mind between the theory of *karma* or bondage—which is an attempt at explaining the ennui-laden life of mankind retrospectively—and the theory of salvation. Indians, by following the Vedic word and the oft-repeated assurances of their elite, have awaited the advent of the enlightenment, or an overnight transition in their view. But in absence of any such advent, they have fallen back upon the give-yourself-up disposition and become fatalists. In Indian life and literature fatalism is a common man's philosophical device. It is also a logical offshoot from the entire hierarchy of faith in *karma* held by millions of Indians at all times. There is no escape, according to this faith, from the weary world, until the arrival of a metaphysical awakening, a seeing of the innermost essence of things. And there is a hope, constantly intensified by the confessions of a handful of the seers, that salvation will finally crown everybody's efforts.

[30] Radhakrishnan, S. (Ed.) : *The Principal Upaniṣads,* p. 197.

Chapter Three

AN APPROACH FROM THE NOTION OF ORDER

UNDER THE RULE OF THE UNSEEN

A CURIOUS concept, somewhat naturalistic in character and yet embodying most of the ethical implications of the theory of *karma,* entered upon Indian philosophy around the third century B.C. with The *Nyāya Sūtras* of Gotama and the *Vaiśeṣika Sūtras* of Kaṇāda, and helped to strengthen the intelligent men's understanding of the subservience of the world to the enormous cosmic process. This is the concept of *aḍṛṣṭa* or Unseen Power. It was held that the merits of good actions and the demerits of evil ones are ordered by the *aḍṛṣṭa,* which is a self-subsisting law with infinite intelligence, foresight and power. The *aḍṛṣṭa* knows and determines all the consequences of an act prior to its actual happening. It causes circulation of water in trees, anabolism and metabolism in animals, desire and aversion, faith and lack of faith in humans.[1] No question of changing or interfering with the *aḍṛṣṭa* arises since it is an omniscient and omnipotent principle regulated by its own inner logic.

For the followers of the Nyāya and the Vaiśeṣika schools,[2] it is the will of God that directs *aḍṛṣṭa.* It is inconceivable, therefore, that the *aḍṛṣṭa* be subject to any fallibility as human beings are. As a matter of fact, the Unseen Power is both an ethical tribunal operating within every acting individual and the code of justice

[1] Ācārya, Udayana: *Kusumāñjali.* E. B. Cowell (trans.), Calcutta, Baptist Mission Press, 1864, I.4.

[2] These two schools originated independently between the sixth and the third century B.C. But they are so alike in their basic contentions that they are traditionally referred to as one Nyāya-Vaiśeṣika school.

pervading the whole of the universe. Roughly speaking, *it* is God Himself displaying His righteousness and sovereignty in the world of animate and inanimate beings. And the very descent of the disembodied soul onto the embryo in accordance with the deeds of the former is supervised by the *aḍṛṣṭa.*

The quasi-metaphysical element in the concept of *aḍṛṣṭa,* unlike the purely hylozoistic *Ṛta* pattern, is obvious from the Vaiśeṣikas' observation that the *aḍṛṣṭa* is an unknown and unseen impetus behind all psychophysical associations. It is not necessary to see in the present context the evolution of Indian consciousness from the theory of *Ṛta* to that of *aḍṛṣṭa.* However, it is quite clear that while the former suggests the single order of Nature akin to the law of the uniformity of Nature, with the latter a highly nebulous idea of a transcendental empirico-ethical regularity came into Indian thought, and belief in it became helpful whenever a rational inquiry into the causes of certain phenomena was conducted. It is also an interesting coincidence in the history of human consciousness that at the time when Indians were delving in such a monistic formula for the understanding of the universe, the Greeks were endeavoring to reduce all reality to one basic Logos or Nous.

Ṛta, which literally means the order of phenomena, denotes that the variety of things in our experience is controlled by an eternal and unchangeable setting. To the Vedic Āryans all the elements in Nature express a fixed arrangement because they are determined by *Ṛta. Ṛta* forms both the efficient and the material cause of the universe; it is a self-motivating divine course of events to which not only mundane beings but even gods of Nature are subject. The Vedic Āryans had thought that no disorder or chaos is seen in the world since *Ṛta* recognizes and executes what is necessary in the scheme of creation. It has the combined status of spiritual and material laws working with absolute precision. The *Ṛg Veda* says, "The dawn follows the path of *Ṛta,* the right path. . . . The sun follows the path of *Ṛta.*"[3] And the whole universe is based on and obeys the rule of *Ṛta.*

The advance of the Indian mind from the notion of *Ṛta* to that

[3] *Ṛg Veda,* I. 24.

of the *aḍṛṣṭa* order surely resembles the transition of the ancient Greek mind from Anaximander's infinite and ageless space-filling substance, which is supposed to maintain an inherent proportion or "justice" in the elements of Nature, to Anaxagoras's archetypal Nous or mind governing the composition of everything throughout the universe. *Ṛta,* like Anaximander's substance, is basically an indefinable cosmic stuff having its own rule. But exactly like the law of *karma,* it represents an authority on human destinies. It seems that the Indian mind at this stage was so engrossed in projecting its ethical sense onto the external reality that it could hardly entertain the notion of an order that was completely divorced from human interests. And this shows that the *Ṛta* and the *aḍṛṣṭa* were not assumptions of a scientifically oriented mind comparable to the mind of the Greeks.

The Vedic sages identified *Ṛta* with the world, and placed their trust entirely in the proposition that whatever happenings one encounters in Nature one's attitude towards them has to be receptive and prayerful. This trust was augmented immensely when the Nyāya and the Vaiśeṣika founders discerned the superior and somewhat abstract norm of *aḍṛṣṭa.* By means of the *aḍṛṣṭa* it was unambiguously shown that the law of *karma* is a superhuman authority ruling over the activity of the entire mankind.

It is not easy to define the exact relation between the *aḍṛṣṭa* and the law of *karma* as it appears in Indian philosophy. Although for all purposes of theological discussions the *aḍṛṣṭa* is equivalent to the law of universal uniformity willed by God or *Īśvara,* it would not be imperative to suppose that it is exclusively a supermundane reality. Of course for the Nyāya-Vaiśeṣika thinkers, the *aḍṛṣṭa* is something unconscious and irrational and therefore requires to be guided by the intelligent and perceptive divine agency. But it could as well be regarded as an autonomous substance, figuring as a unifying force in the cosmic phenomena and yet ever remaining outside the purview of our comprehension. Taken in this latter sense, *aḍṛṣṭa* would be another name for the law of *karma* itself, that is, the law of moral causation, although what it lays stress on specifically is the imperceptible omniscient *élan* (*aḍṛṣṭakāritam*) which makes the law of *karma* to function.

There is, probably, an indefinable unconscious stratum underneath the whole kingdom of conscious activity: a mysterious, indeterminable creative force which influences imperceptibly human destinies and decisions. To a more realistic school than the Nyāya-Vaiśeṣika, the *adṛṣṭa* would represent a self-governing law of universal causation not needing the assumption of any supernatural being at its background. In fact, the reason why the Nyāya-Vaiśeṣika philosophers often characterized *karma* as *adṛṣṭa* might be that according to them the *karma* notion is not so self-sufficient as to explain itself without the help of a basic logic. However, like other theists in Indian philosophy, they could not allude to a reality, i.e. the *adṛṣṭa,* as something acting in absence of a control from God.

THE QUESTION OF NECESSITY

In the *Śvetāśvatara Upaniṣad* there is a query which later on came to be of central importance to the entire gamut of philosophical thinking in India. It asks, "What is the cause? Whence are we born? By what do we live? And on what are we established? Time, inherent nature, necessity, chance, the elements, the womb or the person (should they) be considered as the cause?" [4] It is not difficult to see that this query anticipated not only the concept of *adṛṣṭa* but also a distinct notion of causal order known as *svabhāva-vāda.* The latter, to which a number of allusions are made in the famous epic *Mahābhārata,* signifies that the universe is a self-determining system of necessarily interrelated events. Among the most prominent philosophical problems which engaged the minds of Indian thinkers, the problem of causal order was observed to have direct import on the theory of the bound human existence.

The obvious view for the schools of Indian philosophy to hold with regard to physical and mental phenomena in the universe should have been that just as the hylozoistic *Ṛta* and the quasi-metaphysical *adṛṣṭa* can admit of no accidental happenings, the *svabhāva-vāda* would not make any freedom of the human will plausible. For since it is presupposed that the very emergence of human reality in the world is the result of the *karmas,* it would be

[4] Radhakrishnan, S. (Ed.) : *The Principal Upaniṣads,* p. 709.

difficult to believe that this result would be made to vanish by means of *karmas* themselves. However, the Indian mind exhibits a twofold approach to reality. On the rational plane it asserts the supremacy of a universal and necessary order, a kind of cosmic *norma;* yet on the transcendental plane it trusts that absolute freedom (*mokṣa*) is realizable. The gap between these two planes has always remained unbridged.

Now by showing that the state of being in the world ought to be explained as something resulting from the potency of one's own bygone actions, Indian philosophers proposed a causal thesis. Whether the doctrine of multiple births and rebirths be scientifically tenable or not, the specific hypothesis that one's present life is the effect in a space-time continuum of happenings does have an explanatory significance. Again, the necessitarianism implied by this hypothesis is so broad that almost anything in regard to a subject's experience could be accounted for with its help. Possibly, therefore, the whole causal thesis about the status of man in the world would not have left so great an impression on the thinking of Indian philosophers had it been put forward solely as a self-comforting stratagem of a few despairing souls. There is undeniably an empirical foundation to it, and that is why it succeeded in keeping generations after generations of Indians under a mood of helpless surrender to the cosmic order. As if to lay a special emphasis on the fact that man's bound existence, or the infallible law of *karma,* for that matter, has an empirical justification, Indian thinkers propounded the concept of causal order while asserting at the same time that the spiritual and the transcendental in man is not in any way contained by this order.

CAUSALITY AS TRANSFORMATION

The earliest and epistemologically the most valuable attempt made in Indian philosophy to set up a theory of causal order is that of Kapila (seventh century B.C.), the founder of the Sāṅkhya system. Generally known as *satkārya-vāda,* with its further specification as *pariṇāma-vāda,* this theory states that the phenomena we recognize as the cause and the effect are basically one and the same identical thing. The effect exists in its cause prior to its actual appearance, and the cause potentially contains its effect, so that an effect is only an evolved cause, and a cause is only a latent effect. The theory, which suggests that something is produced as an effect because it was existent already in the form of a cause, has received its name from the fact that *sat* means existent and *kārya* means effect. For instance, the curd preexists in the milk, the statue preexists in the marble and an ornament preexists in gold. The appearance of the effect signifies that a change or transformation (*pariṇāma*) in the internal structure of the cause has taken place and that the cause is now seen as different from what it was.

If we go back to the most primordial cause of the whole universe, Īśvarakṛṣṇa (fifth century A.D.), the most authoritative exponent of Kapila and the author of the *Sāṅkhya Kārikā,* says we would come upon the rigid and unevolved stuff, *prakṛti,* out of which all things have originated.[5] Īśvarakṛṣṇa's concept of causality, known as *pariṇāma-vāda,* is meant to account for the whole of creation by postulating something unmanifested or *avyakta* that is ever pregnant with all that we find ourselves experiencing. Thus causality is a transformation in the state or states of *prakṛti,* and this transformation, observed or unobserved, constitutes the order of the universe.[6]

The qualitative alteration, or *dharmapariṇāma,* of things, including mind, senses, intelligence, the body, etc., does not mean that anything new is brought into existence. What it implies is that through the devising and redevising of the qualitative substratum of things, known as the *guṇas,* different assemblages of physical and mental entities emerge in order to form the world. The ultimate ground of all this process is *prakṛti* or Nature—a self-emanating primeval reality which is both the material and the efficient cause of the universe.[7]

The term "*prakṛti*" is one of those key terms in Indian philosophy which are highly suggestive of a naturalistic approach to the world of everyday experience. As Hiriyanna has said, by coming under the influence of *svabhāva-vāda,* for which the universe is

[5] Davies, John (trans.): *The Sāṅkhya Kārikā of Īswara Krishna,* 2nd ed. Calcutta, Susil Gupta, 1957, p. 8.

[6] *Ibid.,* pp. 21–22.

[7] *Ibid.,* pp. 8–9.

explicable as an internally necessary system, the Sāṅkhya transferred "the capacity to unfold the universe . . . completely to *prakṛti.*"[8] But although *prakṛti* is material and, for all purposes of creation, self-regulating, its capacity to evolve into psychic products, such as intellect (*buddhi*), the ego (*ahaṁkāra*) and the mind (*manas*), would lead one to suspect some nonmaterial agency in it. However, Īśvarakṛṣṇa assures us that the entire activity in and from *prakṛti* is due to a kind of friction among its three constituents, called *guṇas,* namely, *sattva* or that which is fine, *tamas* or that which is rough, and *rajas* or that which is active.[9] It is because of these three mechanically arranged *guṇas* that, regardless of its varied transformation, *prakṛti* cannot be presumed to alter its original material nature.

The Sāṅkhya theory of *satkārya-vāda* does not bring under its range of explanation the transcendental and spiritual entities called the *puruṣas* or selves. Its notion of order is with regard to the world of empirical objects. The *puruṣas,* the Sāṅkhya says, are different from intellect, the mind, the ego, the sensory organs (*jñānendriyas*), etc., since they are pure, eternal and self-sustaining realities uninvolved in and uninfluenced by the worldly changes. They have neither form nor qualities nor a desire for movement. They are of the nature of immaculate awareness and infinite enlightenment. Therefore, no intellectual order could be framed to define their status or functioning.

The Sāṅkhya does not indicate what type of relation prevails between the trans-empirical *puruṣas* and the empirical *prakṛti.* The Sāṅkhya thinkers are in complete accord with the Upaniṣadic thesis that the pure existence or self (*ātman*) is totally independent of and unconditioned by the forms of mind and everything that constitutes the experience of mind. Yet the Sāṅkhya does assert that the whole process of creation emanating from *prakṛti,* which is also called, very significantly, *pradhāna* or the foundation, is due to a contact (*saṁyoga*) between *puruṣas* and *prakṛti.* Thus Ācārya Mādhava, explaining the Sāṅkhya position, remarks that just as iron moves while in proximity of a magnet, so there is a

[8] Hiriyanna, M.: *Outlines of Indian Philosophy.* London, George Allen & Unwin, 1951, p. 268.

[9] Davies, John (trans.): *The Sāṅkhya Kārikā of Iswara Krishna,* p. 11.

movement in *prakṛti* in contact with the motionless *puruṣas*.[10] The "union of Nature and Soul is caused by mutual dependence, like the union of the lame man and the blind man." [11] Nevertheless, from the contact between them one would not be able to argue that the *puruṣas* step into the area of the causal order. The notion of *pariṇāma* or transformation cannot describe the domain beyond that of *prakṛti*.

Had the Sāṅkhya posited *puruṣas* as the motivating principle behind *prakṛti*, and propounded a kind of spiritualistic pluralism comparable to that of Leibniz, it would have found it hard to explain how the transcendence of *puruṣas* and the immanence of *prakṛti* could coalesce into a harmony. But by preserving the purity and the trans-phenomenal self-subsistence of the *puruṣas*, the Sāṅkhya clearly marked the point that if reality is to be viewed from the notion of causal order, only the region of *prakṛti* should be taken into consideration. Not that by making *prakṛti* the final substratum in evolution, the Sāṅkhya has successfully answered the question why and for what end the *prakṛti* has undergone change. It is not easy to know the exact influence of *puruṣas* on *prakṛti*, since, as the Sāṅkhya maintains, even the ordinarily recognized nonmaterial operations evolve from *prakṛti*. It must be said, therefore, that although in their essential being *puruṣas* cannot but be above the order of causality, they should be supposed to have some kind of necessary but incomprehensible connection with *prakṛti* in the enterprise of creation.

As a theory of material evolution, *satkārya-vāda* or *pariṇāma-vāda* is intended to explain the entire field of our mundane experience. Of course the main problem the Sāṅkhya thinkers seem to have been busy with is not so much that of accounting for the order of things in the world as that of finding out why the world emerges in human consciousness at all. For it would be one thing to define the chain of phenomena springing from the unmanifest primeval matter (*avyakta prakṛti*), and quite another to tackle the metaphysical question why pure selves (*puruṣas*) plunge into the world evolved out of *prakṛti*. It is while working out the meta-

10 Mādhava, Ācārya: *Sarvadarśanasaṅgraha*. E. B. Cowell and A. E. Gough (trans.), pp. 228–29.

11 *Ibid.*, p. 229.

physical question about the *puruṣas'* awareness of the world that the Sāṅkhya must have struck upon the idea of causality as transformation, about which it showed remarkable scientific imaginativeness.

CAUSALITY AS EMERGENCE

The intellectual interest of the Sāṅkhya theorists does not seem to have been attracted by the new emergent element in any phenomenon that is related to another phenomenon as its effect. According to their approach everything that belongs to the spatio-temporal world is an unfoldment of one basic principle whose relationship to the multiple material products need not be conceived as one implying a regular continuity. The problem of causation, in the sense in which it engaged the minds of Aristotle, Bacon, Hume and J. S. Mill, never bothered the Sāṅkhya thinkers. And this speaks well for the conspicuous lack of the study of scientific method and research in the history of Indian thought. Being more influential than any other causal theory, *satkārya-vāda* was responsible for shaping the idea of causality of even Śaṅkara, Rāmānuja (eleventh century A.D.) and other Vedāntins.

Besides, in spite of their professed scientific motivation, Caraka (second century A.D.) and Suśruta (fourth century A.D.), in their brochures on medicine and physiology respectively, make no attempt at setting up causal generalizations based on observation. And this is clearly due to the prevalent conviction in their times that causality is merely the actualization of what is potential. The disposition of the Indian mind to feel empirical phenomena as something atrocious must have generated even among scientists in ancient India an attitude of disinterestedness in the pursuit of the empirical knowledge. Writing on some of the physical theories current in ancient India, Basham has remarked that they were "closely linked with religion and theology, and differed somewhat from sect to sect." [12] It is not unnatural, therefore, that when thinkers of old India reflected on the question of cause-effect uniformity, what they primarily applied their mind to was the rela-

[12] Basham, A. L.: *The Wonder That Was India*, p. 496.

tion of the world as a whole to one original source and not the phenomenal orderliness of the experienceable universe.

But around the third century B.C., a few realists, dissenting from the Sāṅkhya, busied themselves with epistemological and logical theories as we understand them today and put forward a totally analytical view of causality known as *asatkārya-vāda* or *ārambha-vāda*. These realists, led by the Nyāya-Vaiśeṣika school, made the world of sense-experience the basis of their investigations; and, in the course of their debates and disputes against opponents, accepted it as a self-evident truth that the phenomena in the spatiotemporal universe are logically explicable. The thinking of an array of Indians—Vātsyāyana of the *Nyāya-bhāśya,* Vācaspati of the *Nyāya-vārttika-tātparya-tīka,* Jayanta of the *Nyāyamañjari,* Gaṅgeśa of the *Tattvacintāmani,* Praśastapāda of the *Padārtha-dharma-saṅgraha,* and Śridhara of the *Nyāya-kandalī,* to mention some—reflected a faith in realism.

The concept of *asatkārya-vāda* contends that a cause is an unconditional and invariable antecedent in relation to its effect. An effect, it says, is a fresh beginning or *ārambha* and, as such, is nonexistent before it is produced. The cause and its effect are distinctly separate in the sense that they figure as independent events manifesting a specific relation of continuity between themselves. Hence, the effect arises due to the working of a certain causal aggregate, a logical and empirical antecedent, a conglomeration of conditions. The Nyāya thinkers argue that if the effect of a cause is not regarded as something different from that cause, the fact of the emergence of the effect as a new phenomenon would remain unaccounted for.

For the Naiyāyikas, there is as if a certain power which holds a cause and its effect together. It is because of this power that only specific causes precede specific effects unconditionally. For instance, the Nyāya realists, like Keśava Miśra and Nīlakaṇṭha, hold that a *kāraṇa* or cause is something that necessitates an effect.[13] Indeed, the power in the cause that makes its effect necessary is not external to the cause. It is the essence of the cause, that is *it* being

[13] See for comments on these and other Nyāya realists Radhakrishnan, S.: *Indian Philosophy*. London, George Allen & Unwin, 1966, Vol. 2, pp. 96–98.

given, the effect must follow the cause and the cause is inferable from the effect. Thus the relation between a cause and its emergent effect is described by the Nyāya as one of unconditionality or necessity (*ananyathāsiddha*), invariability and inductive determinability. No two phenomena could be said to be causally related unless the one which appears antecedently and that which appears consequently are logically and empirically conceived as tied together, and neither of them is regarded as likely to occur in isolation. Thus what Vātsyāyana states deserves our attention.

He holds that in the case of every ordinary happening, not only the cause is perceived as something being there, but also the effect is discovered as something possessing qualities analogous to the qualities of its cause. Neither of these two things can be possible in regard to an "eternal" phenomenon. Nor can one deny, Vātsyāyana argues, that there is a perception of the cause and that of the "production" of the effect. And these perceptions must have an actual basis in the world of objects. Vātsyāyana concludes from this that the effect is the "product" of the cause which is "brought into existence" in the style in which the cause itself was brought into existence.[14]

The Naiyāyikas, like J. S. Mill, defined cause as a sum total of necessary and invariable conditions (*kāraṇasāmagri*). As regards the conditions which remain accidentally present when the effect occurs, they classified them into various types. For instance, when a potter manufactures a pot, the color of his stick, the health of his father, etc., are not causally related to the making of the pot. In the same way, there may be a number of coeffects which either precede or accompany a phenomenon, but they are not in any way unconditional in relation to it. Then the potter's stick or wheel invariably makes a sound while the pot is built, and this sound moves the atmosphere; and the potter keeps a donkey tied to a pole nearby while his work is in progress. Yet all these things have no necessary relation to the pot. They are, therefore, merely contingent so far as the effect is concerned.

The Nyāya mentions three kinds of causes: the material cause

[14] Jha, Gangānatha (trans.): *Gautama's Nyāyasūtras* (*With Vātsyāyana's Bhāṣya*). Poona, Oriental Book Agency, 1939, pp. 429–30.

(*samavāyi*), the nonmaterial cause (*asamavāyi*), and the efficient cause (*nimitta*). The material cause of a thing constitutes that stuff out of which the effect emerges. For example, the clay in relation to the pot, and the threads in relation to the cloth are material causes. The nonmaterial cause denotes the particular arrangement or conjunction—somewhat like a saturation point—in the material cause. Just as the symmetry of the threads is the *asamavāyi* of the cloth, and the color of the threads the *asamavāyi* of the color of the cloth, God's workmanship is the *asamavāyi* of the production of the world. The third cause, the *nimitta,* denotes the agency that brings about the effect. Thus the potter is the *nimitta* of the pot.

From the differentiation the Naiyāyikas make between the relevant and the irrelevant circumstances in the causal relation, and the way they characterize various causes, it can be seen that they displayed a highly observant and critical method in the study of the constituents of knowledge. While the Vaiśeṣika school was guided principally by the purpose of developing a theory of reality somewhat similar to the one the Greek atomists had, the Nyāya had concentrated on the problems of knowledge with a view to dissecting the rules and conditions of intellect. Kanāda, the father of the Vaiśeṣika system, had propounded a pluralistic realism in which the whole universe was explained as having emerged from nine *dravyas* or substances objectively real and eternally undergoing combinations. The Nyāya took this explanation for granted and endeavored to work out the epistemic conditions which enter the very subject-object connection.

Thus the concept of causality in the Nyāya realism is the result of a spirit of scientific interest, rather uncommon in the evolution of Indian philosophical thinking. Indeed it would not be correct to say that the Nyāya-Vaiśeṣika movement could disregard or be uninfluenced by the basic motivation of the philosophization in ancient India, namely, the quest of absolute freedom from the weary state of being in the world. It suggests in many contexts that the ultimate objective of all intellectual pursuits is to facilitate one's final release or *apavarga.* "When there is a relinquishing of the birth that has been taken and the non-resumption of another, —this condition, which is without end (or limit) is known as

Final Release, by those who know what Final Release is." [15] However, the intellectual zeal with which the Nyāya-Vaiśeṣika realists stayed busy with the study of the furniture of knowledge and of the world noticeably beclouded their transcendental search, and eventually put them on the philosophical map of the world as seekers of the scientific explanation of the universe.

The most oblique departure of the *ārambha-vāda* from the *satkārya-vāda* doctrine, which was so deeply ingrained in the monistically oriented mind of India, cannot be easily explained. Not only does the former represent a logico-empirical approach to the whole question of reality, but it even suggests that the effect is as concrete as and belongs to the same order as that of the cause. Clearly, *ārambha-vāda* has nothing metaphysical about it. It shows no inclination to define that primordial ground or order which kept *satkārya-vāda* preoccupied most of the time.

For the *satkārya-vādins* causality is not a *relatum* between phenomena but something that hinges on the presence of the perceiving minds, which, by the very fact of their limitations, are not able to see that the cause and the effect are forms of one and the same thing. It must be said, therefore, that there cannot be any common basis for comparison of the two theories except that to both of them the universe is explicable if we approach it from a notion of uniformity. The antagonism between them amounts to the antagonism between two views of reality: one refusing to admit that there can ever be a thing which is not preexistent in some other thing, or which is not a transformation of it, and the other taking it almost as a truism that the cause and the effect are real events in an order of continuity. *Satkārya-vāda* is an intellectual theory, having necessarily a trans-empirical extension; *ārambha-vāda* is a self-contained logico-empirical analysis. They are formulations of the cause-effect relationship, with distinct degrees of emphasis on the perceptible qualities of the world.

A METAPHYSICAL UNDERTONE

There is a point at which the *asatkārya-vādins* or *ārambha-vādins* shed their empiricistic and dispassionately logical outlook

[15] *Ibid.*, p. 46.

by alluding to a sort of abstract and indeterminate principle at the bottom of the perceptible cause-effect relationship. And such an allusion is more prominent in their treatment of human actions than physical happenings. As it has been stated earlier, the Nyāya-Vaiśeṣika held that the effects of man's voluntary acts are determined by *adṛṣṭa,* an unseen universal order directly under the authority of God. Although, otherwise, the threefold doctrine of causality of the Naiyāyikas contains no explicit statement of any such order, it could be shown that the *adṛṣṭa* has its counterpart in the *asamavāyi* or nonmaterial cause.

The *asamavāyi* is the inherent power of a cause and determines what sort of effect would emerge from it. Ordinarily the chain of material causes and their respective effects would face an *infinitum regressus* if every cause needed to be accounted for by means of an antecedent cause. Perhaps more than any other *ārambhavādin,* Udayana Ācārya, an important Naiyāyika of the tenth century A.D., became aware of this so far as the sphere of ethical phenomena is concerned. He wrote that if we wish to prove the existence of an omniscient and indestructible being, we must necessarily take into account the appearance of effects, the combination of atoms, the "support of the earth in the sky" and all compositions and decompositions of elements. He said that the earth would need a maker because it is an effect like a jar from the raw material. As a matter of fact, every combination is an action, and the action which produces the combination of atoms and launches the process of the universe must have behind it the volition of an intelligent being.[16] Thus for Udayana Ācārya the existence of a supernatural cause, or *adṛṣṭa,* is self-evident.

Now had this reasoning been carried further to establish that the fundamental impetus behind all cause-effect relationships in the universe is an invisible nonmaterial substance (*asamavāyi, adṛṣṭa*), it would have inevitably given rise to a metaphysics close to that of Rāmānuja's. Of course the *asamavāyi* as a nonmaterial cause is too restricted and too structural an entity to present any close resemblance between itself and God or *Brahman.* But the very fact that there was an inclination among the later Naiyāyikas

[16] Ācārya, Udayana: *Kusumāñjali.* E. B. Cowell (trans.), p. II, 6.

to acknowledge the insufficiency of a realistic explanation of the world and to revert to an abstract force, or even to God, is an evidence of the tilting of the Nyāya mind towards metaphysical speculation.

It is rather astonishing that the analytical and initially positivistic thought of the Nyāya-Vaiśeṣika school could not stay altogether uninfluenced by the transcendentalist core of the Vedic-Upaniṣadic *Weltanschauung*. The *asatkārya-vāda* view of reality has not cast more than a scant impress on the growth of Indian consciousness. Rather, the whole of the Nyāya-Vaiśeṣika movement must have started, as Stcherbatsky has said, out of the art of effective debating at intellectual meetings and seminars. And, therefore, the scientific discipline it tried to sow in India with remarkable enthusiasm proved to be without an internal transcendentalism. It was a passing phase, a provisional technique of argumentation on the periphery of the vast spiritually inclined ethos of India. As Ninian Smart remarks, it did not have "an inner religious logic, so to say, which determines its main structure." [17]

It is only in the last few decades that some of the sparks of genius of the Naiyāyikas have been brought forth by scholars and worked upon in the light of contemporary logic and epistemology. But we shall comment on this question later.

WHAT IS *APŪRVA*?

While Udayana Ācārya's *Kusumāñjali* in the Nyāya school and Prasastapāda's *Padārtha-dharma-saṅgraha* in the Vaiśeṣika school are eminent examples of the Indian attempt to posit God as the pilot of the universal order of things, Jaimini's *Mīmāṁsā Sūtra* and Kumārila Bhaṭṭa's *Ślokavārtika* in the Pūrva Mīmāṁsā school (fourth century B.C.) are confessions of the view that such an order need not be controlled by any supernatural being. Kumārila Bhaṭṭa in his notably atheistic treatise argues against the very necessity of the idea of God for the apportioning of *dharma* or merit and *adharma* or demerit to the deserving ones.[18] By pointing out

[17] Smart, Ninian: *Doctrine and Argument in Indian Philosophy*. London, George Allen & Unwin, 1964, p. 96.

[18] Bhaṭṭa, Kumārila: *Ślokavārtika*. Gangānatha Jha (trans.), Calcutta, Asiatic Society of Bengal, 1909, pp. 355–56.

that the recommendation of awards and punishments to the good and evil characters respectively would require no supposition about a divine agency, Kumārila rules out the possibility of there being any way of knowing such an agency even if it existed. Before anybody lived, he asks, who was there to perceive God, and if it is said that He cannot be perceived, how can we find out that He acts?[19]

The Mīmāṁsakas are extremely cutting when they remark that if *adṛṣṭa* or *karma* is conceived as being under the supervision of God, it would be reduced to an insignificant category. And on the other hand, if God is regarded as being dependent on some force other than Himself, i.e., *adṛṣṭa,* it could be inferred that He is not entirely free in His judgments. Therefore, the infallible law by which *dharma* and *adharma* are assigned to worldly beings could better be regarded as self-subsisting and as operating eternally under its own inner necessity. It is in this sense that Jaimini, the founder of the Pūrva Mīmāṁsā system, explains the principle of regularity regarding the specific effects of specific actions and names it as *apūrva* or transcendental potency.

The notion of orderliness involved in the principle of *apūrva* can be easily understood. The word *apūrva* suggests that the law of *karma* pervades the consciousness of all individuals in the form of a transcendental potency. Because of this potency every action that emanates from an individual remains tied to its effect, which may appear sooner or later. Apart from its significance to the code of rites and rituals on which the Pūrva Mīmāṁsā system put a great deal of emphasis, the *apūrva* was conceived with specific import to the explanation of our varied worldly situation. Maintaining, in consistency with the main current of thought in ancient India, that all embodied souls live a life of bondage generated by and in tune with their performances in the previous lives, the Mīmāṁsakas said that every human action, ritualistic or otherwise, contains the potency of producing its own effect.

Somewhat with a wider intent Pārthasārathi, a Mīmāṁsaka, contends in his *Śastra-dīpikā* that the potency of an action is its unmanifest energy or *śakti,* and that almost everything in the uni-

[19] *Ibid.,* p. 355.

verse must be said to possess it. He says that even words are pregnant with *śakti;* otherwise, they would not have figured as the means of communicating meanings. For Jaimini this *śakti,* or *apūrva* for that matter, enjoins actions on man. And although the actions themselves come to an end, their effects are as if held up in heaven and continue to linger there till they appear on earth in some concrete form. Never will the effects of actions vanish; nor will there be actions which are free from *apūrva.*

With the notion of *apūrva,* it may be noted, the Mīmāṁsā school ventured the assumption of a reality, an order which, unlike *adṛṣṭa,* could be cognized as being different for different persons suiting the nature of their deeds. While, as with the Naiyāyikas and the Vaiśeṣikas, God could be looked upon as the *modus operandi* of *adṛṣṭa,* His existence becomes superfluous in relation to the individually working *apūrva.* For even if we believe with theists that God's presence is necessary for the process of the universe, it need not be thought that *apūrva* comes under His influence in any particular manner. Thus it becomes a transcendental potency, a self-contained tribunal, reigning over all conative consciousnesses and creating the aftermath of their actions.

The theistic element in the law of *karma,* which is the law of the uniformity of moral causation, is totally abolished by the Mīmāṁsakas; and consequently, some sort of indeterminate momentum is admitted as individualizing itself in every one of human lives. Indeed the Mīmāṁsā thinkers, like other orthodox thinkers of their times, did accept the supremacy of the Vedic injunctions regarding the law of *karma.* However, their unique contribution in this respect consists in indicating that it is the *apūrva* (literally meaning never before) of an action that constitutes as if the cushion of the law of *karma,* that is the law of *dharma* and *adharma.* Looked at in this way, *apūrva* represents a self-directing potency measuring every action and storing up its appropriate reaction.

ORDER AND FREEDOM

Insofar as *karma, adṛṣṭa* and *apūrva* can be seen to have otherworldly allusions and to be principles superimposed on the connection between acts and their results, they would suggest, although only apparently, a fatalism of the most discouraging kind. Strictly speaking, all these principles emphasize the absolutistic nature of the order of human destinies and invigorate the central Vedic-Upaniṣadic thesis that a person's good and bad deeds bring into being certain amount of inertia, which endures under the supervision of some transcendental "Reason" until their fitting consequences transpire. The actual appearance of these consequences cannot be interfered with even by the gods of Nature or the Lord of living things, called Visvakarman.

In spite of the authoritative status of any of these principles, however, Indian thinkers have maintained that the urge for absolute freedom can act against the whole domain of moral causation and bondage, and throw the exit to *mokṣa* open. Man's being in the bound world is conceived as a causally explicable phenomenon, an event in accordance with a universal order; but it is not denied that considering the prospective free choice he is capable of making, the bound existence will some day be annulled. The strictly logical query, namely, whether the actual expression of such a free choice is not itself subject to *karma* or *adṛṣṭa* or *apūrva* need not interest us here. Of immense significance as this query is to the discussion of what a *mokṣa*-directed conduct is and how it is to be learnt, it may be stated in its regard here that according to Indian thinkers the notion of order—whether in the shape of *karma* or *adṛṣṭa* or *apūrva*—is valid on the intellectual level; the notion would make no sense when one realizes the transcendental level.

No Indian sage has successfully explained the origin of human bondage, that is the riddle why and how the first *karmic* contents are formed and why and how they descend upon one's fundamentally pure and trans-empirical consciousness. There is no reason to suppose that human consciousness would indulge in any activity in spite of its inherent knowledge that activity is bound to plunge it into a wearisome and bound existence in the world. But the mystery takes place somehow, and the pure consciousness becomes worldly. Indeed to all orthodox Indian philosophers the cause of man's being in bondage is his ignorance or *avidyā,* a sort of naïve perspective he builds about the world of his.

Chapter Four

THE THESIS OF AN ANTI-INTELLECTUALISM

THE DOCTRINE OF THE MANY VIEWS

IN THE whole of the history of Indian thought, the most vivid instance of shelving the very issue of establishing a single intellectual theory of the universe is found in Jainism. The metaphysics of the Jainas is so averse to constructing scientific or objective knowledge that at no time it seems to have argued in support of a universal and absolute truth. The Jainas put forward a pluralistic conception of reality known as *anekānta-vāda* or the doctrine of the many reals with its counterpart in logic called *syāda-vāda* or the doctrine that all knowledge is probable.

According to the Jainas, the universe consists of an infinite number of material and spiritual units, *ajīvas* and *jīvas,* each of which is as independent and self-contained as a monad in Leibniz's system. Every one of these units, again, possesses innumerable attributes, modes and configurations which no finite intellect can exhaustively comprehend.

There are attributes of a thing which change, and there are those which do not change. The former are called by the Jainas *guṇas,* and the latter, *paryāyas.* Any given thing, therefore, is a complex of immutable and mutable qualities, a many-in-one and one-in-many, a permanence at the basis but a flux at the surface. It is impossible to imagine that the knowledge one has of a thing at any particular time could contain all of its qualities en masse. Śri Malliṣeṇasūri (thirteenth century A.D.), one of the most talented Jainas, says that "the real simply is composed of infinite attributes, that existence otherwise than so is not easily justified."[1]

[1] Malliṣeṇasūri, Śri: *Syād-vāda-mañjari.* F. W. Thomas (trans.), Berlin, Akademie-Verlag, 1960, p. 132.

What one's mind can grasp of a thing at a particular point of time is a partial view, a *naya,* of the thing. Such a partial view or *naya* is merely a fraction of the wholesome being of the thing. Now an infinite number of *nayas* are possible about one and the same thing, or even about one and the same attribute of a thing. But if any one of the *nayas* of a thing is taken as its whole being, a fallacy called *nayabhāsa* would occur. Consequently, we can never claim to know a thing in all its objective characteristics or in its entire past, present and future being. Thus, Śri Malliṣeṇa explains, "Only that which appears in the present moment has the form of an entity, not the past or the future. Because the past, as having perished, and because the future, as not having attained to its own-being, are of a form void of all potency. . . ."[2]

So to know something is to know it from one of its numberless points of view, each of which is relatively true and relatively false. Never is it possible to make a statement expressing what a thing in all its objective and constantly changing condition is. The same statement could be true from one point of view but false from another. This particular feature of what can be termed as epistemological relativism is known in Jainism by the name *syāda-vāda* because of its inherent emphasis on the thesis that since all knowledge is piecemeal, it is subject to error and hence never more than probable.

A highly relativistic and epistemologically uncertain and skeptical approach to the nature of reality, as one preached by the Jainas, would reduce any concept of order, causal or otherwise, about the universe to an invention. If no two subjects can obtain identical percepts of the same thing, and if the subjects are so distinctly situated from each other and in relation to the thing that what one of them perceives is never perceived by the other, then no observation or statement embodying an interphenomenal connection would be conceivable. Both the *pariṇāma-vādins* and the *ārambha-vādins,* despite their divergent philosophical interests, have tacitly adhered to the opinion that the relation between one event and another, or between a cause and its effect, is not only knowable but also definable and generalizable. To both these groups causality is a relation that governs the very stuff of the uni-

[2] *Ibid.,* p. 155.

verse. Neither is it subject to alteration or modified interpretation from individual to individual, nor is it such that as and when perceived by one individual, it may be crossed by the perception of some other individual.

Reference to any law of absolute relationship between objects does not form even indirectly the intention of the Jainas. They do not recognize that if a comparison between any two aspects (*nayas*) of the same object is attempted, it is possible to evolve a common basis for the comparison. They do not see, as the Sāṅkhya and the Vedānta thinkers for instance see, that the relativism of knowledge is only a superficial characteristic of the world in time and space, and that as soon as one begins to account for it, an allusion to something absolute would become inevitable.

Of course while explaining how the material world came into being, Jainism does maintain that it is a product of the combination of *aṇus* or atoms. Atoms of matter (*pudgala*) arrange themselves in different ways, increase or decrease the volume of material things on account of their inner capacity, and thereby create the world. The Jainas also say that the influx of the *ajīvas* or material units into the *jīvas* or spiritual units starts *karmas* and the *saṁsāra* (the circuit of births and deaths). However, what the Jainas specifically emphasize is that whatever the types of the combinations of atoms, and whatever the relations among these combinations, they are all viewed partially. That is to say, what is grasped as permanent from one point of view will not remain so from another point of view. In short, no assertion about anything or about any relation between one thing and another can ever be wholly true or wholly false. And therefore, the fact remains, the Jainas state, that whatever we perceive or know about the world is true or false, certain or uncertain, valid or invalid, only in a way.[3]

It is on account of his inadequate and undeveloped capacities that man has to endure a plurality of views about the world and be subjected to uncertain, partial and probable knowledge. The highest goal of man is to reach that immaculate state of awareness at which all possible perspectives or *nayas* the world might mani-

[3] *Ibid.*, p. 137.

fest are brought within the field of vision. No conceivable interference with one's enjoyment of absolute intellectual certainty is likely to appear at this state. The Jainas call this uppermost stratum of knowledge by the name *kevala-jñāna* (Universal Vision).

IN SEARCH OF THE INCOMPREHENSIBLE

One of the most curious leaps one witnesses in the history of Indian consciousness is from the epistemologically constructive and world-affirming attitude of the Nyāya-Vaiśeṣika thinkers to the utterly negativistic and world-denying attitude of the followers of an unbelievably esoteric sect of Buddhism called the Mādhyamika in the second century A.D. It would be worthwhile to see here how the Mādhyamika system explained the phenomenal world and put forward a philosophy of intense nihilism. Our present discussion, however, will remain limited to the epistemology in this system and leave its ontological aspect for later treatment.

So far as the explanation of man's life in the world is concerned, the basic sayings in Buddhism center around the doctrine of *pratītyasamutpāda* or Dependent Origination. As it was shown already, the underlying principle of this doctrine is one of psychophysical causality working in a circle and accounting for the phenomenon of human suffering (*duḥkha*). But since Buddha himself was least concerned with any epistemological or logical inquiry for its own sake, he stated the *pratītyasamutpāda* doctrine as a commonsense axiom for the misery mankind undergoes in the world rather than as an empirical analysis claiming universal import. It was some centuries after the death of Buddha (*circa* 483 B.C.) that Buddhism grew into a host of very interesting epistemologies. The most profound among these is one by Nāgārjuna (second century A.D.), the first systematic expounder of the Mādhyamika movement.

The Mādhyamika or the Middle School is widely known as the Shūnya-vāda because of its voidist style of thinking and its total distrust in intellect. For a Shūnya-vādin nothing that forms the object of intellect, or nothing to which the categories of intellect are applied is itself real. Intellect is often deceptive, subject to delusions, misgivings and errors, and can never give us a full and trustworthy knowledge of the universe. Aśvaghoṣa (fifth century

A.D.), about whose life and works scholars know very little, tells us, in consistency with the voidist logic, that the function of intellect through judgments, definitions and deliberations is to facilitate limited enlightenment. Intellect is not able to give us, he says, the true vision of the real; it can only make one imagine vaguely what reality would be like.[4]

Aśvaghoṣa contends that intellectual constructions are arbitrary formulations whose observational and descriptive powers do not go beyond the world of sense perception. Whatever is accessible to intellect is rigid, partial, relative, mundane, and therefore only a finite aspect of the real.[5]

Nāgārjuna's anti-intellectualism is of the most extreme type. He reached a point in voidism much further than that of Aśvaghoṣa's when he tried to show that since intellect is analytic, discursive and critical, the most genuine insight into Being, which is the indescribable (*avāchya*) foundation of all worldly things, cannot be attained through it. Whatever is intellectually apprehended is contingent and cancellable.

Nāgārjuna's conception of Reality (*tattva*) takes us to a kind of absolutism which cannot easily be characterized in terms of any of the traditional labels in philosophy. Usually known as Shūnyavāda or nihilism, it attributes to Reality every conceivable negative expression, probably to suggest that what is ultimately real is, in contrast to what belongs to the world, forever unidentifiable, indeterminable and nonaccessible to reason. Reality is *prajñāpārimitā,* in the sense that it is the nonconceptual intuition of the most integral object.[6] If we take any entity in the world and try to seek its perfect transcendental genesis, we would find that its worldliness soon dissolves in appearance. Thus the true nature of a thing is not revealed to intellect.

The basic form of a thing, according to the Mādhyamikas, is nonrelative and transcendent to thought. Intellect or thought and

[4] For a treatment of Aśvaghoṣa's anti-intellectualism, see Suzuki, T. D.: *Aśvaghoṣa's Discourse on the Awakening of Faith in the Mahāyāna.* Chicago, Open Ct., 1900, pp. 7–9.

[5] *Ibid.*, pp. 110–113.

[6] See for a detailed discussion of this concept, Murti, T. R. V.: *The Central Philosophy of Buddhism.* London, George Allen & Unwin, 1960, pp. 224–28.

its counterpart, the universe, are real insofar as they respond to the practical dispositions of human life. It is impossible to grasp the embryonic source of our existence itself unless we exercise a mystic vision and ascend to the purest and altogether trans-empirical level of awareness. For the Mādhyamika, as Murti points out, "the Absolute . . . is not known in the way that particular phenomena are known . . . it does not possess any attribute of its own; but its presence can be 'indicated' even by an ascribed mark. . . ." [7]

In his renowned work, called *Mādhyamika Kārikās,* Nāgārjuna states his anticausal theory of *śūnyatā* or *śūnya* (literally, devoid of any conceptual distinction). The theory is a bold attempt to shift the direction of old Buddhism from a commonsense and ordinarily accepted view regarding the cause of human misery to the thesis that if we view existence from the transcendental standpoint, we would realize that all interphenomenal relations are unreal. The shift was definitely initiated by Nāgārjuna and later on intensified by a number of Mādhyamikas, such as Ārya Deva (third century A.D.), Buddhapālita (fifth century A.D.) and Chandrakīrti (seventh century A.D.). All Mādhyamikas have reached the conclusion that causality is an intellectual hypothesis for the understanding of the empirical world. It would cease to be useful the moment we pass beyond this world and intuit the very essence of it.

Nāgārjuna thoroughly criticizes all important concepts of causality. According to him a transcendental view of the universe would convince us that nothing can ever be really produced or ruined. Nothing rises from within itself; nothing emerges as new. There is no movement, no creation, no disappearance, no causation. "Origination, existence and destruction," remarks Nāgārjuna, "are of the nature of *māyā,* dreams or fairy castle." [8] What is real is beyond deliberations, and no predication is possible about it. Reality is neither existent nor nonexistent, neither one nor many, neither pure nor impure, neither something nor nothing, neither at rest nor moving, neither responsive to doubt nor

[7] *Ibid.,* pp. 231–32.
[8] Quotation *Ibid.,* p. 177.

to belief. It transcends all duality, definability, linguistic expressions, theories and speculations.

To know Reality is to know *śūnya,* argue the Mādhyamikas, for any assertion which alludes to Reality is empty of the exact content. The Jainas had shown that every judgement reflects an individual mind's pose, an opinion, a perspective, a *naya.* And to the Mādhyamikas, to state something about the real is to thrust one of the intellectual categories on it and to cause a limitation with regard to its wholeness. Thus Nāgārjuna's reasoning against the *satkārya-vāda* and *asatkārya-vāda* conceptions of causality follows from his central proposition that the very distinction between cause and effect is founded on intellect, and as such, amounts to an attempt to bring Reality down to the tier of mundane experience. He says that if the effect is only a self-expression of the cause, there is no reason why the two should be regarded as distinct; and if, on the other hand, the effect is a new creation by the cause, no common ground between them would be determinable.

The conclusion Nāgārjuna draws from his clever treatment of the theories of order in the universe is that we can speak of neither continuity nor distinction nor any other connection between events. Phenomena are what they are; they can be neither identified nor differentiated. As Stcherbatsky, while elaborating upon this point, puts it,

> A reality which is stripped off from every relation and every construction, which has neither any position in time and space nor any characterizing quality, cannot be expressed, because there is in it nothing to be expressed, except the fact that it has produced a quite indefinite sensation. . . . To maintain that ultimate reality, the thing as it is in itself, can neither be conceived nor named means that it cannot be cognized by consistent logical methods. . . .[9]

Phenomena are connected or causal, from the point of view of our day to day living or *saṁsāra;* but they are also absolute and free, from the point of view of the ultimate transcendental Being. To attribute to Reality, therefore, what we perceive or conceive with regard to phenomena is to delimit it.

So at the same time and to the same individual consciousness,

[9] Stcherbatsky: *Buddhist Logic.* New York, Dover, 1962, Vol. 1, pp. 185–86.

Reality is both Being and Nothing, or neither Being nor Nothing. Suppose we say that it is *x*. This would indeed be its description from a certain aspect or consideration. From some other aspect or consideration it would be not-*x*. Just as it could not be described as plenitude, it could not be described as even nullity. In this sense, the Buddhist logic tries to denote it as "point-instant of reality," "pure object" (*śuddha-arthaḥ*), "own essence" (*sva-lakṣaṇa*), neither "non-zero" (*aśūnya*) nor "zero" (*śūnya*).[10] The dialectic is unavoidable since looking at it from no specific angle, Reality would be neither *x* nor non-*x*. What can one say about it then? Just nothing, *śūnya,* silence.

It must be known that for Nāgārjuna the phenomenal world is an intellectual construction and hence unreal or illusory, or it is a contingent expression of what is in itself transcendental and pure, though not in the sense in which it is so for Śaṅkara and other Vedāntins. Nāgārjuna's Shūnya-vāda tends to deny the very thesis, prevalent in Śaṅkara and, for that matter, in all absolutistic trends in philosophy, that the ultimate reality is a full, perfect and eternally positive idea that is seen or thought of as piecemeal, finite and spatiotemporally extended being. It appears that the main reason why Nāgārjuna rejects the notion of order or of positive rational structure in any of its conceivable forms is that according to him Reality is a formidable domain of chiaroscuro unamenable to intellect, perpetually mystifying, and neither like nor unlike the world. To stake any intellectual explanation of such a thing is futile.

[10] *Ibid.*, pp. 181–83.

Chapter Five

THE REALM OF TRANSCENDENTAL REALITY

TOWARDS AN INWARD-SEEING SENSIBILITY

IN INDIAN philosophies the notion of the order in the universe figures as a nexus connecting the fact of human bondage and the ethics of salvation (*mokṣa*). Generally on the kind of the theory of universal order a philosophy propounds depends the attitude of that philosophy towards life, the world and salvation. Leaving the materialistic Cārvākas, for whom all phenomena including consciousness are simply the results of the combinations of elementary physical constituents and therefore constitute a mechanical product rather than a purposive program, no school of Indian thought has denied the desperate state of man's being in the world and failed to show its primordial cause.

Jainas' epistemological relativism and Mādhyamikas' nihilism have discarded the intellectual aspect of the cause-effect relationship, even while diagnosing the weary worldly situation. But they did it primarily with a view to demonstrating that although causality is empirically and practically verifiable, its contingent character would become obvious when one transcends intellectual categories by an inward-seeing process. As a matter of fact, nowhere have Indian thinkers preserved the analysis of the phenomenal order wholly self-contained. Everything had a relevance to our recognition of the ultimate aim of ripping off the circuit of bondage and realizing freedom. And this is as much true of the pre-eminently epistemological and realistic movement of the Nyāya-Vaiśeṣikas as of the utterly atheistic and esoteric negativism of the Mādhyamikas. To speak from the point of view of the theory of knowledge, the Nyāya-Vaiśeṣika preoccupation with the conditions of knowledge and, the Jaina and the Mādhyamika distrust in all discursive knowledge represent extreme limits between which Indian intellectualism seems to have oscillated. However, the seriousness of attaining the realm of transcendence nowhere lessened. Salvation through transcendence is the pivot around which Indian interests moved.

At no time has real division between intellectual search and metaphysical speculation occurred in the history of Indian consciousness. Speaking of the eminently logico-epistemological investigations of the Nyāya school, it could be said that although a desire to shape the effectiveness of their rhetoric compelled the Naiyāyikas to concentrate their attention primarily on the rules of intellect, they did admit the subordinate nature of this task in relation to the intrinsic desirability of salvation. There was always something basically purposeful behind whatever intellectual endeavors Indian philosophers engaged themselves in, and the purpose was nothing short of an absolute liberation from suffering and worldliness.

This is why the original efforts of the Naiyāyikas to inaugurate logic in India and the very valuable researches of Udayana Ācārya and Gaṅgeśa (twelfth century A.D.) did not leave any discipline on the conduct of the Indian mind comparable to that of Aristotle's logic on the Western mind. Generally, Indians are one of the most metaphysical, ambiguous and fuzzy-headed species on earth. And, therefore, apart from the fact that this characteristic has been and still is the main hindrance in the path of their success in practical life, it has acted as a fuel for their spontaneous and emotive representations in transcendentalism, mysticism, aestheticism, literature and poetry. Ambiguity is an inseparable accompaniment of the inward-seeing consciousness.

Not only the usually held opinion by Western authors that Indian philosophy has sprung from mysticism and profound faith in the otherworldly, but also the restricted and largely consoling theory held by a few that the traditional thought in India did attempt to surpass idealism or spiritualism are distinct renderings the whole ambiguous expression of Indian consciousness is open to.[1] Except the Cārvāka and some very sparsely spread anti-idealistic trends, all schools of Indian thought have reflected a most intense ambiguous mentality and, further, made themselves amenable to multiple nuances and commentaries, many of which are not without an underlying essay to overrate certain ideas firmly settled in the tradition.

Ambiguity or even ambivalence is not always a demerit of philosophy. In fact, when a philosophical school straightens itself to such a shape that it contains itself inside the requisites of a strict formal structure, it becomes insular and operates in a fixed logical complex. Not only is such a philosophy deprived of the spontaneity of feeling and transcendental flights, but also it comes to own wares which show utter indifference to man's inward-seeing sensibility and suprarational tensions. Tacitly ambiguous expression is invariably the sign of a great turmoil concealed underneath. Indeed an ambiguous consciousness finds an outlet through ambiguous philosophies. And the former is nothing but a certain *Weltanschauung,* whose identification with either discursive thought alone or plastic affective self alone is out of question. Philosophies in India have sustained an extremely ambiguous temper, insofar as they have harbored an ambivalence, a chasm, within the consciousness of Indians and have hardly been motivated by a scientific interest.

Intellectualism, or a purely scientific consideration of things, was never coherently adhered to by any of the schools of Indian philosophy. It always has had, as perhaps even today it happens

[1] The theory that the traditional thought in India did try to set forth a strong anti-idealistic movement is held, among others, by Ruben, Walter: *Geschichte der Indischen Philosophie*. Berlin, Deutscher Verlag der Wissenschaften, 1954; Roy, M. N.: *Materialism*. Calcutta, Renaissance Publishers, 1951; Riepe, Dale: *The Naturalistic Tradition in Indian Thought;* Damodaran, K.: *Indian Thought: A Critical Survey*. Bombay, Asia Publishing House, 1967; and Sankrtyayan, Rahul: *Darśan Digdarśan* (Hindi). Alahabad, Kitab Mahal, 1961. A rather unusual estimation that "Indian thought exhibits a deep intellectual passion for clarity, precision and explicitness" and that "the anti-intellectualism inherent in the revelatory conception of truth is the darker side" of Indian thought, is made by Rege, M. P.: Some Reflections on the Indian Philosophical Tradition, *Quest, 44:* 9–24. However, a fairly controlled view that "it is by no means claimed that by piecing together the healthier elements of . . . different anti-idealistic trends one can reach a satisfactory and integrated outlook" is put forward by Chattopadhyaya, Debiprasad: *Indian Philosophy: A Popular Introduction*. New Delhi, People's Publishing House, 1964.

to have, a limited following in India. It has neither roots in India's tradition nor fully devoted supporters. As Will Durant has sharply shown, the most vivid lesson that the seers of the Upaniṣads teach their followers is the inadequacy of the intellect. "How can this feeble brain, that aches at a little calculus, ever hope to understand the complex immensity of which it is so transitory a fragment?" [2] Even the interests of the most realistically and analytically minded Nyāya and Vaiśeṣika thinkers were ultimately drifted by the central conception of Indian philosophy towards trans-empirical realities, such as *aḍṛṣṭa,* God, immortality and the unincarnate state of the liberated souls.[3] Allusions to these entities have evidently affected the seemingly rebellious intellectualism of the Nyāya-Vaiśeṣika system.

In India intellectualism figures as scantily situated spots across a land of profound transcendentalism on the one hand, and of puerile regressive superstitiousness on the other. Both have their origin in the Indian tradition, to the extent to which they repel the supremacy of intellect. However, while it is superstitiousness that is on the wane and desirably so, even with the advance of education and reformation through mental training, transcendentalism remains the very essence of Indian consciousness. The quest of transcendence becomes the sole shaper of India's relation with herself and with the rest of the humanity. As Durant suggests, to a transcendentalist adhering to the core of the Vedic-Upaniṣadic teaching, intellect is not useless but has its modest place, because it is useful when it deals with relations and things but "falters before the eternal, the infinite, or the elementally real." [4]

But in our own time the challenge which India has come to face is from an urgent need to equip herself intellectually, to build herself scientifically and technologically, in order to surmount the obstacles to her material well-being. The promise of a salvation through the exit into a world other than the one we ordinarily

[2] Durant, Will: *Our Oriental Heritage.* New York, Simon and Schuster, Inc. 1954, p. 412.

[3] For the Nyāya-Vaiśeṣika deliberations on the trans-empirical entities, see Sankrtyayan, Rahul: *Darśan Digdarśan* (Hindi). pp. 585–94, pp. 631–38. Sankrtyayan makes a feeble attempt to show that despite these deliberations the Nyāya-Vaiśeṣika thinkers were pronounced intellectualists.

[4] Durant, Will: *Our Oriental Heritage,* p. 412.

value has ceased to beckon the practically-minded thinkers, mostly because the fantastic material achievements of the West, professedly wedded to scientific advancement, are greatly inviting. Nevertheless, the *mokṣa*-laden history, through which the Indian mind has journeyed all these past centuries, has established a peculiar type of sensibility in it. It is this sensibility that has stayed most prominent in the Indian approach to things.

To this sensibility praxis does not count at all. Being sharply inward-seeing, it embodies an intense longing for the worship of the Vedic-Upaniṣadic past, a loyalty to it and to those who represent it, a lack of interest in the future, a steadily but effectively growing awareness that the Absolute or God is all-embracing, and above all, a deeply ingrained mood that enmity towards human existence is the eternal rule of the phenomenal world. Nowhere else was this sensibility given more direct and uninhibited an expression than in the lives of the Vedāntins, yogis and Hindu mystics. In a way, existentialists in the West today—the most uncompromising antirationalist metaphysicians of an age that can claim nothing akin to the psychic state of early Hindus, Jainas and Buddhists, except perhaps a sense of nausea at the "ritual" of everyday living—could be regarded as the closest assimilators of this sensibility.

The Indian transcendentalists' preoccupation with the question of salvation (*mokṣa*), understood as absolute freedom, becomes vastly clear when we consider also the fact that they, like existentialists, were melancholic personalities, extremely conscious of the incidents of absurdity, despair and ennui in life. And this particular quality of the Indian mind explains its habit of subordinating thought to intuition, clarity to ambiguity, precision of expression to abundance of nuance, the commonsense use of the world to the metaphysical negation of it. The originally empirical issue of the cause-effect relationship and for that matter almost every other issue was made to evolve into some sort of ontology [5] as soon as Indian sages cast their reflections on it. For in the context of the perspective or perspectives Indians took of anything in

[5] Fundamentally speaking, *pariṇāma-vāda, ārambha-vāda,* Śaṅkara's outwardly causal theory called *vivarta-vāda, pratītyasamutpāda,* etc., are ontological suppositions.

the universe, nothing could be left limited strictly to its empirical or logical boundaries. Everything had to have its genesis in the trans-empirical domain; everything had to have natural affinity to that unknown sphere to which access is possible through transcendence alone.

There is not much poignancy, therefore, in the oft-made accusation that the attempt at philosophizing in ancient India is loaded with mysticism and poetry, when it is observed that it was a nauseating and weary feeling of being in a world where suffering is the prime law of all living beings that drove Indians to an inward cloister invariably lost to clear and articulate thought. Cloistering oneself was desirable as a means of escape from the world of bondage and boredom. It was a procedure towards the attainment of the final goal, a *sine qua non* of the absolutely *real* existence.

THE CONDITIONING MILIEU

Philosophical thinking in traditional Inḍia appeared as a flight of the savants from the day-to-day act of living. In general, the process of survival for Indians, in the time when the Upaniṣads and their highly elucidatory commentaries were composed, must have been dull and even squalid. Besides the peculiar contrast in the geographical conditions[6] found characteristically from the Himalayas downwards and across the Ganges, the irksome problems of survival and occupations, vis-à-vis the native fighters of the land, must have disturbed the very stability of Indians' mind and body and moulded the Indian temperament—the most melancholic temperament in the history of mankind.

Philosophic creativity in India in the past reflected this temperament. Rather, the temperament generated the philosophic creativity, which further helped the temperament to mature and harden and sustain itself against the onslaughts of foreign cultures in later times. The whole mass of Indian consciousness is as if mesmerized by this temperament, initially transfused into it by

[6] Hollow azure sky with mystic colored horizons, vast and vacuous land ascending upwards to become soaring Himalayas, deep black nights studded by echoing cries of fierce animals, gushing waters of flooding rivers or none at all, are some of the features of the geography of North India where the Upaniṣadic thought sparked off. See also Basham, A. L.: *The Wonder That Was India*, pp. 2–4.

the sages gifted with a transcendental vision, and is convinced of the futility of its continuance in the mundane world. As Bergson has correctly observed,

> From the most remote times, the Hindu speculated on being in general, on nature, on life. But his effort, sustained through many centuries, has not led, like the effort of the Greek philosophers, to a knowledge susceptible, as was Greek science, of unlimited development. The reason lies in the fact that to him knowledge was always rather a means than an end. The problem for him was to escape from life, which he felt to be unremitting cruelty.[7]

There is such a thing as the orientation of every born Indian to this temperament; and despite internal variations in things Indian and their gradual modernization, the orientation persists, forms the essential postulation of Indian reasoning, feeling and acting, has made way into the Indian scheme of education and politics, and functions even in the Indian outlook towards the future of humanity. Indians, not even in their industrialized urban milieu and semi-Westernized ways of living, have remained free from this orientation.

As a matter of fact, the orientation of Indians to lessons in the melancholic temperament starts as early as their days of childhood. Almost all agencies of training and information inside and outside home which are bound by the world-negating tradition excel in their power of impressing upon the young the virtue of renouncing all material comforts and leading an austere manner of life in search of transcendental peace. Indian school texts, storybooks, songs, movies, festivals, popular versions of original religious accounts, pastime sermons by elders and priests, are a constant reminder to the young and the old alike that the real goal of life is its total abnegation. It is a conditioning process, a kind of subtle initiation spread over past many centuries, and though gradually on decline at present due to the sway of Western ideas and of course the practical needs of the moment, has certainly reserved a potentiality to channel Indian interests over years to come.

As always in respect of individuals face to face with life's in-

[7] Bergson, Henri: *The Two Sources of Morality and Religion.* R. Ashley Audra and Cloudesley Brereton (trans.), New York, Doubleday Anchor, 1954, p. 224.

herent hardships, Indians, when shaken by every sort of unopportune occasions, had to adopt a poise against them. What exact factors in the life of a people determine this poise is not easy to know. Again, it is not something that results from a careful calculation and judgment. Perhaps the poise is a contrivance, at times conducive and at other times not so, for the general physical continuance of the people. While in the West this poise has always been one of confidence in the authority of human endeavor over cosmic forces and has produced science and technology, in India it has refused to regard the bodily well-being with any enthusiasm and attachment.

The antagonism between the Western and Indian poises is an antagonism between the resoluteness of the former to bring about a change in human destiny and the self-surrendering spirit of the latter, between mechanically pedalled reason and *mokṣa*-directed transcendentalism, between an unambiguous effort to annihilate or convert menacing forces of the universe and a humility of mind and heart before the will of the beyond. William Haas highlights this antagonism when he contrasts the "unswerving self-assurance" of the Western mind with the "grandiose and ghastly system" invented by the Indian mind to demonstrate to itself the "futility and nothingness of . . . all existence."[8] What would most immediately strike the observation of a critical student is the attachment, almost addiction, of Indian consciousness to transcendental abstractions. Through them Indian consciousness has sought to lift itself up the drab and mortifying phenomenon of the world, to grasp the very foundation of it, and to dissolve itself in the realm of the Absolute or *Brahman*.

BRAHMAN AND *ĀTMAN*

To the inspiration of the authors of the Upaniṣads, the transcendental ground of all existence, material and mental, is *Brahman*. The word *Brahman,* which derives from the root *bṛh,* meaning to gush forth, to burst forth, or to grow, denotes that first embryonic reality from which the entire universe of our experience has sprung up. It is suggested that the word, if traced down

[8] Haas, William S.: *The Destiny of the Mind*. London, Faber and Faber, 1956, p. 52.

to the root *bṛih* or *vṛih,* which signifies to talk, must have originally meant prayer, but was later on taken to mean the single omnipresent and omniscient soul manifesting itself through human consciousness and the world. All over the literature interpreting Indian philosophy, *Brahman* has been defined as Supreme Reality, transcending the entire phenomenal universe, self-caused, self-dependent and self-controlling. Originally, the *Ṛg Veda* had referred to one single monotheistic Being (*ekaṁ sat*) as the primordial essence of all created things.

The Upaniṣads affirm that *Brahman* is the Reality of all real things, the ultimate principle of all forms of consciousness, the highest fusion of truth, knowledge and eternity, *satyam-jñānam-anantam,* the underlying unifying spirit of all particular beings, and the ontological mover of life and its activity. Even contradictory characteristics are often ascribed to *Brahman*. For instance, the *Bṛhad-āraṇyaka Upaniṣad* says that it is "light and no light, desire and absence of desire, anger and absence of anger, righteousness and absence of righteousness and all things"; [9] for the *Kaṭha Upaniṣad* it is "smaller than the small, greater than the great," sitting and yet moving, lying and yet going everywhere; [10] and for the *Śvetāśvatara Upaniṣad* it is to be known as "a part of the hundredth part of the point of a hair divided a hundredfold, yet it is capable of infinity." [11]

There is nothing that does not depend on *Brahman,* that has not emerged from it, that is not finally reducible to it. *Brahman* is the intelligent governor or *antaryāmin* of all phenomena; and as such, it is above them all. Intelligence, matter, space, time, causation, change and all those categories through which we discern the reality of the world, we are told, have their abode in *Brahman*.

With a quasi-theological vein the Upaniṣads mention three distinguishable states of the evolution of *Brahman: Virāt,* or the cosmos, *Hiraṇyagarbha* or the soul of the cosmos, and *Īśvara* or the self-conscious *Brahman*. Indeed these states must not be understood as forming a spatiotemporal passage through which *Brah-*

[9] Radhakrishnan, S. (Ed.) : *The Principal Upaniṣads,* p. 272.
[10] *Ibid.,* p. 617.
[11] *Ibid.,* p. 741.

man evolves. They are rather empirical situations attributed to *Brahman* by us on account of our comprehending the connection between it and the world. By itself *Brahman* does not play any part in the creation of the universe. It is absolute, pure, abstract, eternal, and of the nature of unmixed *ānanda* or delight. However, as a substratum pervading behind the visible matter, it is *Virāt;* and as the propelling energy of *Virāt,* it is called *Hiraṇyagarbha.* The only distinguishing point between *Virāt* and *Hiraṇyagarbha* is that while the latter denotes an all-comprehensive potency ever seeking its own expression, the former is the stuff of the entire physical existence. But the state which is closest to *Brahman,* and the one through which *Brahman* becomes a self-conscious person in the perspective of man in the world is *Īśvara.*

One might remark that when looked at from the mundane point of view, the complete and integral *Brahman* begins to emit three aspects in none of which it suffers a debasement. Again, *Virāt, Hiraṇyagarbha* and *Īśvara* do not constitute an inner representation of *Brahman;* they are conceptual characteristics that we according to our religious perception establish in it. The transcendental nature of *Brahman* is unaffected by these characteristics. *Brahman* eternally remains the highest self-identical consciousness, irreducible to thought and inexpressible through any of the rules of creation and evolution. It is subject to no change, although every change in the universe is to be accounted for by means of an allusion to its self-fulfilling urge.

The essential individual consciousness, which is only an expression of *Brahman,* is called by the Upaniṣads the *ātman.* The word *ātman* comes from the root *an,* meaning to breathe, and has been used to indicate the most fundamental being of the individual. For all philosophic purposes, the *ātman* (the Self) is identical with *Brahman* (Supreme Being). It is the innermost reality in man to which the phenomenal world figures as a superficial but inevitable experience.

On the ontological level there is no separation between Supreme Reality and the Self, although to every individual his own empirical existence is the source of distinct and unique experience. In a remarkably expressive though figurative style, the authors of the Upaniṣads have shown that the *ātman* forms the essence of all that one is, and that its intuitive knowledge is the highest among all forms of knowledge. *Ātman* is the inner light, the self-knowing subject, the self-revealing spirit, and approaches, as far as its trans-empirical character is concerned, the subtlest and the deepest experience one can attain during one's inward-directed seeing.

There are frequent suggestions in the Upaniṣads that *ātman* cannot be satisfactorily described because it is the final subject of all conceptualization. It is pure consciousness, pure transcendence, pure subject-object identity and pure existence. When we are awake, the Self functions as the primordial motivation beneath our intellect, feeling and action. When we are asleep, it resides as a passive life-force capable of exhibiting itself through diverse experiences. The *ātman* is the eternal substratum in all actual and possible states a person may pass through during his present and future existences, or might have passed through his past lives. It is as if the locus wherefrom the entire universe has sought to emerge and become spatiotemporal.

THE ĀTMALOGICAL PRONOUNCEMENT

India's traditional philosophy is a formidable superstructure founded on a complete and uncompromising ontological subjectivism, which we have called ātmalogy. No challenge other than that from the superficial epistemological objectivism of the Cārvākas and the logical analysis of the Naiyāyikas can be seen to have arisen against it in the entire history of Indian thought. Initially, ātmalogy is the Self's return to its own original abode with a view to figuring out its total domain, when it is stirred up by the conviction that human life in the world is a permanent victim to forces generated by its own inherent deficiencies and ignorance. While the expression of this attitude is most direct and poignant in the Upaniṣads, in Buddhism, in Sāṅkhya, in Yoga and in the Vedānta, the attitude itself pervaded under the outward colorful polytheism even through the *Ṛg Veda*.

Ātmalogy could be the designation of a philosophical system, to which *ātman* or the individual spirit cannot be equated with what man empirically experiences but with what he is prior to any experience whatsoever. At the level of pure and transcendental existence, the *ātman* and *Brahman* are one and the same principle. But at the level of worldly existence, the *ātman* finds itself to have lost its identity with itself and with *Brahman* and fallen in a bound state. To an ātmalogist the spiritual essence of man is entirely different from his contingent being; and therefore, for the realization of the former the latter ought to be suspended or annihilated.

There is obviously a difference between the type of ontological subjectivism, characterized as ātmalogy, and the epistemological subjectivism of Bishop Berkeley. The follower of Berkeley's subjectivism is not committed to a method of salvation but to a method of knowledge. In other words, while to an ātmalogist it is one's trans-empirical intuition that would finally determine the inauthentic nature of one's knowledge of the world, to a Berkeleyan the very occurrence of perception is an empirical phenomenon in which the attributes in the perceiver are imposed on the perceived. Berkeley, unlike the ātmalogists, affirmed the existence of the world even when he called it "mental" or "in the mind." He showed no inclination to doubt the sensations arising from the world.

The ontological subjectivism of Indian thinkers, like the transcendentalism of phenomenologists and existentialists, is both an attitude and a method. Both are the reflection of a predominantly egocentric and inward-seeing consciousness. And the intensity with which they have arisen is clearly due to a sort of mental equipment, the larger part of which is drawn by the feeling of the weary spectacle of the universe and the destiny of human beings in it. Ātmalogy has refused to confine itself to objectivity and drab mechanical intellect. Its search is trans-phenomenal, in the sense that it is directed towards the profoundest region of individual consciousness, towards an explorative examination of the genesis and the destination of the ego. Ātmalogy in Indian philosophy is the only legitimate outcome of the original Vedic-Upaniṣadic preoccupation with the potentialities of I-consciousness.

As it was said before, ātmalogy engaged the attention of all Indian sages except the Cārvākas and the Nyāya-Vaiśeṣika logicians. Although it has in no other school of Indian thought reached so great a height as in Buddhism and Yoga, there is absolutely no ethical and metaphysical tendency in the Indian tradition where it has not figured in some form or other. When abstracted from all its sociopolitical implications, ātmalogy remains a transcendental quest for the foundation of consciousness and, as such, declares itself as the first and the final endeavor to map out the expanse of the ego.

Really speaking, the philosophy of the *Brahman-ātman* relation or more accurately of the *Brahman-ātman* identity is inspired by the most direct encounter of man with his own being. This encounter might be remotely conditioned by the physical and social milieu, namely, the economico-politico-social factors, or the excess of desires and ambitions producing a psychic depression and even unfavorable geographical changes. But when one observes the conditioning power of all these things, one need not shift the emphasis away from the fact that the essential structure of a philosophy conceals a not exhaustively explicable presupposition, a *Weltanschauung,* that has a self-sustaining capacity irrespective of the modifications in the milieu and in a mysterious way influences the milieu itself.

Therefore, any strictly causal explanation ventured, for instance, by Marxists and Freudians of India's unique *ātman*-directed search, although illuminating scientifically, would not conclusively account for the metaphysical import of the search itself. As Ernst Cassirer has aptly put it, "All human works arise under particular historical and sociological conditions. But we could never understand these special conditions unless we were able to grasp the general structural principles underlying these works." [12] To look upon human consciousness as an a priori given, the source of all experience, and to concentrate on it in order to find a solution to the riddle of existence are the task of a philosophy much more withstanding than the empirically oriented studies. And for such a philosophy empirical happenings form only a setting for consciousness whose dynamic search for its own meaning is something intrinsically self-oriented and therefore genetic in relation to all phenomena. "A 'philosophy of man'," Cassirer

[12] Cassirer, Ernst: *An Essay on Man: An Introduction to a Philosophy of Human Culture.* New Haven, Yale, 1962, p. 69.

writes, "would . . . be a philosophy which would give us insight into the fundamental structure of . . . human activities, and which at the same time would enable us to understand them as an organic whole."[13] What ātmalogy, or the ontological subjectivism, preeminently aimed at is the statement of the metaphysical justification of this insight.

Hardly elsewhere have Indian philosophers shown the rigor of their metaphysical discipline so powerfully as when they tried to penetrate through the layers of consciousness towards the region where the individual *ātman* and the universal *Brahman* become indistinguishable from each other. This is the region where the *ātman* is perceived as the essence of *Brahman*. The transcendental method involved in ātmalogy is not an epistemological method; it is the method of a "seeing" or intuitively possessing the universal truth within the essence of one's own self. Such a "seeing" has notably emanated from the transcendental purpose to which Indian philosopher-saints,[14] not less than the Vedic-Upaniṣadic *ṛṣis* or seers, have remained absolutely faithful.

Indian metaphysics is not a rigid intellectual exercise. It centers around a cosmic view, a Reality-intuiting method whose absolute infallibility is felt before it is articulated, a kind of moral passion to "see" the gravity of the very worldliness of human consciousness. It is not so much the ātmalogists' language as the integral impact they have created through their intense longing for transcendental experience that has proved to be tremendously suggestive. In fact, what Wittgenstein has modestly said about the activity of his statements, in the *Tractatus Logico-Philosophicus,* can be put in the mouth of any of the ātmalogists from Yājñavalkya, the enlightened Upaniṣadic teacher, to Śri Aurobindo (1872–1950), the neo-Vedāntin:

> My propositions serve as elucidations in the following way: anyone who understands me eventually recognizes them as nonsensical, when he has used them—as steps—to climb up beyond them. (He must, so to speak, throw away the ladder after he has climbed up it.) He must

[13] *Ibid.*, p. 68.

[14] What Indian philosopher-saints experience is, to use Unamuno's expression, "the hunger of immortality." See Unamuno, Miguel de: *The Tragic Sense of Life*. London, The Fontana Library, 1962, pp. 54–71.

transcend these propositions, and then he will see the world aright. What we cannot speak about we must consign to silence.[15]

ĀTMALOGY AS A TRANSCENDENTAL PHENOMENOLOGY

It may be shown that ātmalogy and Edmund Husserl's transcendental phenomenology [16] reflect the same sort of metaphysical tendency inasmuch as they both represent a distrust in the world of sense-perception and a profound desire for self-exploration by means of radical trans-empirical concentration.

A phenomenologist begins with the total suspension (*epoché*) of all the usual conceptions about the nature of the world. The suspension or bracketing, as it is named in phenomenology, of our everyday awareness with regard to the phenomenal existence is a deliberately chosen attitude. Such an attitude, psychologically speaking, amounts to a reversion of the act of experiencing. Its final purpose is to carry consciousness to its preexperiencing state, and to examine therefrom the emergence of experience itself. For phenomenologists, the *epoché* is not a logical activity but rather an inward-seeing practice directed towards seeking the prereflective domain of consciousness. It is maintained that the *epoché* implies the operation of grasping the essences or *Eidos* of things with a view to evolving a new vision of existence as such.

Man's ordinary understanding of the universe is conditioned by numerous presuppositions, interests, motives and dogmas. We are constantly influenced by our sociocultural habitat, logical and linguistic inheritance, intellectual and emotional commitments and in general by the entire inner and outer milieu in which we live. The rules of meaning and expression, of selection and elimination in perception and intellection, the act of interpretation and valuation, totally govern our contact with the world. Some sustained reflection would convince us that though our full being is involved in this contact, there is nothing necessary about the nature of the contact itself. Not only is it modifiable, but even its *raison d'être* can be revised. The phenomenological attitude ap-

[15] Wittgenstein, Ludwig: *Tractatus Logico-Philosophicus*. D. F. Pears and B. F. McGuinness (trans.), London, Routledge & Kegan Paul, 1961, p. 151.

[16] Edmund Husserl (1859–1938), one of the most gifted German thinkers, was the first to call his profoundly ego-searching philosophy *Phänomenologie*.

pears as soon as a thinker focuses his attention on the ordinary understanding of the world and disconnects himself from this understanding by cancelling from within himself the complete bulk of world-impressions.

The phenomenological attitude in the Husserlian sense has the single purpose of reestablishing the world within the domain of consciousness on an absolutely indubitable ground.[17] Thus to look upon the world phenomenologically is to posit it in one's consciousness uninhibitedly in one's own way, to penetrate through the diverse furniture of empirical knowledge with a view to intuiting the precognitive and pure self, to rest in the essential or *eidetic* domain. It is in this sense that the main objective phenomenologists have before their mind is a complete organization of the cognitive consciousness based on the direct perception of one's own ego.

According to Husserl, pure consciousness and its reflections are at the background of our contact with the external world. So just as the phenomenological suspension (phenomenological *epoché*) of the empirical or objective consciousness is the first step of the method of ego-searching, the transcendental suspension (transcendental *epoché*), which puts one exclusively within the domain of pure consciousness, is the next step. By achieving the suspension of the empirical ego par excellence, one eliminates oneself as sensing, desiring, representing, acting and, in general, as a consciousness environed by spatiotemporal reality. And by achieving the suspension at the transcendental level, one attains a "realm of absolute being." [18]

It is this latter realm that Husserl by his transcendental phenomenological reduction, and Indian metaphysicians by their ātmalogy posited as the most authentic goal of their methods. For Husserl held that consciousness, considered in its "purity," must be cognized as a "self-contained system of Being," as a "system of Absolute Being," which has no spatiotemporal manifestation and which cannot be penetrated through by the categories of empirical

17 For an extremely lucid treatment of this point, see Farber, Marvin: *The Aims of Phenomenology*. New York, Harper, 1966, pp. 63–78.

18 See Farber, Marvin: *Naturalism and Subjectivism*. Illinois, Thomas, 1959, p. 133.

knowledge.[19] And Aurobindo Ghose, who as one of the greatest mystic-ātmalogists in India attempted a synthesis between the infinite and the finite in experience, argued that the supramental being would descend to a universal awareness and figure as a harmony between the individual self and the total self, between the individual will and the total will, or between the individual action and the total action.[20] Śri Aurobindo was of the view that the evolution of gnostic consciousness entails a transformation of our "world-consciousness and world-action," for it extends the power of awareness to include the inner and the outer.

That the ātmalogical movement has recommended a severe intellectual discipline of the withdrawal of one's consciousness from the total empirically given world is universally known. A cessation of the discontentedness which all of us experience with our being here and now is the fundamental motivation of ātmalogy. Ātmalogists reflect a temperament that is wholly attracted towards the otherworldly. And since nothing in the realm of mundane existence is able to appease it, this temperament has inevitably evolved into a subjective engagement with transcendence or *Brahman*. A totally unrestrained and world-denying *Brahman-ātman* identity where the highest constitutive background of all experience is grasped is the professed aim of the entire tradition of Indian thinking.

It should be observed, however, that ātmalogy does not figure as a dispassionate endeavor to reach the foundation of consciousness for its own sake. It represents an internally generated, urgent need to find an exit to the wearisome fact of man's worldly being. The valuation of any activity in terms of its significance to man's salvation (*mokṣa*) has always remained central to ātmalogists' philosophization. Therefore, far from having any constructive knowledge-building program similar to that of transcendental phenomenology, and far from even suggesting that its intellectual enterprise might possess immense value to epistemological and psychological researches, what ātmalogy was bent on achieving is

[19] Husserl, Edmund: *Ideas.* W. R. Boyce Gibson (trans.), New York, Collier Books, 1962, p. 139.

[20] Ghose, Aurobindo: *The Life Divine.* American ed., New York, Greystone, 1949, pp. 865–68.

the reduction of human self to its formless (*nirguṇa*) bottom. For the formless *Brahman-ātman* unity, the pure and transcendentally intuitible ego, is the genesis of everything and, hence, the sole end of life's activity.

The phenomenological procedure in ātmalogy must be regarded as specifically value oriented because of the ideal of *mokṣa* or absolute freedom ātmalogy has all the time entailed. Keeping their eyes on the domain of transcendental Reality, ātmalogists cast doubts on the very existence of the spatiotemporal universe and often condemned it as an obstruction to man's spiritual advance towards his self-realization. While Husserl and the Husserlian phenomenologists have consistently maintained that the sphere of pure and trans-empirical consciousness is one where essences are perceived with absolute certitude and the whole amount of empirical knowledge is reestablished, to ātmalogists the highest and the most desirable mode of existence devoid of world's weary being dawns in this sphere. It will be seen in the next two chapters that there is something characteristically existentialist and negative in the way this sphere has been described by the famous Buddhist and Vedānta systems. The uniform inclination in all of them is to a kind of transcendentalism, which, considering its remoteness from man's obvious trust in the empirical world and day-to-day demands, has proved to be sublime but totally lacking in practical utility.

Chapter Six

THE PROBLEM OF BEING AND NOTHINGNESS

CONSCIOUSNESS AS MOMENTARY FLASHES

When Buddha was reflecting on the sorrowful condition of mankind, the first and foremost truth that emerged in his mind is that individual consciousness is momentary (*anitya*). Momentariness is consistent with contiguity of experienceable point-instants, and so to ascribe it to self is to imply that self is an eternally enduring flux without any permanent substance or identity underneath. That Buddha was mystified by the Upaniṣadic idea of unchangeable *ātman*, or the Self, and the idea of God, and that he refused to commit himself to any characterization in definitive terms of what the ultimate essence of existence is, is pretty well known.

Buddha's curiosity, like Bergson's and A. N. Whitehead's curiosity, to follow the constantly fleeting impressions on the Psyche was so dominant that he could not be drawn to the view that something stagnant and invariable need be postulated behind these impressions. Everything in the universe, Buddha said, is in a change. Things come into being and pass away. They never are; they always become. They are without any essence or substance or Being. Instability, disintegration, impermanence, succession, transitoriness, characterize all existence. Hence Nāgasena, a talented Buddhist dialectician of the second century B.C., replying to a question from King Milinda whether there is anything unchanging outside our physiological structure, makes it clear as Buddha himself would have done that there is no permanent soul residing in matter or body. Human soul, he says, is a bundle of five aggregates or *skandhas:* matter (*rūpa*), feeling (*veḍanā*), perception (*sāmjñā*), disposition (*saṁskāra*) and consciousness (*vijñāna*). Nāgasena reduced the self of man to an uninterrupted flow of moments.[1]

Buddha's introspective discovery that what we perceive within ourselves is eternally diverse cognitions was only apparently opposed to the Upaniṣadic theory of *ātman*. Metaphysically inclined minds, even while following Buddha's message of the impermanence of human consciousness, have recognized the region of existential identity (*tādātmya*) as the center of their searching analysis. Nevertheless, an attempt to cancel the notion of a stable and durable *ātman* was bound to extend one's imagination beyond the edge of positivity. This happened to no lesser measure in the case of Buddhists than in that of certain Western philosophers in whom the deepening of self-awareness attained an abyss of no return.

Schopenhauer, for example, in the face of the phenomenal world which he characterized as one vast will embodying wickedness, evil, suffering, antipathy, selfishness, misery and failure, craved for the total extinction of will and the attainment of non-existence. Nietzsche, despite his passion-laden aphorisms against Western values and culture, was himself unable to evolve any value, and ended in becoming a condensed nihilist. He confessed that he could never throw over the "iceberg" of incurable futility and save himself. For Eduard von Hartmann "the Unconscious," that is the spiritual principle at work behind Nature, is the primordial basis on which the world depends. All negative values emanate from "the Unconscious," a complete surrender to which, says Hartmann, would signify the final worth of life.

Thus, when Aśvaghoṣa, the Shūnya-vādins Nāgārjuna and Chandrakīrti, and the Vijñānavādins[2] or Yogāchāras Asaṅga and Vasubandhu, both belonging to the fourth century A.D., directed their observation and transcendentally unrestrained quest towards inner subjectivity, what they ostensibly contributed to the spirit of Indian thought is a philosophy of existence that did not funda-

[1] See Radhakrishnan, S.: *Indian Philosophy*, Vol. 1, pp. 391–92.

[2] They were the followers of Vijñānavāda, the tendency of subjective idealism that developed in Buddhism around the fourth century A.D. They were also called Yogāchāras, because of their practice of *yoga*.

mentally deviate from the ātmalogical heritage but proved to be extremely evolutionary, subjectivist and voidist. In a sense, Buddhism aimed at carrying ātmalogy to its furthest point, where the very experience the Vedic-Upaniṣadic sages hypostatized as the Self (*ātman*) could be seen as the non-Self or *anātman*. Hence the concept of *anātma-vāda,* claiming that there is no immutable core in things, or the doctrine that everything is momentary (*anitya, kṣaṇika*) should act as the Buddhists' extension of the metaphysics of the Upaniṣads.

Consciousness according to Buddhism is only an "intermittent series of psychic throbs, associated with a living organism, beating out their coming-to-know through one brief span of life." [3] It is by some kind of habit of recognition that one acquires the capacity to refer to oneself as a soul, a self, a mind. Consistent with their eminent theory of instantaneous or momentary Being called *kṣaṇika-vāda,* the Buddhists argue that the whole universe of our experience consists of moments following one another, and that in some mysterious fashion these moments figure as a principle of self-identity.

THE EXPERIENCE OF NOTHINGNESS

The philosophy of non-Self (*anātman*) is presented by different Buddhists in different ways. Aśvaghoṣa, the brilliant expounder of the Mahāyāna school of Buddhism, has named non-Self as *tathatā* or suchness, in order to suggest that whatever it be, it is the ultimate and absolute meaning of everything. For Nāgārjuna, it is *śūnya* or *śūnyatā,* the basic unreality of things. And for all Buddhists in general, it is *nirvāṇa,* that is, something standing beyond all attributions and predicaments. What was emphasized by Buddha himself is that the universe and individual consciousness have emerged as real and "solid" in our experience from a noumenal-transcendental and incomprehensible region of absolute nullity. The non-Self appears as the Self; the total emptiness appears as the act of creation; and the trans-phenomenal Nothingness appears as the manyness and diversity of positive entities.

Tathatā, like *Brahman,* is the ultimate Being about which no

[3] As quoted by L. de La Vallée Poussin: *The Way to Nirvāṇa.* Cambridge, Cambridge U. P., 1917, p. 48.

precise assertion is possible. Aśvaghoṣa contends that *tathatā* is beyond the subject-object duality, beyond internal variations of consciousness. As the metaphysical ground of all experience, it is supreme, indefinable and self-evident. It is the source of all that is free, peaceful, lovable, wise, perfect and serene. "It is neither that which is existent, nor non-existent . . . neither one nor many. . . . It is altogether beyond the conception of human intellect, and the best way of designating it seems to be to call it suchness."[4]

In fact, two aspects of *tathatā* are distinguished by Aśvaghoṣa in the *Mahāyāna-shraddhotpāda-shāstra* (*The Awakening of Faith in the Mahāyāna*). When considered in its ontological status, it is the intrinsic nature of all things, and as such, it is so pure and unaffected by vicissitudes of the world that it is most appropriately called *bhūtatathatā* or thatness of existence. Thus the infinite and unconditional character of *tathatā* would posit it as sheer absence of predicates, a kind of metaphysical blankness underneath total positivity.

However, had *tathatā* remained as pure and transcendental reality amenable to no reference whatsoever, it would have been senseless even to mention it meaningfully. There is another aspect of suchness, therefore, which is accessible to intellect and rooted in man's day-to-day existence. As an original foundation of the universe, *tathatā* is free from every qualification; it is as full and as comprehensive as it can be. Also it symbolizes highest self-consciousness, most encompassing spiritual realization and even ceaseless change. But somehow it conditions itself and becomes manifest as *saṁsāra,* the "wheel of births and deaths." Plurality and variegatedness, creation and decay, Aśvaghoṣa says, pertain to *saṁsāra,* which is only a mode of suchness. It is in *saṁsāra* that *tathatā* attains the unfoldment of its innate spatiotemporal potentialities, and consequently offers itself for predication and judgment.

In all its philosophic implications, *tathatā* is the ontological principle equivalent to Nāgārjuna's *śūnya.* Indeed, while *tathatā* has been described by Aśvaghoṣa with some positive stress on its

[4] As quoted by Humphreys, Christmas: *Buddhism,* pp. 148–49.

plenitude, *śūnya* is viewed as void and without any substance experienceable by human agency. There was clearly too much of nihilism in Nāgārjuna's approach to ultimate existence to make him allude to its fullness. Although on many an occasion he does state that *śūnyatā* or Nothingness is a state different from both Being and non-Being, Self and non-Self, he is reluctant to confer upon it the amplitude of that divine ideal one comes across in Parmenides's *is,* Spinoza's *causa sui,* Bergson's *élan vital,* Josiah Royce's *Absolute* or even ātmalogists' *Brahman* or *ātman*. Nāgārjuna's *śūnya* is a cipher, indeterminable, unutterable, and occult to the entire range of actual and possible knowledge.

The basic metaphysical conception with which Buddhism was preoccupied was the ultimate essence of human life shorn of all relativity and contingency. It was the search for an elementary and independent reality which incomprehensibly descends to the level of empirical existence and becomes the subject of perspectives, interest and purposes. As Stcherbatsky explains, nothing short of the full totality of all relations, "the Universe itself viewed as a Unity," the trans-phenomenal ground of all phenomena, could be regarded as ultimate reality.[5] But since the search for such a reality was to start from one's being in the spatiotemporal domain, Nāgārjuna does not hesitate to characterize *śūnyatā* or Nothingness as the abode of the worldly and yet beyond the worldly, the fleeting stream of momentary flashes and yet no-Self or no-Substance. This is why, Nothingness as an ontological entity is for him an unidentifiable principle owning a power of transmitting itself to the mundane world.

No wonder, therefore, recognizing that the essenceless and amorphous ultimate substratum of existence is beyond the grasp of mortals if they do not exercise a peculiar mystical intuition, Buddha after his enlightenment chose to communicate to others the profoundest silence of the soul with a view to enabling them to hear their own "inner voice." *Śūnyatā* and *tathatā* denote the cancellation of all statements, all views, all opinions. Even to say that *śūnya* is beyond affirmation and negation, Nāgārjuna remarks, is to speak of something which is so vague and so unquali-

[5] Stcherbatsky: *Buddhist Logic,* Vol. 1, pp. 7–8.

fiable that it cannot but stay remote from the ultimate. Thus what words and thoughts crave for defining is the element of the elements (*dharmadhātu*), absolute calmness (*śānta*), that which cannot be apprehended by any process other than nonintellectual insight, coolness, or extinction (*nirvāṇa*).

Surendranath Dasgupta points out that it could at times be objected that if all experiences are fundamentally void or *śūnya,* there would be no ground for the differentiation between moral rightness and wrongness, truth and falsity, and even between answering a philosophical question and not answering it.[6] For everything would not only be devoid of all acceptable distinctions but also inexpressible as regards its ultimate existence.

The objection, however, loses its force when it is observed that any differentiating process is valid only on the intellectual plane. For the Shūnya-vādins, a *tathāgatgarbha* (one who has attained *śūnya* or Nothingness) has completely merged in the silence of absolute existence and made himself immune from intellectual distinctions. Being the domain of uninterrupted tranquility, the experience of Nothingness, Shūnya-vāda holds, satiates all doubts, posits all reality in its proper mental setting, and transfers to the individual a sense of transcendental establishment.

The terms *tathatā, śūnyatā* and *nirvāṇa* point out a sphere of experience incompatible with any of the spheres human intellect can conceive. It is so overwhelming that it places consciousness in its entire being into total self-containment and consummation. In this sense, *śūnyatā* posits one as the center of all Being. In an attempt to map out the exact expanse of the ultimately real in Buddhism, Stcherbatsky says that the unique reality, although held to be uncharacterizable (*anirvacanīya*), has been variously named as the element of elements (*dharmadhātu*), as thisness (*idamvtā*), as the relation of elements to thisness (*idaṃpratyayatā*), as suchness (*tathatā*), as the suchness of existence (*bhūtatathatā*), and lastly as the cosmic body of the Lord, or Buddha's *Dharmakāya.*[7]

Thus to a person who has concentrated his mind on the funda-

[6] Dasgupta, Surendranath: *A History of Indian Philosophy.* Cambridge, Cambridge University Press, 1957, Vol. 1. pp. 139–40.

[7] Stcherbatsky: *The Central Conception of Buddhism and the Meaning of the Word "Dharma."* London, Royal Asiatic Society, 1923, pp. 96–99.

mental meaning of human life, the world or *saṁsāra* consists of innumerable impressions floating on absolute Nothingness. To know this Nothingness in its entire blankness is to seize the innermost sense of one's self and one's being in the world. So despite different descriptions of the region of transcendental Nothingness one meets with in Buddhists' writings, what one is led to intuit by them all is the heart of the universe, the non-Self central to the Self, the vast hollow expanse at the bottom of positive "reals."

The peculiar sort of the helplessness and impotency of verbal expression Buddhists might have felt while putting across the exact content of the *śūnya* situation is understandable when we see that life's ultimate essence is inaccessible to ratiocination. Not a few Western thinkers have given expression to what can be called the unclear innermost kernel hidden behind ratiocination itself. For instance, Bergson, with an endeavor to examine his "person in its passivity," finally comes to explore deep down himself and writes that there is at least one experience which we all grasp from within. This is the experience of "our own person in its flowing through time, the self which endures." [8] We seize ourselves, according to Bergson, as a continuity of flow ever running rich and intense. Like Buddhists, Bergson must have been overwhelmed by the succession of states in consciousness, each of which anticipates what would follow next. Man's inwardness, Bergson says, is the "unrolling of a spool." There is no living being who does not find himself reaching along the end of this spool. And however intense is one's grasp of this spool, no image or expression would communicate it.

And A. N. Whitehead, characterizing the essence of things as "process," "intentional act," or "intentional freedom," holds that what the inwardness of the subject aims at is not intellectual but affective. The subject tends towards the "lure for feeling," that is, a kind of lucid and self-creative region in which the mental acts emerge and are defined. For Whitehead, the "lure for feeling" is the main power guiding the "concrescence of feelings" by which the multifold datum of the physical happenings is collected into

[8] Henri Bergson: *The Creative Mind*. Mabelle L. Andison (trans.), New York, Philosophical Lib., 1946, pp. 79–81.

the unity of the final fulfilment of feeling.[9] It is through the "lure of feeling," Whitehead remarks, that an amorphous mental stratum, an inexplicable rhythm of objects, and finally propositions and universals attain meaning.

Again, what Camus regarded as something unlike "an infinite number of shimmering fragments . . . offered to the understanding" has utmost Buddhistic ring in it.

> . . . if I try to seize this self of which I feel sure, if I try to define and to summarize it, it is nothing but water slipping through my fingers. I can sketch one by one all the aspects it is able to assume, all those likewise that have been attributed to it. . . . This very heart which is mine will for ever remain indefinable to me. Between the certainty I have of my existence and the content I try to give to that assurance, the gap will never be filled. For ever I shall be a stranger to myself.[10]

It was mentioned that the Buddhist conception of *anātman* or non-Self was a full stretching of the Upaniṣadic conception of *ātman* or Self. There is therefore an obvious parallel between what Buddhism regards as the primitive essence of all existence and what ātmalogists would conceive as the content of *Brahman*. Thus whenever Shūnya-vādins in general and Nāgārjuna in particular sometimes warned their followers against equating *śūnyatā* with sheer vacuity, they might have meant to suggest that by the very fact that statements are made about *śūnyatā* even by those who have attained a direct intuition of it, it must be regarded as a logical and grammatical subject like *Brahman*. Any reference to *śūnyatā* would confer on it an affirmative status, a "hard" positivity. However, when *śūnyatā* qua *śūnyatā* is referred to as something intellectually inexpressible, it would be left as the negative Universal, as diehard extinction, as almost death. Nothingness in Shūnya-vādins' philosophy represents the climax of a stiff and ontologically unrestrained ātmalogy. From its eternal pervasiveness spring up instantaneous flashes of Being experienced by us as consciousness and the world. To retrace all positivity to this Nothingness was, for Buddhists, the sole way of fulfilling life's commitment.

[9] Whitehead, A. N.: *Process and Reality* (An Essay in Cosmology). Cambridge, Cambridge U.P., 1929, pp. 30–35.

[10] Camus, Albert: *The Myth of Sisyphus*. Justin O'Brien (trans.), p. 22.

Both the theory of *tathatā* and the theory of *śūnya* must be looked upon as philosophical approaches gravitating towards the thesis of ontological subjectivism so deeply ingrained in the Upaniṣadic *Weltanschauung.* The overtly affirmative characterization of suchness and the negative one of Nothingness need not constitute, as a matter of fact, any antagonism within the Buddhist approach to ultimate reality. The underlying thought in the entire system of Buddhist metaphysics is that Reality is so dynamic, abstruse and irrational that intellect can know it only as an abstraction. In a specifically mystic sense, one could remark that the primordial source of all existence is an amalgamation of Self and non-Self, Being and Nothingness, or rather Being in Nothingness and Nothingness in Being. Such an occult substratum, wholly emptied of positivity, and strangely, even of negativity, is the only correct constituent a wise man (the Buddha), the Buddhists hold, "sees" as the foundation of the phenomenal world.

Nāgārjuna in his commentary on the *Prajñāpāramitā Sūtras,* a work whose authorship is much debated by scholars, reports on what Buddha had thought regarding the nature of the supreme essence of the universe.

> The Tathāgata sometimes taught that the *ātman* exists, and at other times he taught that the *ātman* does not exist. When he preached that the *ātman* exists and is to be receiver of misery and happiness in the successive life as the reward of his own *Karma,* his object was to save men from falling into the heresy of Nihilism (Ucchedavāda). When he taught that there is no *ātman* in the sense of a creator or perceiver or an absolutely free agent, apart from the conventional name given to the aggregate of the five *skandhas,* his object was to save men from falling into the opposite heresy of Eternalism (Śaśvatavāda).

"Now which of these two views represents the truth?" Nāgārjuna asks, and states, "It is doubtless the doctrine of the denial of ātman . . ." [11] So whether it is alluded to as *tathatā,* or as *śūnya,* or as *nirvāṇa,* what is indicated is the same identical experience, namely, the deepest layer of one's own inner being and that of the universe.

[11] As quoted by Jadunath Sinha: *History of Indian Philosophy.* Calcutta, Central Book Agency, 1952, Vol. 2, p. 294.

It is interesting to note that Chandrakīrti (seventh century A.D.), whom Stcherbatsky describes as "the great champion" of the school of Mādhyamikas,[12] reaffirms in his commentaries on Nāgārjuna that the absolute, the vacuous bottom of all existence, cannot be cognized by logical methods. He shows that the world or *saṁsāra* is the false image of this Nothingness, which should be grasped only in "mystic intuition." The position Chandrakīrti did not hesitate to adopt, much in supersession of the early Buddhist logic, was of condensed skepticism, criticism and destructivism. Intellect, he says, gives us the account of what happens in common life, of our contact with objects, of our enjoyment of objects. But on establishing a rapport with what is behind the veil of objects, with their "transcendental source," the empirical reality ought to be rejected.[13]

AN EXISTENTIAL UNDERCURRENT

One cannot fail to notice an amount of very striking resemblance between the Mādhyamika view of existence and the much discussed existentialism of some of the contemporary philosophers. Indeed, there are factors peculiar to the two schools of thought that would restrain any farfetched comparison between them. Yet Mādhyamika Buddhism and existentialism are preeminently philosophies of life founded on an extremely overt anti-intellectualism. For both, human existence is so authentic a "feeling" or "awareness" that unless it is seized in all its immediate and transparent moods, one would not know its distinct metalinguistic nuance. Apart from the fact that the existentialists, like Buddhists, have given expression to a temper rarely to be found in the general rationalistic tradition of the West, the common ground that would bring the two sets of thinkers together is their determination to evolve the concept of trans-phenomenal Being or Nothingness. It would not be, therefore, out of place in the present context to dwell upon the principal metaphysical thesis that clearly establishes a concord between the two lines of thinking.

As a matter of fact, Bergson towards the beginning of this century had systematically embarked upon solving the "mystery" of

[12] Stcherbatsky: *Buddhist Logic,* Vol. 1, p. 45.
[13] *Ibid.,* p. 63.

Nothingness. At the outset he admitted that existence "appears . . . like a conquest over nought." [14] He wrote,

> . . . if something has always existed, nothing must always have served as its substratum or receptacle, and is therefore eternally prior . . . (Being) may have always been there, but the nought which is filled, and, as it were, stopped up by it, pre-exists for it none the less, if not in fact at least in right.[15]

But Bergson suspected something deceptive in the very content of such a substratum. For he said it is impossible for one to form an idea of Nothingness, to posit it in all its emptiness, to grasp it as a thing.

Finding that the mystery of Being and Nothingness is somewhat like an entanglement from which one can never get free, Bergson further said, ". . . once negation is formulated, it presents an aspect symmetrical with that of affirmation . . ." and ". . . if now we analyse this idea of Nothing, we find that it is, at bottom, the idea of Everything." [16] There is no doubt, therefore, about the fullness, the universal pervasiveness of such an entity. "It is an idea eminently comprehensive and full, as full and comprehensive as the idea of All, to which it is very closely akin." [17] Bergson asserts that what is really primordial to our experience is positive states of consciousness appearing moment after moment, and not nought par excellence.

The fundamental assumption with which Martin Heidegger, Husserl's pupil and one of the greatest shapers of existentialism, starts is that the question of Nothingness, however alien to science, is the main question philosophy should be preoccupied with. According to Heidegger, Nothingness can be "felt" at the basis of every form of logical negation. Unlike Bergson, Heidegger suggests that it is because of the ontological status Nothingness enjoys that the "revelation of what-is as such" takes place. He, like Nāgārjuna, repudiates logical approach to the question of ultimate reality, and represents that with him the whole problem of seek-

[14] Bergson, Henri: *Creative Evolution.* Irwin Edman (trans.), New York, Modern Lib., 1944, p. 300.

[15] *Ibid.*, pp. 300–301.

[16] *Ibid.*, pp. 321–22.

[17] *Ibid.*, p. 322.

ing the genesis of positivity in the transcendental realm of negativity has met with a rediscovery.

All existentialists in an open revolt against rationalists maintain that our awareness of the fact that we exist is prior to and untranslatable into logical thoughts. Man's situation in the spatio-temporal world, they say, is not a phenomenon that can be scrutinized scientifically and analytically. The transient manner of explaining logically different factors constituting human life inevitably ignores something mysterious and fleeting, vast and empty, fundamental and trans-empirical. While Kierkegaard, the Danish existentialist and the first systematic expounder of extreme anti-intellectualism, defined human existence as something alienated from its original source, namely, Being, Heidegger characterized it as nothing (*Nichts*). It is the endeavor of existentialists, much like that of Buddhists, to bring into focus the complete negative ground on which our awareness of positivity is founded. Despite diverse designations of this ground by different existential authors —Kierkegaard calls it Being and God, for Karl Jaspers it is Existenz and transcendence, for Gabriel Marcel it is the trans-phenomenal mystery—what they finally allude to is the rationally inaccessible core of human existence.

Thus Heidegger rejects the commonly accepted authority of the logical method for proving or disproving ontological reality. Since his principal concern is to explore reality through the exploration of the inwardness of the living subject, he employs a technique that is not very unlike the general Buddhist technique of "Be a light unto thyself (*ātmadīpo bhava*)." That this technique has only led him to the theory in *What is Metaphysics?* that Nothingness is the sole matter that is worth a philosophical investigation represents the nihilistic goal of his philosophization. Heidegger has opposed all absolutistic tendencies in metaphysics before him as vigorously as Nāgārjuna had opposed the Upaniṣadic tradition stressing the eternity and infinity of the *Brahman-ātman* identity. And for Heidegger, as for Nāgārjuna in particular and the whole Mādhyamika school in general, Nothingness takes the place of Being, Being conceals itself within the truth of Nothing, Being dissolves itself in Nothing. The possibility of a direct intuition of Nothingness as the condensation of one's own awareness is the nucleus around which Heidegger's existentialism and the Mādhyamika Shūnya-vāda are built.

The concept of Nothingness, in Heidegger's philosophy, emanates from what he describes as the key mood of dread (*Angst*). The entire universe of positivity is as if unable to hold on to itself, he thinks, and "slips away" into a limitless empty field.[18] When one is in dread, one feels the coming of Nothingness, of a sort of utter baselessness of everything, and eventually one is put on the course towards a transcendental vacuum. The fading away of what-is becomes so imminent that one's subjectivity proper gets involved in that very process, leaving behind a fuzzy aftermath of essencelessness and indescribability. For Heidegger, this happens but as a pointer signifying the supremacy of basic "nihilation," [19] for the genuine comprehension of which logical thought is a hindrance.

As a phenomenologist, Heidegger has held that the roots of logical creativity disclose themselves to a consciousness when the latter is grasped as the end of the "nihilation" process. "Only in the clear night of dread's Nothingness," he says, "is what-is as such revealed in all its original overtness. . . ." [20] Thus, our sense of what-is springs from an a priori negativity manifest in all logical and extralogical situations. Neither is there any ultimate what-is, nor is any instance of logical validity tenable trans-empirically. There is no absolutely "solid" fact, no feeling of absolute safety. The very movement of human consciousness towards its future or towards freedom is the expression of Nothingness at the center of human reality.[21]

Heidegger's Nothingness, like Nāgārjuna's *śūnyatā,* would not submit itself to any satisfactory articulation. It does not entail any reference to objects in the perceptible universe. It is the only experienceable domain at the background of positivity and totality. As for the essences of things of our ordinary perceptions, they telescope into this Nothingness and let their meaning fade away

[18] See Heidegger, Martin: *Existence and Being.* Introduced by Werner Brock, London, Vision Press Ltd, 1949, pp. 365–66.

[19] *Ibid.*, p. 366.

[20] *Ibid.*, p. 369.

[21] For a discussion of this question, see Sinari, Ramakant: *Reason in Existentialism.* Bombay, Popular Prakashan, 1966, pp. 64–67, 228–31.

into its infinite and ever incomprehensible compass. And so Heidegger, like Chandrakīrti the Shūnya-vādin, argues that although whenever we turn to what-is, we ignore the region of Nothing, Nothingness does not really cease to thrust itself on the act of experiencing and to plunge us into vacuity.[22]

Already a good deal of speculation prevails on what the Mādhyamikā thinkers might have referred to by the term *śūnya* or *tathatā,* and also on whether the term does not posit Nothingness as some sort of absolute reality. Although, as a matter of fact, for one's task of determining the Mādhyamikas' ethical position a complete analysis of the content of *śūnya* or void is indispensable, such an analysis would not throw any light on our understanding of what Nāgārjuna calls "the awareness of the hollowness" or "an absolute non-relational entity." As a quasi-epistemological and quasi-psychological concept, *śūnyatā* would imply Being and non-Being, or the Self and the non-Self at the same time. Looked at from this point of view, the concept is akin to not only Heidegger's *Nichts* but also to Jean-Paul Sartre's *Néant* and Merleau-Ponty's "pre-human flux."

While giving an extremely suggestive explanation of the aim of the assumption of negation in Buddhism, Zimmer remarks,

> . . . the concept of emptiness, the void, vacuity, has been employed in the Mādhyamika teaching as a convenient and effective pedagogical instrument to bring the mind beyond that sense of duality which infects all systems in which the absolute and the world of relativity are described in contrasting, or antagonistic terms.[23]

Thus, with Nāgārjuna, among all Mādhyamikas, the notion of *śūnya* appears to denote the fullest negativization of everything including *śūnyatā* itself. It is in this elementary sense that *śūnyatā* and *Nichts* have for their intensional range the whole field of ontologically intuitible emptiness, where Nothingness itself is found to nihilate itself.

Heidegger's condemnation of logic is quite consistent with his

[22] Chandrakīrti, much like Heidegger, said, "Since all logical concepts are relative and unreal, there must be another, non-relative, absolute reality, which is the Great Void." See Stcherbatsky: *Buddhist Logic,* Vol. 1, p. 539.

[23] Zimmer, Heinrich: *Philosophies of India.* New York, Bollingen Foundation, 1953, p. 523.

systematic attempt to prove that all affirmative statements in respect of ultimate reality notably miss this emptiness, that is, the primordial Nothing on the surface of which positivity seems to buoy. And in this condemnation Nāgārjuna would join hands with him. Insofar as Nāgārjuna's anti-intellectualist passion for the pursuit of life's meaning is concerned, he can be regarded as a worthy precursor of the whole movement of existential metaphysics. But his motivation, namely, to seek an exit for man from the wearisome and futile function of living in the world, is uniquely Oriental and stands in no comparison with the largely descriptive procedure of existentialism.

It is well known that for all Buddhists as for Buddha himself, no encounter of man with the world is without pain (*duḥkha*). To the Buddhist *Weltanschauung,* as indeed for the Vedic-Upaniṣadic *Weltanschauung,* the very man-and-the-world nexus entails misery and bondage. There is no aspect of this nexus which to Indian consciousness does not arouse rancor and resignation on our part against all that is phenomenal. In order to put an end to this state of affairs, one must transcend the universe and be fused with *śūnya,* which would seal all further possibilities of one's continuance in the world. Nothing short of this step, Indians have believed, could place one in perfect equanimity.

One may say that just as for Aśvaghoṣa and the Shūnya-vādins *duḥkha* or suffering reveals *tathatā* or *śūnya* at the basis of all existence, for existentialists the instances of futility in life reveal transcendental Nothingness. The "despair" and "sickness" of Kierkegaard, the feeling of "shipwreck" in Jaspers, the "nausea" of Sartre, the sense of "absurdity" in Camus, for example, are proclaimed to be the expression of a universal nought. "Dread reveals Nothing,"[24] says Heidegger with the same mood with which Buddha had prophesied that sorrow reveals that everything is founded upon *nirvāṇa* (extinction). So as moral diagnosticians of the condition of man in the world, neither Mādhyamika Buddhists nor existentialists lose sight of the fact that the very knowledge of the ultimate foundation, i.e. Nothingness, of the universe would transform our view of existence. For both these sets of

[24] Heidegger, Martin: *Existence and Being.* Introduced by Werner Brock, p. 366.

thinkers, preeminently metaphysically oriented as they are, transcendental vacuity runs forth throughout human lives. Man becomes aware of his innermost being as pure Nothing. It is this Nothing that he puts himself face to face with whenever he creates or suffers situations of anxiety and failure.

BEYOND FUTILITY?

There is an astonishing resemblance between the Mādhyamikas' and Sartre's voidist interpretations of human life. In fact, it must be observed that a way is carved for the philosophy of existence of these thinkers by the sociocultural milieu when they place themselves in relation to the world so acutely that they are unable to find anything permanently good in the purpose of existence. While both Shūnya-vāda and existentialism are, fundamentally, configurations of an inward-seeing sensibility that finds itself hindered by the phenomenal world, they sustain and propagate themselves in the eras of frustration and ennui. This is why the Shūnya-vādins like Nāgārjuna and Chandrakīrti, and the existential philosophers like Heidegger and Sartre have reasoned in a style peculiar to human consciousness thrown vis-à-vis the spatio-temporal universe, and transmitted a mood of utter pointlessness about life.

Pointlessness or futility of life has been predominantly an Eastern lamentation—a lamentation of Jainas, Hindus and Buddhists. For traditionally it was believed to be alien to the Western attitude stimulated by work, hope and lust for life. However, the fact that such a lamentation has extensively hued the nineteenth and twentieth century literature of the West shows that underneath its urge for adventures in scientific and technological planning, the West hides an unmitigated sense of insignificance regarding the ultimate purpose of life in the world. "The whole of existence is poisoned in my sight, particularly myself," wrote Kierkegaard.[25] "Consciousness is 'unhappy consciousness.' Consciousness is subject to law, which takes cognizance of the common but not of the individual. . . . The very structure of consciousness readily produces slavery," says Nicolas Berdyaev, the

[25] Bretall, R.: *A Kierkegaard Anthology*. Princeton and Oxford, Princeton and Oxford U. P., 1946, p. 11.

Russian philosopher of religion.[26] And Sartre makes Mathieu, the hero of *The Age of Reason,* utter, "A life is formed from the future just as bodies are compounded from the void." [27]

Now while existentialists with the Christian faith have not carried their view about life's pointlessness to its extreme limit but have restrained it by positing Being or God as the absolute destination of the "act of existing," Sartre more than any other modern thinker has stretched the theory of the melancholic consciousness to a point from which it can achieve a reversion only arbitrarily. He cognizes Nothingness not so much as an ontological principle unrelated to the concrete realities encountered by man; he sees it in the very functioning of the intercourse between human awareness and the world. Like Nāgārjuna, he reads the immaculate vastness of Being as void. For Sartre says, "The being by which Nothingness comes to the world must be its own Nothingness. . . . Nothingness can be conceived neither outside of being nor as a complementary, abstract notion, nor as an infinite *milieu* where being is suspended." [28] And Nāgārjuna remarks, almost in the same sweeping vein, "There absolutely are no things, / Nowhere and none, that arise (anew), / Neither out of themselves, nor out of non-self, / Nor out of both, nor at random." [29]

By going much farther than Heidegger, Sartre declares that it is because man is fundamentally a nullity that there are samples of annihilation and negativity spread over the seemingly positive situations in the world. Our negative experiences (*negatités*), such as those of absence, change, distance, regret, repulsion, loss, bad faith, have their origin in the universal and eternal Nothingness. Every being is "fragile," comments Sartre; he asks what fragility would amount to if not the probability of nonexistence of a specific entity in specific circumstances. Thus no object can escape the possibility of its annihilation or not-being. Nothing-

[26] As quoted by Maurice Friedman: *The Worlds of Existentialism.* New York, Random House, 1964, pp. 155–56.

[27] *Ibid.,* p. 138.

[28] Sartre, Jean-Paul: *Being and Nothingness.* Hazel E. Barnes (trans.), New York, Philosophical Lib., 1956, pp. 22–23.

[29] Radhakrishnan, S. and Moore, Charles A. (Ed.): *A Source Book in Indian Philosophy.* Princeton, Princeton U. P., 1967, p. 341. (Stcherbatsky's translation of Nāgārjuna's *Mādhyamika-sāstra*).

ness descends on every positive situation, on account of the inherently flexible human agency present in it.

After one of the most profound explorations in his *Being and Nothingness* through the extraordinary regions of the human Psyche, Sartre arrives at the theory that the discovery of transcendental Nothingness begins with the samples of negativity in the empirical sphere. It is from the phenomenon of inanity secreted by human selves that negativity originates and becomes real. Sartre's nihilism comes noticeably close to Nāgārjuna's voidism when he, like the Buddhist extremist, shows that distinctly negative experiences like suffering, misery, frustration, disappointment, death, etc., universally characterize human existence and thereby point out the intrinsic hollowness of all Being.

Insofar as the undeniable fact of man's life in the world is concerned, what Sartre emphasizes all along his writings is the sense of total futility man is condemned to bear as a result of his being exposed to the very world of objects where he finds no fixity, no substantial motivation for living. It is obvious that the subtlety of the existentialists' comprehension of human reality and of its complex socioethical issues cannot be looked for in the Mādhyamikas' way of thinking. However, existential ontology portrays identically the same supraintellectual domain as that ascertained by the Mādhyamikas. The fact that the atrocious forces of negativization lift up their heads constantly, even in the seemingly most hopeful circumstances as though to demonstrate that the whole idea of positivity buoys on Nothingness at the bottom, is acknowledged with equal intensity by Sartre and Nāgārjuna.

Through phenomenology and existentialism several twentieth century thinkers in the West have definitely taken a turn towards a type of philosophy that is in fundamental agreement with Eastern trans-phenomenalism. The future might reveal a growing closeness of feelings between the West and the East supported by the metaphysical concept of Being and Nothingness intuitible as a single unqualifiable expanse. The question whether any constructive social theory can be elicited from such a concept is not so pertinent to the present context. While even according to the atheistic existentialists, and especially according to Sartre, an all-embracing humanism could be set up on the basis of transcendental Nothingness, Buddhism has not so far produced any world-affirming concrete plan of human welfare. Nevertheless, to Buddhists as to existentialists, the most authentic experience around which all intellectual theories center and from which they acquire their meaning is that of being placed in a universe marked by innumerable vicissitudes.

Logically speaking, the theory of transcendental Nothingness would render contingent any program of thought or action. And if still a theory of social good, as that propounded by Sartre through his vindication of Marxism, is installed on it, it is bound to smell of arbitrariness and practical expedience. To what extent, therefore, such a theory is justifiable within the system of ultimate negativity would pose a problem to the Heideggerians and Sartrians, but not to the Mādhyamikas, who have consistently maintained in a note of overwhelming existential pathos that nothing short of the absolute extinction of world awareness is to be finally desirable.

FROM NOUGHT TO IS

One of the most puzzling developments in the history of Indian philosophy is the appearance of a division among Buddhists after the death of their Master. The Hīnayāna school with its main ramifications, the Vaibhāṣika and the Sautrāntika, and the Mahāyāna school with its offshoots, the Vijñānavāda and the Mādhyamika, sprang as distinct metaphysical movements—the former assuming that the external world is real and objectively perceptible, and the latter explaining it as an indescribable emergence from the fundamental nought.[30] Apart from the significant distinction recognizable between them as far as Buddhism in practice is concerned, the Hīnayāna and the Mahāyāna embody divergent suppositions. The Vaibhāṣikas and the Sautrāntikas are realists; the Vijñānavādins and the Mādhyamikas are transcendental idealists. To the former the only cause that can be con-

[30] "Hīnayāna" means the small carrier which is able to lead only a limited number of people towards salvation. "Mahāyāna" means the large carrier which can take many people to the same goal. The Vaibhāṣikas or direct realists and the Sautrāntikas or indirect realists are world-affirming Buddhists. The Vijñānavādins or subjective idealists and the Mādhyamikas or nihilists are world-denying Buddhists.

ceived for the origin of the representations in our consciousness is the existence of the spatiotemporal world; to the latter there is no object or impression that does not have its ultimate source in the sphere of pure and transcendental consciousness.

Despite the obvious impact of the Upaniṣadic thought on the main current of the Buddhist metaphysics, the individual attitudes of Buddhist reformers must have been responsible for the realistic doctrines of the Vaibhāṣikas and of the Sautrāntikas. By holding that things are real per se whatever be the nature of the cognitive mind, these thinkers could infer the prevalence of the results of past and present actions unified within the same consciousness. Realism was a reaction to the extreme thesis that the self consists of flashes or moments, of a continuity of impermanent points, none of which would be related to the other necessarily and intelligibly. The main contention of the Hīnayāna Buddhism that everyone has to shape the path of his own salvation would hardly stand if it does not entail a guarantee that it is the same identical consciousness that passes from bondage to salvation and the same objective world that is "suffered" and forsaken. Realism was felt to be necessary by those Buddhists who were wedded to the recognition of experiential identity.

It must be emphasized that the already mentioned concept of the nonreality of the self stays not only as the unique contribution of the Buddhist metaphysics to the sweepingly world-opposing theory of the inward-seeing Indians, but also, with the logically unrestrained negativism in the Vijñānavādins' and Mādhyamikas' reasoning, it attains an abyss of absolute nullity. Attention has been given in these pages to the Mahāyāna schools with a view to bringing out the hypothesis that it is they that clearly show the signs of immense influence of the Upaniṣadic *Weltanschauung* and, further, prove to be unavoidable in the Vedāntins' reckoning.

Vijñānavādins and Mādhyamikas are propounders of a theory of consciousness with several facets: transcendentalism, solipsism, existentialism, subjective idealism and an uncompromising pessimism. They do not admit, as the realist Vaibhāṣikas and Sautrāntikas do, the independent and external being of matter, of the elements of the mind, of sensations, or of the worldly phenomena. Their interest is not concentrated on the analysis of the universe as something objectively given. And contrary to the Vaibhāṣikas' and Sautrāntikas' conviction that the final destination of man, namely, *nirvāṇa,* is a state of indefinite and uninspiring ideal, they have looked upon transcendental experience as the highest flight of human soul, as the profoundest zero-consciousness, as an essenceless abode of pure I-ness. No important commentator on the Upaniṣadic teaching, as for instance, Gauḍapāda, Śaṅkara, Rāmānuja, could have helped taking a serious notice of their philosophical intention and program. Even otherwise, transcendentalists of all times might have found something appealing about their allusion to Nothingness as the foundation of life.

Whereas the Mādhyamikas as Shūnya-vādins are somewhat blunt in declaring their nihilistic ontology, the Vijñānavādins or Yogāchāras,[31] much like ātmalogists, shroud it behind a persistently conducted epistemological inquiry. The Vijñānavādins contend that everything inside and outside mind has its origin in the Cosmic Consciousness or Universal Mind called *ālayavijñāna.* The *ālayavijñāna* is the trans-phenomenal principle in the process of objectifying itself and as such is capable of an infinite number of phenomenal manifestations. Whatever physical or psychical nature we experience consists wholly of the mind-stuff; and it is on account of some inherent defect in perception that this mind-stuff is felt as the world. The Cosmic Consciousness (*ālayavijñāna*) alone is real; the knower-known distinction is apparent and non-existent.[32]

The phenomenal manifestations of the Cosmic Consciousness amount to a superimposition of the immanent on the transcendent, of the apparent on the real, of Is on Nought. The *ālayavijñāna* is the abode of pure, eternal, unchangeable, unthinkable, indeterminable, homogeneous and undifferentiated existence akin to the unconscious. In its ultimate constitution it is like *śūnyatā* or qualityless (*nirguṇa*) *Brahman.* It is the foundation of the illusory universe—a hypothesis which the Vijñānavāda has put forth in order to suggest that the world is not a product of pure consciousness as such but has its source in the intellectual process of individuation or dispersion. The most outstanding Vijñānavādins,

[31] The Vijñānavādins evolve a logic rooted deeply in their ontology.

[32] See Murti, T. R. V.: *The Central Philosophy of Buddhism,* pp. 104–5.

namely, Maitreyanātha (fourth century A.D.), who is credited with having established the school, Asaṅga and his brother Vasubandhu (fifth century A.D.), Dinnāga (sixth century A.D.), Dharmakīrti (seventh century A.D.), Śāntarakṣita and Kamalaśila (eighth century A.D.) have all adhered to this hypothesis.

According to the Vijñānavādins, the spatiotemporal world is not there at all. It is an emergence from thought and other mental dispositions. At the transcendental level, consciousness is unobstructed and free from the knower-known duality. Its transition to the phenomenal world, the Vijñānavādins hold, is a sort of deception suffered by man on account of his unenlightened selfhood. However, much like the Mādhyamika Buddhists, the Vijñānavādins could find no satisfactory explanation to the riddle, ever insoluble in transcendental idealism, as to what makes *ālayavijñāna* or pure consciousness manifest itself as empirical beings and individual minds.

Maitreyanātha mentions three levels of knowledge: illusory or imagined (*parikalpita*) knowledge, empirical or causal (*paratantra*) knowledge and absolute or metaphysical (*parinispanna*) knowledge. It is at the last level that enlightenment or *prajñā* dawns and the eternity of consciousness becomes transparent and self-evident to one's intellect. Empirical knowledge never entails any intrinsic certainty. It is many a time self-contradictory, conventional and refutable. It is only of ordinary (*laukika*) use; and as one approximates to the level of *prajñā,* one becomes more and more aware of its contingent and practical nature. Maitreyanātha, however, has no answer to the question why pure consciousness falls from its original trans-empirical state to the day-to-day worldly state.

Maitreyanātha's disciple Asaṅga emphasizes his Master's view that an insight into absolute consciousness is to be attained by means of a leap beyond conceptual knowledge. But even when one attains this insight, he says, one is not able to characterize absolute consciousness in decisive terms. In other words, for Asaṅga, the ontologically self-luminous *ālayavijñāna* is of the nature of one continuous intuition comprehending the noumenal basis of all phenomenal existence. To experience phenomena, therefore, as they are given to senses, i.e. without their foundation in the transcendental, is to be misled by naivete and superficiality. At the same time, once the fullness of the experience of the noumenal is grasped, the futility of the everyday objects becomes obvious, and then one's task is confined to eliminating whatever is phenomenal as essentially devoid of ultimate truth.

Asaṅga at times describes ultimate reality as *tathatā* or suchness, signifying that it is neither existent nor nonexistent, neither pure nor impure, neither finite nor infinite, neither Being nor Nothingness. It is clear that all that the world amounts to, in his opinion, is a positive manifestation of what is in itself linguistically indescribable.

A synthesis of positive and negative assertions about the ultimately real is most conspicuous in Vasubandhu's doctrine of pure consciousness. Vasubandhu was a convert from the Sautrāntika to the Vijñānavāda school and therefore represents an absolutism that tries to bridge the empirical and the trans-empirical so systematically that one would find him to be an admirable precursor of the entire tradition of Advaita (nondualist) Vedāntins from Gauḍapāda (fifth century A.D.) to Swami Prabhāvananda.[33] He supports Asaṅga's conviction that the trans-empirical reality is an intellectually ungraspable spiritual principle perennially running at the root of the universe, and that the entire plurality of subjects and objects is a stir and movement within this principle.

In his *Vijñāpti-Mātratā-Siddhi: Vimshatikā,* Vasubandhu remarks that the external world is generated by mind, like a hair lingering in the atmosphere or like a double moon which are not there are generated by the eye. All objects are the expression of pure consciousness. They have no independent reality; they are as fictitious as happenings in a dream. Vasubandhu shows that they figure mostly as projections of certain deeply rooted dispositions (*vāsanā*) of human mind. Although it is a fact, therefore, that we perceive external things as beings "outside" us, an insight into the genesis of our consciousness will convince us, Vasubandhu says, that they are the product of mind's self-observation.

[33] Swami Prabhāvananda is a renowned monk of the Ramakrishna Order. He is the most faithful exponent of the Vedānta thought, a leader of the Vedānta Society of Southern California, and the author of *The Spiritual Heritage of India* (with the assistance of Frederick Manchester). New York, Anchor Books, 1964.

Unlike Nāgārjuna and other Mādhyamikas for whom nihilation or nought is the essence of all things, Vasubandhu recognizes the appearance of all entities as mental creations. From this point of view, the Cosmic Consciousness (*ālayavijñāna*), which forms a link between blank Nothingness and the world, becomes the universal and innermost stuff of all that is. Otherwise why should our awareness of the world run into a qualityless indefinable expanse, and the latter again concretize itself as individual consciousnesses? When Vasubandhu assumes the absolute self-transforming character of pure consciousness, he is careful to indicate that man's actual sensations do not emanate from pure consciousness per se. There is a strange influence of ignorance or *avidyā* on pure consciousness, as a result of which the whole chain of mind's impressions of things starts and is perceived as real.

The spirit reflected by Vasubandhu is, in all its essential aspects, the spirit of the Upaniṣadic philosophy. In fact, he should go down in the history of Indian philosophy not only as an absolutist closely comparable to some of the well-known Western absolutists (Spinoza, Hegel, F. H. Bradley, Bosanquet, Josiah Royce, for example) but also as a forerunner of Guaḍapāda, the first systematic expounder of the ātmalogical metaphysics. Without deviating from Buddha's message of non-Self in the least, and without at the same time committing himself to Mādhyamikas' extreme voidism, he tried to steer clear in the direction of a type of transcendentalism which found its completion in the spiritualist monism of Śaṅkara.

Not that Vasubandhu has answered all the queries which pertain explicitly to his theory. For instance, if the spatiotemporal world is as false as a dream, what makes our normal and day-today consciousness adhere to it and accept it as indubitable? How does the same object present basically the same properties to all perceivers? Supposing that the world emerges as a superimposition on pure consciousness, how to account for the origin of this superimposition? These and several other questions would arise the moment we assume that whatever is offered to the empirical self is *ipso facto* contingent. The burden of tackling these questions, however, does not fall on Vasubandhu alone. Vasubandhu is one of the links in the chain of the shapers of Indian consciousness whose main aim has been to demonstrate that the world of our commonsense experience has a seeming reality against the eternal and absolute world of the ontological experience. For Vasubandhu, as for Indian idealists in general, therefore, between the two levels of reality—the transcendental and the immanent—the latter is a show put up by a mysterious universal power, namely, *māyā* or illusion.

Like all Buddhists Vasubandhu recognizes the distinction between practical or mundane truth and transcendental or absolute truth. Incidentally, while some Buddhists have called the former *saṃṛti satya,* others have referred to it as *vyāvahārika satya.* The absolute truth in the same way has been named as *paramārtha* and *parinispanna satya.* It is quite probable, as V. Bhattacharya has pointed out, that this theory of two truths was borrowed by Śaṅkara from the Buddhists through their influence on Gauḍapāda.[34] Vasubandhu likewise places especial emphasis on the transcendental truth, and in contrast with Nāgārjuna's *śūnyatā* and Aśvaghoṣa's *tathatā,* posits transcendence as an all-comprehensive substantial entity, a concretely realizable domain of peace and joy, whose reflection in the universe we ordinarily experience is inauthentic and totally misleading. Man is a victim to this inauthentic experience. It is just there, Vasubandhu says, like a false elephant created by a magician's wand. Indeed the mystery is how consciousness from one tier shifts on to the other tier, and how while functioning on the transcendental tier, it develops the notion of falsity with regard to that which happens to it empirically.

Vasubandhu's influence on later Buddhists is considerable. For about three hundred years subsequent to Vasubandhu's period, however, Buddhism might have felt a tremendous need of logicians who could withstand the growing challenges from the debaters holding orthodox or dissenting metaphysical views. For around this time a movement for establishing and defending Buddhism as a school of logic—acknowledged widely as Svatantra-Vijñānavāda [35]—appeared on the scene, and with its four most

[34] As quoted by T. M. P. Mahadevan: *Gauḍapāda: A Study in Early Advaita,* p. 189.

[35] So called because of its acceptance of the Vijñānavāda metaphysics, and its casting it in a new pattern to suit logical requirements.

original thinkers, Dinnāga, Dharmakīrti, Śāntarakṣita and Kamalaśila, it waged a philosophical war against the Naiyāyikas and the Mīmāṁsakas. Although all these four thinkers accepted Vasubandhu's doctrine of pure consciousness (*ālayavijñāna*), they redefined it by reverting to the doctrine of momentariness (*kṣaṇika-vāda*). It may be mentioned that the four-pronged Buddhist ontology of non-Self (*anātman*), Nothingness (*śūnyatā*), pure consciousness (*ālayavijñāna*) and Universal Flow came to an admirable articulated shape with the Svatantra-Vijñānavāda movement and became a lasting contribution to the Indian logic.

In a sense the Svatantra-Vijñānavāda represents an exceptional success Buddhism attained towards its last days in India. It constructed a theory of knowledge too amorphous to be refutable, and by its help it advanced one of the most dynamic and intuitionist pleas for subjectivism. Yet nothing could help arrest the rapid declining of the impact of Buddhism on Indians; and by the time Kamalaśila's career had come to an end, Buddhism must have begun to feel the shortage of scholars.

Indeed one of the mysteries in the history of Indian philosophy that has not been fully explained so far is the defeat of the Buddhist thought against the intellectual onslaughts of ātmalogists, and its eventual disappearance from India. As a matter of fact, the central philosophy of Buddhism is not antagonistic to the Upaniṣadic metaphysics. On the contrary, one can venture to state that not only Buddha himself but also his followers had exhibited in their doctrines an inward-seeing sensibility so akin to that to be found in the Upaniṣads.

Apart from the distinctive features of their basic assumptions, the ground of similarily between the *Weltanschauung* of Buddhists and that of Hindus is so vast that one finds it difficult to conceive that the two sets of thinkers might have come to an open clash. Of course, at a certain juncture they must have awakened to their own institutional interests and desired the extinction of their opponents. But could these interests have been so stringent as to lead one group expel the other?

At least in two ātmalogists, it appears, the elements of dissension with the Buddhist transcendentalism happen to be at their minimum: Gauḍapāda and Śaṅkara. Neither Gauḍapāda nor Śaṅkara is a chaste ātmalogist. They are fine amalgamations of Nāgārjuna's nihilism and Vasubandhu's absolutism and the Upaniṣadic ātmalogy, with a heavy bent towards the last. It is quite probable that had Gauḍapāda and Śaṅkara not descended on the scene of Indian philosophy, Buddhism would have taken firm roots in India and by subtly converting the ardent adherents of the Vedic-Upaniṣadic idealism, would have absorbed them into the nihilistic metaphysics.

Chapter Seven

THE VEDĀNTA VIEW OF BEING AND THE WORLD

GAUḌAPĀDA

THE earliest systematic treatment of the principal thesis of the Upaniṣads that "*Brahman* or the Absolute is alone real and all else is *māyā* or appearance" is contained in Gauḍapāda's commentary on the *Māṇḍūkya Upaniṣad.* Gauḍapāda (fifth century A.D.), a teacher of Śaṅkara's teacher and an ardent student of Mahāyāna Buddhism and of the Upaniṣads, is the real precursor of Śaṅkara's *māyā-vāda.* A great part of the force of Gauḍapāda's metaphysics is again the result of his extreme reliance on the Buddhist schools of Shūnya-vāda and Vijñānavāda. And it is because Gauḍapāda has openly manifested this reliance in his works that he has stayed a subject of controlled admiration on the part of the passionate followers of the Upaniṣads.

However, Śaṅkara is ostensibly receptive whenever he refers to him. Besides, the impact of Gauḍapāda's reasoning on Śaṅkara is so great that, as Mahadevan has said, Śaṅkara must have found in his words the spring of eternal life.[1] But it can be shown that the ideas of nonorigination and nonbirth (called *ajāti-vāda*), attributed to Gauḍapāda and noticeably embodied by Śaṅkara in his theory of causality, have their seeds in the non-Upaniṣadic tendencies prevalent at the time.

Gauḍapāda, like Parmenides of Elea, argues that we cannot speak of the origination or transformation of anything in the world. For to speak in that vein is to presuppose that whatever is, was not there before it came into existence. Things have no origi-

[1] Mahadevan, T. M. P.: *Guaḍapāda: A Study in Early Advaita,* p. 240.

nation, no birth, no beginning. They just are; and all the conceivable distinctions, such as those between mind and matter, the knower and the known, the nonexistent and the existent, the beginning and the end, bondage and release governing them are illusory. One's seeing such distinctions, Gauḍapāda remarks, is like seeing the footprints of birds in the sky.

Everything that is, is *aja;* origination (*utpāda*) is inconceivable. Gauḍapāda commands the metaphysical acumen reminiscent of Parmenides's when he demonstrates his nonorigination idea by means of four main truths: (1) The nonexistent cannot have the nonexistent for its cause; (2) the existent cannot have the nonexistent for its cause; (3) the existent cannot be the effect of the existent; and (4) the existent cannot be the effect of the nonexistent.[2] Therefore, the entire domain of spatiotemporal beings and psychic impressions is a massive panorama of illusions—the effect of *māyā.* The very attachment we have to things that surround us is based on our naive regard to contingency and practical utility. We must know, says Gauḍapāda, that the world of which we have experience consists of innumerable unreal constituents and relations emerging like a chain of imaginations and fantastic designs. They constitute a dread-like smoky veil over the pure and self-luminous transcendental principle of *Brahman,* whose real nature becomes transparent when one rips off the bubble of immanent consciousness.

In the *Māṇḍūkyakārikā,* Gauḍapāda mentions three expressions or levels of consciousness: (1) consciousness as a wakeful perceiver of worldly occurrences, (2) consciousness as an experiencer of dreams, and (3) consciousness at the deep level, where no concrete object is perceived. Consciousness at this third level is essentially closest to the most ideal fourth tier, which according to Gauḍapāda is not accessible to any rational description or understanding. Self-awareness at the highest tier comprises the most integrated subject-object unity enduring beyond time and space. Within this unity is involved the wholesome realization of the self—the realization of an infinite emptiness, which is also seen as the foundation of all phenomenal beings. When this germinal

[2] See *Ibid.,* p. 143.

experience springs up, the entire creation is discovered to be *māyā,* a massive dream, and all our psychophysical reactions to it are dispassionately identified as the imagination of the worldly soul or *jīva.*

Ingenious interpretations of the ideas of past thinkers have always formed an important part of the discipline of philosophy. And amidst different tendencies in Indian philosophies, when one examines the development of the Vedānta, one comes to note that it is a philosophy wholly in this sense. The Vedāntins' thoughts telescope into the Upaniṣadic presuppositions so completely that they give a semblance of originality. Thus the entire class of Vedānta thinkers constitutes one single movement, admitting of diverse shades inside it but never digressing from the essential sayings of the Upaniṣads. Even Śaṅkara, the most influential in the whole bulk of old speculative thinkers, and Aurobindo Ghosh, the most articulate Vedāntin of the present century, so far as the motivation of their idealism is concerned are merely expounders of Upaniṣadic consciousness as it is found interpreted in Gauḍapāda's writings.

ŚAṄKARA ON REALITY AND APPEARANCE

Śaṅkara (A.D. 788–820), the most remarkable rationalist India has ever produced, criticized the Sāṅkhya school for its reluctance to look upon the *Puruṣa* of *puruṣas,* or the Self of selves, as the final mover of *prakṛti* or Nature.[3] He accepted the Sāṅkhya doctrine of *satkārya-vāda,* but reset it in such a manner that he explained the effect as only an appearance (*vivarta*) of the cause. By positing the Supreme Being (*Brahman*) as the ultimate cause of all existence, and by annulling the very reality of the world, he propounded a theory which has come to be known as *Brahma-vivarta-vāda.*

It is this theory that has left an unerasable influence on the Indian mind by offering it some kind of defence mechanism and consolation against the total disagreeable worldliness man is condemned to. At all times the Indian populace has been impressed by the belief that since all happenings in the world are unreal, one

[3] Shankarāchārya: *Shāriraka-Bhāsya.* N. L. Shastri (Ed.), Bombay, Nirnaya Sagar Press, 1927, II, 2, 2.

need not take life with any significant attachment. One's goal lies in the attainment of what is at the root of appearance, namely, *Brahman.*

According to Śaṅkara, the universe has appeared as the effect of something which is absolutely real (*satyam*), eternally conscious (*jñānam*) and infinite (*anantam Brahman*). The universe is a variegated pattern and cannot have originated from a cause which is not absolutely perfect and self-caused. This self-caused cause, namely, *Brahman,* Śaṅkara says, expresses itself through an infinite number of things (*nāma-rūpa*), all of which are appearances. The nature of an appearance is such that it is true in practice (*vyavahārika*), but has no metaphysical (*pāramārthika*) status. And yet the fact is that all these appearances depend upon and are internal to the Supreme Spirit (*Brahman*), which is their material cause (*upādāna-kārana*) and efficient cause (*nimitta-kārana*).

Thus the Sāṅkhya imagination that *puruṣas* are completely free from the process of creation and that they are intelligent but silent seers of the world is rejected by Śaṅkara. His causal theory, unlike that in the Sāṅkhya, is strictly for the elucidation of the link between spatiotemporal existence and the spiritual impetus lying underneath. Actually, Śaṅkara moulds *satkārya-vāda* to suit his purpose of explaining the gulf between the transcendental and the empirical, the eternal and the temporal, the supremely real and the dubitable. The result is that he gives us a notion of causality in which the cause and the effect do not belong to the same category, that is, the cause is real and the effect is only apparent.

It might have appeared to Śaṅkara that if *puruṣas* are what the Sāṅkhya describes them to be, they would never have fallen into bondage and suffered the conditions of birth, suffering, death and ignorance. There is no reason whatsoever why *puruṣas* should prompt themselves to have a contact (*saṁyoga*) with *prakṛti,* and thereby should create a situation from which they must liberate themselves. By confining *satkārya-vāda* to the domain of *prakṛti,* and by leaving the influence of *puruṣas* on *prakṛti* utterly mysterious, the Sāṅkhya thinkers inevitably resorted to some kind of esoteric abstractionism. Perhaps by recognizing the fact, therefore, that the plurality of such *puruṣas* carries no specific importance insofar as the nature of their relation to *prakṛti* is concerned, the

Sāṅkhya commentaries like Vāchaspati's *Tattvakaumudī,* Gauḍapāda's *Sāṅkhya-kārikā-bhāṣya* and Vijñānabhikshu's *Sāṅkhya-pravachana-bhāṣya* have implied that the *Puruṣa* can be conceived as one single Spirit. That Śaṅkara heavily leaned on this implication while constructing his own concept of *Brahman* hardly needs any especial emphasis.

Śaṅkara's basic assumption that *Brahman* and the world would not be seen as the cause and the effect respectively had man been at once gifted with a supernatural and unalloyed insight to perceive transcendence qua transcendence is essentially a restatement of Gauḍapāda's position. From Śaṅkara's explanation it would follow that the *Brahma-vivarta* (the appearance of *Brahman*) is manifest only to ordinary human consciousnesses or *jīvas;* and so, the former is what it is perceived to be because of the presence of the latter. His renowned argument that *Brahman* appears as the world because of *avidyā* or ignorance must be understood to mean that it is the element of naïveté, the unenlightened common sense, that deprives consciousness from grasping the exact structure of the Real, i.e. the foundation of the worldly.

Śaṅkara was too inward-seeing a subjectivist to have signified by such terms as *vivarta, māyā* and *pratibhāsika* (all meaning, appearance or illusion) something objective and empirical arising out of *Brahman.* Looked at from the ontological point of view, therefore, *Brahman* is not the cause of anything. (The category of causality does not apply to it.) Śaṅkara finds it necessary to infer, however, that *Brahman* is the cause when he seeks to justify his initial postulate that the world in time and space is dependent on *Brahman.* Nevertheless, it would be highly bewildering to suggest that *Brahman* as the cause creates itself as the apparent effect. Scores of questions would arise from such a statement: why and how does *Brahman* produce its appearance? What would be the disposition of *Brahman* towards the world? Is *Brahman's* transition into the world as necessary to *Brahman* as the dependence of the world on *Brahman* is necessary to the world?

Śaṅkara erects his system on the basis of his experience that the Supreme Reality symbolizes *sat-cit-ānanda* (being-intelligence-joy)—the trans-empirical origin and destination of all phenomena. Consequently, he is compelled to resort to an intellectual explanation as to how *Brahman* becomes the world. That is why the relation construed by him between the worldly and the otherworldly, or the immanent and the transcendental, has so much in common with the monistic metaphysics in the West—a metaphysics rooted in the basic intellectual need to show how the phenomenal world issues forth from Being. Śaṅkara sees, as Hegel, F. H. Bradley, Kierkegaard, Josiah Royce and Karl Jaspers have seen, that the philosophical imperative preeminently figures in the form of a logical demand to justify the universe in relation to the beyond.

Incidentally, Nāgārjuna has not felt an imperative of this kind. Not only did he condemn intellect, but he also goes to the extent of considering all that is thought of as referring to the inauthentic and the superficial. For the entire Mādhyamika thought, despite its frequent ingenious vindications that it is a nonnihilist view of existence, the ultimately real is nothing else than the unqualifiable. And as it has been shown already, in holding that Nothingness, or the incomprehensible void is the absolute ground of the universe, the Mādhyamika much more than the Vedānta has come to have today a remarkable resemblance to atheistic existentialism.

ŚAṄKARA AND BRADLEY

There is an impressive similarity in Śaṅkara's and F. H. Bradley's assumptions regarding the status of the world and regarding the relation of the world to Being. In the first part of his *Appearance and Reality,* Bradley attempts to show that the ordinarily experienced phenomena, or rather categories of phenomena, such as time, space, cause, things and the self, do not belong to the Real. Reality, he says, does not consist of things which we think to be real. Indeed, to say that something is not real does not amount to saying that it is unreal but that it is appearance.

Bradley's reasoning becomes highly poignant when he goes to indicate that the expression "appearance" is an "implied metaphor" and therefore capable of being misunderstood.[4] His remark should be pertinent to our understanding of the same word in Śaṅkara's philosophy. For much of the confusion prevalent in the

[4] Bradley, F. H.: *Appearance and Reality.* London, Swan Sonnenschein & Co. and New York, Macmillan, 1908, pp. 485–86.

traditional interpretations of Śaṅkara must be attributed to the unwanted rigidity with which his conception about the position of the world has been viewed. For Śaṅkara, as for Bradley, Reality is the cause of the world in the sense in which for modern physicists the bunches of corpuscles or waves in front of me are the cause of what appears to me as a table, a notebook, a pen, a heap of papers, etc. The emergence of these articles is true to my perception; however, they do not have any reality per se, that is, they are only the manifest forms of something discrete and vacuous.

Śaṅkara could not possibly be unaware of the logical implication that if *Brahman* is not subject to causal determination, then the world, for whose being *Brahman* forms the ground (*adhiṣṭāna*), also ought to remain free from causality. Yet, it cannot be denied that we perceive the world as universally governed by the sequence of causes and effects. To show, therefore, that the causal order of the universe is quite compatible with the non-causal Supreme Being is the principal endeavor of Śaṅkara's system. And fundamentally, he, like Bradley, succeeds in this endeavor inasmuch as he regards our world-experience as having no status beyond the confines of our ignorant or naive selves. Being inseparable from our bondage-oriented life, the world responds to our natural dispositions, and makes us incur punishment on ourselves according to the deeds done by us.[5] For Śaṅkara, the appearance of the world has a moral significance. It is as if the result of our being alienated from the Absolute.

THE INDIVIDUATION OF THE ABSOLUTE

According to Śaṅkara, the universe is there not as an ontological extension of *Brahman* but as an aspect of it perceptible by man's empirical view. Śaṅkara's most misunderstood reasoning that the world is like an illusory snake seen in a rope does not attribute to the world total nullity. The world results from the fact of man's beclouded intellect—an intellect to which what is ultimately and everlastingly real is inaccessible.

Strictly speaking, Śaṅkara sidetracks the whole issue of the rec-

[5] For a particular emphasis on this point, see Introduction to *Shankar-Brahma-Sūtra-Bhāṣya* (Marathi). Vasudevshastri Abhyankar and D. T. Chandorkar (trans.), Poona, D. E. Society, 1957, pp. 16–18.

onciliation of the transcendental *Brahman* with the causally bound universe by making the latter hinge solely on the limitedness of man's perspective. Thus the theory of causality in his system takes for granted the bound state of the souls, the individuation of *Brahman,* and the dispersion of Being through births and rebirths. Were there no bound souls, there would have been no world. However obvious may be its reality to our day-to-day perception, the world would just cease to exist as soon as all souls merge within their absolute abode, namely, *Brahman.*

It has been shown already that Śaṅkara is a strong upholder of the Upaniṣadic thesis that man's life in the deceptive, fictitious, dreamlike and fleeting world, which is totally inauthentic in comparison with the domain of indeterminable and qualityless *Brahman,* is his fall. The indubitable truth, Śaṅkara says, is that the pure and self-luminous sphere of the Supreme Spirit is not grasped by our practical reason but by the suprarational and metaphysical power inherent in everyone. This power is the power of the *ātman,* the individuated form of *Brahman.* This power enables *ātman* to know itself.

In what relationship towards individual selves (*ātman*) does *Brahman* stand? Moreover, does Śaṅkara, who is regarded by some critics as a Nāgārjunite or pseudo-Buddhist, imagine unqualified *Brahman* to be ontologically commensurate with the ultimate reality pursued by the Buddhists?

Considered wholly as the domain of extraordinary otherworldly intuition, the reality which Buddhists have termed as *tathatā, śūnyatā ālayavijñāna* or *nirvāṇa* (literally, blowing out) is the same as that which Śaṅkara has characterized as the intellectually indefinable *Brahman.* Therefore, whenever a difference between the two concepts is observed in a somewhat marked manner by some Śaṅkarites by attributing to *Brahman* pure consciousness, pure being, pure blissfulness, etc., and by attributing to *nirvāṇa* pure negativity, stress is given on the linguistic aspect of these concepts. In fact, *Brahman* like *nirvāṇa* is a sphere to which thought has no access. It is the residuum obtained on the cancellation of all that is ratiocinated and intellectually understood. Like Buddhists' "glow" of momentary consciousness, it is said to be apprehended through the process of inward-seeing and at a level where the empirical domain no more figures as something real.

It was shown earlier that Śaṅkara carried forward Vasubandhu's golden mean between the spiritualism of the Upaniṣadic sages and the extreme voidism of the Mādhyamikas. This can also be inferred from the fact that Śaṅkara nowhere characterizes *Brahman* in wholly unambiguous terms. Even when he assumes that *Brahman* is an absolutely uncontaminated essence in relation to which the whole spectacle of worldliness would be seen as a fiction, he seems to voice the combined view of Nāgārjuna and Gauḍapāda. What is the essence of *Brahman* then if no logically satisfying assertions about it are possible?

According to Śaṅkara, our recognition of the phenomenal or *vyāvahārika* existence gives us only the empirical and pragmatic reality. The standpoint to which we are accustomed in our ordinary life originates not from our transcendental or *pāramārthika* being but from a misguiding and deluding agency, called *avidyā* or ignorance, operating in us. *Avidyā* inauthenticates *Brahman* or *ātman,* and reduces it from the trans-empirical (*pāramārthika*) to the empirical (*vyāvahārika*) tier.

Now, to say that *Brahman* is twofold—*pāramārthika* and *vyāvahārika,* or *nirguṇa* (qualityless) and *saguṇa* (having qualities)—is to imply that both authenticity and inauthenticity, transcendence and immanence can be predicated of it. Of course, the two characteristics of *Brahman* respond to two distinct points of view. Understood as the innermost subjectivity perceived from within, *Brahman* or *ātman* constitutes a region about which contingent statements make no sense. As a matter of fact, the term *jīva* (soul) suggests in the whole Vedānta tradition the condemnation of *Brahman* or *ātman* to worldliness, to the mundane process of births and rebirths, to bondage. Even a cursory glance at the Vedic literature would indicate that problems of great complexity have arisen in Indian philosophy from the attempts to understand the why and the how of this condemnation. The very assumption, however, that the *jīva* represents the inauthentication of *Brahman* really means that in its essence, in its *ātman,* every *jīva* is *Brahman* itself.[6]

The question of the *Brahman-ātman* relation or, more precisely, of the *Brahman-jīva* relation has proved to be central to the specu-

[6] *Ibid.,* p. 9.

lations of most of the post-Śaṅkara thinkers, particularly to those of Bhedābheda-vādins, Rāmānuja, Madhva, Nimbārka, Vallabha and, in our own time, of Aurobindo Ghose. This is obviously due to the fact that they, like Śaṅkara, adhere to the *ātman-jīva* distinction in the Upaniṣadic spirit by positing *ātman* as itself *Brahman* or the Universal Self, and *jīva* or the individual ego as its inauthentication.

The distinction between *ātman* and *jīva* is clearly reason oriented. But when this distinction is looked at from the standpoint of subjectivity or inwardness, both *ātman* and its inauthentic form *jīva* appear as two aspects of the same transcendental consciousness. The *jīva,* from this standpoint, sinks almost to nonexistence or *māyā*. Not that by this method the problem of the transcendence-immanence relation is dissolved to the satisfaction of intellect. It is certainly freed from developing into an impasse and is brought down to an experiential or existential level. That is why for the Vedāntins and Buddhists, as for the phenomenologists and existentialists, the contingent nature of the phenomenal world is established as soon as our penetration into the necessary and self-evident transcendental domain becomes a fact. The *jīva* is then found to be a creation of naïveté, a superficial *imagerie,* a sequence of commitments generated by the deeds of the past lives.

Some more reflections on this problem would belong to what I have later called the phenomenology of *māyā*—a sort of explorative egology seeking to describe various configurations of consciousness. When viewed in the light of this, transcendental consciousness or *Brahman* posits itself as a domain of inward-seeing to which nothing positive would be ascribable. The most embarrassing feature of our conceiving this domain, however, would be to know why the plurality of egos should emerge from the immaculate expanse of eternal consciousness. The relation of the *ātman* to the *jīva* does not become logically warranted even from the fact that the latter is the worldly being entered into by the former due to its action-oriented status.

REALITY AS DIFFERENCE AND NONDIFFERENCE

Śaṅkara died in the Himalayas at the age of thirty-two. He had extraordinarily combined in himself severe discipline, missionary zeal, tenderness, rebelliousness against the regressive social mores, and a spirit of detachment from the concerns of the world. His dedication to the task of social reformation despite his action-precluding metaphysics, reminds one of Socrates. Perhaps such a dedication, a kind of compassion-laden humanism, resulted from the doctrine of the meaninglessness of the worldly life which Śaṅkara had fully imbibed within himself.

One of the most significant effects of Śaṅkara's philosophic mission was that Southern India of the sixth and seventh centuries witnessed Hinduism as a powerful movement in the face of rapidly spreading Buddhism and Jainism. It cannot be doubted that so far as the Indian scene is concerned, Śaṅkara's ambiguous and yet grandiose, hypnotic and robust transcendentalism was too influential for even Rāmānuja (eleventh century A.D.), a popular theist, to surpass. And for that matter, it remains unrivalled even to this day by any of the world-affirming tendencies India imitates from the West.

Like Śaṅkara, a chain of thinkers, although none so original as Śaṅkara, have taken up the question of the *Brahman-jīva* relation, and reasoned in a manner that has left his cleverly construed nondualism (*advaita*) partly corrected and partly condemned. Bhāskara's and Yādavaprakāsha's doctrine that unity and plurality in the universe are equally real, Rāmānuja's idea of the nondualism of the distinct many (called *viśiṣṭādvaita*), Madhva's dualism (*dvaita-vāda*), Nimbārka's all-inclusive dualistic nondualism (*dvaitādvaita-vāda*) and Vallabha's pure nondualism (*śhuddhādvaita-vāda*) portray causality to suit their own specifically metaphysical requirements. We shall see in what way each of these theories has pushed Being or the transcendental to a sphere of experiential necessity.

Bhāskara (A.D. 1000), in his commentary on the *Brahma-Sūtra* known as the *Bhāskarabhāṣya,* put forward the view that *Brahman* is a unity and identity. And yet, he argued, it effects the universe as its own diversification and plurality. *Brahman* in its evolved form appears as the world consisting of an infinite number of characteristics. The latter, therefore, are as real as *Brahman,* and their limitations represent the limitations of *Brahman* itself.[7] The

[7] Radhakrishnan, S.: *Indian Philosophy,* Vol. 2, pp. 670–71.

handicaps (*upādhis*) we witness in the world around us, Bhāskara says, are handicaps of *Brahman* itself. The world and *Brahman* cannot be conceived to function on two different tiers. The material nature of the world, the suffering state of the *jīvas,* the law of *karma,* the experience of bondage, are all there in *Brahman.* Thus, *Brahman* is *bhedābheda,* that is, difference and nondifference within one and the same absolute Being.

Bhāskara is a forceful critic of the theory of the nonexistence of the world. His endeavor is to establish a synthesis between the absolute and the immanent without labelling any aspect of Being as *māyā* or illusion. *Brahman,* he says, is one and many, identical with itself and diversified within, and otherworldly and worldly at one and the same time. It forms the underlying spirit of the whole domain of differentiation and plurality. Just as the waves are manifestations of the potentiality of the sea, and the same sea appears to be different when it is in the form of waves, so the universe is the manifestation of the same identical (*abheda*) *Brahman,* which appears to be different (*bheda*) in its spatiotemporal status.[8]

There is no thing that does not form a part, a facet, an expression of *Brahman.* Indeed, we should not infer from the imperfections of various entities in the world that *Brahman* is itself imperfect. Bhāskara believes that the world is neither absolutely identical with *Brahman* nor absolutely different from it. Although no region of human experience, however inconsistent and absurd and limited, can lie outside the Absolute, it would not be legitimate to say that therefore the Absolute shares the ignorance (*avidyā*) of its manifest forms, namely, *jīvas.* According to Bhāskara, the *jīvas* are created by *Brahman* and finally absorbed by it as, for instance, the sun's rays are created and absorbed by the sun.

For Bhāskara, as for Yādavaprakāsha (A.D. 1100), another famous bhedābheda-vādin, every *jīva* is made to descend to the state of ignorance because it is to suffer limitations and handicaps imposed upon it by its past deeds. But ignorance cannot hold the *jīva* in bondage forever; for being primordially infinite and pure, it is bound to free itself from its mundane condition. A *jīva* and

[8] Dasgupta, Surendranath: *A History of Indian Philosophy,* Vol. 3, p. 6.

its world are themselves *Brahman* temporarily shrouded by mind's dispositions. *Brahman*'s transformation into beings in the world, Bhāskara remarks, does not amount to *Brahman*'s being exhausted or polluted.[9] The transformation proves that all worldly beings are fundamentally spiritual. And in this lies both *Brahman*'s apparent suffering and *jīvas'* perennial will to thrust themselves towards transcendental selfhood.

As a matter of fact, it is not with Bhāskara that the *bhedābheda* concept of Reality comes into currency for the first time. Two centuries before him Śaṅkara had mentioned and criticized the *bhedābheda-vāda* of one Bhartṛprapancha, according to whom *Brahman* is one and many, cause and effect, nondifference and difference at one and the same time. Still, Yādavaprakāsha has something interesting to contribute to the *bhedābheda-vāda.* He agrees with Bhāskara in maintaining that *Brahman* has produced the world, in the sense that the world is really a change internal to *Brahman.* But he contradicts Bhāskara in maintaining the fundamental purity of *Brahman.*

Yādavaprakāsha argues that material things and human consciousness are states (*avasthā*) of Supreme Reality and as such they simultaneously represent oneness and variety, nondifference and difference within *Brahman.* Subscribing to the doctrine that the world is the transformation of *Brahman* (*Brahmapariṇāma*) which his pupil Rāmānuja further developed, Yādavaprakāsha inserts within the *bhedābheda* conception a kind of two-order notion without in any explicit way suggesting a dualism of Supreme Reality and the universe. Consciousness (*cit*), matter (*acit*) and God (*Īśvara*), and through them various phenomenal changes, Yādavaprakāsha says, are transformations of *Brahman.*[10] However, the fact that we do not have a clear comprehension of these transformations proves that we are subject to a mysterious functioning of ignorance (*avidyā*) in us.

With only the extinction of ignorance we can hope to see the exact relationship of *Brahman* to its differentiations and forms. To be in the world, to be a *jīva,* is thus to be condemned to finitude. In order to overcome this state, Yādavaprakāsha holds, one

[9] *Ibid.*, p. 10.
[10] Ibid., p. 301.

must bring one's *ātman* back to its original self-luminous and everlasting composure. To Yādavaprakāsha, *Brahman* and God are one and the same Being.[11]

An absolutism of the Leibnizian variety—a kind of spiritualistic pluralism, with every entity stationed in it with logical and existential necessity—is perhaps the most balanced and popular form Śaṅkara's *māyā-vāda* could anticipate within the framework of the Vedānta philosophy. The man who showed utmost awareness of such a form with an admirable degree of inventiveness in it is Rāmānuja, at first a follower and later a rebel of Yādavaprakāsha's teachings.

THE DUALISM OF THE DISTINCT MANY

Rāmānuja is more like a saint than a philosopher. As the founder of a theistic metaphysics—which, incidentally, has an elegance about it comparable to that of Thomism in the West—he has left an unerasable impact on pious Hindu minds. He is ever revered as a flawless believer in the meaningfulness of worldly action.

Rāmānuja's initiation into public life as a preacher started suddenly when his master Yamunāchārya died. The story goes that Rāmānuja, as he approached Yamunāchārya's corpse, found three fingers of its right hand folded. The phenomenon was interpreted as symbolizing that Rāmānuja was to fulfil three wishes of the dead master, the most significant being to prepare and propagate a treatise on the *Brahma-Sūtra*.[12] Thus unlike Śaṅkara, Rāmānuja was roped into the task of interpreting the *Brahma-Sūtra* by some kind of accident.

Rāmānuja's treatise on *Brahma-Sūtra,* called the *Śribhāṣya,* stands a testimony to the experience of those raptures of religiosity for which he was famous. It is said that what he recorded in the *Śribhāṣya* were the sayings of God that were directly communicated to him. Nowhere in his philosophy can one find the stark

[11] *Ibid.*, p. 302.

[12] *Brahma-Sūtra,* also called the *Vedānta-Sūtra* or *Śāriraka-Sūtra,* embodies the doctrine of the unqualified Supreme Reality or *Brahman* and explains the relation between *Brahman* and the world. The authorship of the *Sūtra* is attributed to Bādarāyaṇa, who systematized in it the philosophical thought of the Upaniṣads.

nihilism of the Mādhyamika brand. He considers no aspect of human experience as illusory or unreal (*māyā*). His is a way of thinking we frequently come across in those whose hearts secrete perennial love towards things and men by thinking that all these are forms of God. *Brahman* or God, he says, is the Supreme person (*purusottama*) who expresses Himself through an infinite number of modes and attributes.

According to Rāmānuja, it is wrong to characterize *Brahman* as indeterminate (*nirguṇa*) and determinate (*saguṇa*), corresponding to its pure or transcendental and empirical states respectively. For *Brahman* is always in possession of absolute knowledge (*jñāna*) and supreme power (*śakti*), both of which jointly figure in regard to the universe as its generating, preserving and destroying *élan*. *Brahman* and God are identical. Having created the universe out of Himself, God or *Īśvara* has introduced His own image into it in the form of souls, entitling them to rewards and punishments deserving their deeds. Thus all souls descend to the world from their pure selfhood because of their innately *karma*-determined nature. It is only by their descent that *ātmans* become souls (*jīvas*), identifying themselves with bodies and developing an impression of belonging to the world. This impression is false; it is the result of *ajñāna*.[13]

In his doctrine of the nondualism of the distinct many known as *viśiṣṭādvaita,* Rāmānuja attributes to the Supreme Reality an internal variegatedness so that both the inanimate and the animate things could be regarded as the elements of and being within Supreme Reality itself. For him, as for Īśvarakṛṣṇa of the Sāṅkhya, the spatiotemporal universe is explainable as an actual product (*pariṇāma*) of the hidden potentialities of *Brahman:* it is not to be regarded as an appearance of *Brahman.* The world of our experience consisting of human beings (*jīvas*) and matter (*acit, jaḍa*), Rāmānuja says, is a modification of *Brahman,* which is eternally in the process of self-manifestation and yet stays unqualified (*nirguṇa*).[14] Both the world and *Brahman* are real, although the former has its being grounded in the latter.

[13] *The Vedānta-Sūtras,* with the Commentary of Rāmānuja, George Thibaut (trans.), Sacred Books of The East, Vo. XLVIII, pp. 427–29.

[14] *Ibid.,* pp. 473–74.

In his epistemological theory, known as *satkhyāti,* Rāmānuja suggests that just as while we perceive a shell as silver neither the shell nor silver can be said to be nonexistent, in our observation of Supreme Reality as the world neither of the two is fictitious. However, the connection between Supreme Reality and the world is that the former acts upon the latter, is embodied in the latter, suffers a kind of inward dispersion (*svagatbheda*) and becomes the latter.

Rāmānuja's account of the causal relation between *Brahman* or *Īśvara* and the universe, although traditionally described as one of a *satkārya-vādin,* differs from that of the Sāṅkhya in one important respect. The *puruṣas* or sẹlves, in the system of Kapila, occupy no understandable position whatsoever in the system of creation. One has a suspicion that since *puruṣas* are never involved in the phenomenal world, originating from *prakṛti,* they are ever free and pure and do not in any real sense come into contact with it. At the same time, when stretched to its final logical extremity, Rāmānuja's theory is found to postulate no reality outside the self-transforming *Brahman,* which is both the material and the efficient cause of creation.

The *jīvas* or worldly consciousnesses of Rāmānuja's system are clearly within the domain of causal occurrences. Although they are basically manifold monadic forms of Supreme Reality, they are affected by matter, psychical dispositions (*vāsanā*), ignorance, etc., and have to strive to get off the causal chain in order to regain their original transcendental status. They are not immune from the whole show of existence (*saṁsāra*) as *puruṣas* are. The very fact that the *jīvas,* for Rāmānuja, constitute body-mind complexes shows that their descent from otherworldliness to worldliness incarnates them and creates a disposition in them to liberate themselves.

Rāmānuja conceives of *Brahman* as a superintellectual reality capable of expressing itself in intellectual and subintellectual forms. But he does not basically improve the difficult philosophical situation we meet with in the Saṅkhya or, for that matter, in the entire Vedānta tendency. He states that *Brahman* is the Supreme Self, God, self-luminosity, omnipresence, eternity and perfection, and asserts at the same time that it causes the *jīvas* and the phenomenal universe to appear. Consequently, the type of causal relation speculated here hangs on two *relata,* of which one is metaphysical and the other empirical. The peculiar sense bestowed on the notion of causality by Śaṅkara and Rāmānuja, therefore, pulls cause apart as something requiring no entry into any relationship with the spatiotemporal world—the world being as if on the remotest periphery of *Brahman.*

Indeed, it is true that for Śaṅkara and Rāmānuja, *satkāryavādins* as they are, *Brahman* as the cause of the world is pregnant with the world. Hence we must presuppose between *Brahman* and the world a continuity and not a hiatus. Further, for such a continuity to be logically intelligible, one has to assume that while *Brahman* is nonspatial, nontemporal and nonsensible Being, the world is totally subject oriented. Perhaps Śaṅkara's reasoning that the world exists only to the practical (*vyāvahārika*) point of view but is nonexistent basically is more tacit than the world-affirming "dualism of the many" (*viśiṣṭādvaita*) of Rāmānuja's. For to hold with Rāmānuja that the world is the actual outcome (*pariṇāma*) of *Brahman* is to leave unexplained the very *raison d'être* of *Brahman*'s mutation. Why is *Brahman* not identical with itself? Why does it undergo actualization and individuation, or actualization through individuation? Why does it *become* the world?

Once cause and effect are regarded as pertaining to no different orders, it is only arbitrarily that we can attribute more reality to one than to the other. Why do the Supreme Reality and the world differ in their genuineness? It could be supposed that there is no causal connection between the two, and that it is man's commonsense awareness that generates the world as the most primary reality. *Brahman,* the ungraspable extremity far and beyond the phenomenal world, is unconditioned by the phenomenal world. As a matter of fact, *Brahman* and the world are neither of the same existential order nor of distinct orders—one metaphysical and the other mundane—but two aspects of the same Being. Both Śaṅkara and Rāmānuja seem inclined to assert that the only thing that can be said to be all-comprehensive is *Brahman,* the world being its finite manifestation. Yet Śaṅkara, by putting the world out of the domain of ontological reality and by clinging to the theory of *māyā,* has proved to be more thoroughgoing than Rāmānuja.

FOR A POPULAR RECONCILEMENT

Strictly speaking, Rāmānuja's rather facile way of reconciling the empirical with the metaphysical and of regarding the former as an inner dispersion (*svagatbheda*) of the latter is more faith oriented than rational. He reminds one of Thomas Aquinas, who considered God as the first cause of all material and mental things, as the fullest unmixed spirit, as the eternal and necessary basis of all beings. Rāmānuja's description of *Brahman* or God as Unity-in-Difference (*viśiṣṭādvaita*), like Aquinas's faith in Him as the highest Being responsible for the world at every moment, suggests that what is uncaused and transcendental figures as causal and mundane.

In the dispersion of Himself through the world, God maintains a composure, an identity, absolute simplicity and perfection. Rāmānuja believes in the Supreme Being or *purusottama* as a being completely unaffected by the transitions of lives in the world. But it may be asked, if God creates the universe out of his very flesh, and if the diversity of things in the world is an integral quality of Him, could not His remaining above all limitations shared by His creation be doubted? It is perhaps by visualizing this difficulty that Bhāskara defined *Brahman* as *bhedābheda,* that is, as something in which difference and nondifference are so fused that *Brahman* is neither free from the shortcomings of the world nor can leave the world as an incoherent and spiritless system. In any case, Rāmānuja's *viśiṣṭādvaita* invigorated the thesis of the internal oneness and variegatedness of ultimate reality, but it did not tacitly show how to bridge the gulf between such a reality and the world.

The Vedāntin triumvirate on whom Rāmānuja's theistic metaphysics had left a profound influence consisted of Madhva (twelfth century A.D.), Nimbārka (twelfth century A.D.) and Vallabha (fifteenth century A.D.). Despite their belonging to an age reverberating Śaṅkara's overwhelming monistic absolutism, they held positions oscillating between nondualism and dualism and initiated an ambitious philosophy of reconcilement of the One and the Many. Again, like Rāmānuja, they directed their efforts towards disproving Śaṅkara's conception of *māyā* and, as V. S. Ghate suggests, sometimes even thought that Śaṅkara was only a disguised Mādhyamika.[15]

Madhva, perhaps the only Vedāntin who went as far as banishing all nondualists (*advaitins*) as "deceitful demons," puts forward a dualism in which God, soul and the world constitute the whole of Reality. According to him there is an eternal difference between *Brahman* and the individual soul, and again between *Brahman* and the physical world. God or *Brahman* does not create the souls and the world. Being perfect and supreme, He is independent of them. He can express Himself in an infinite number of qualities and modes without identifying Himself with any of them. God transcends all immanent things, and yet He is the source of all mental and physical happenings. Madhva says that *Brahman* rules the world through His incarnations (*avatāras*), through His presence in all souls in the capacity of their inner ruler (*antaryāmin*), and creates, maintains and destroys the world through his consort Laksmi.

What is consistently in support of dualism (*dvaita*) in Madhva's philosophy, is his emphasis on *Brahman* as the ruler of the universe, which is materially there and cannot be created from or reduced to nothing. Madhva seems to underline the fact that everything depends on God for its functioning, but nothing represents imperfection or voluntariness on His part. As supreme intelligence, purity and perfection, and as the highest creative force embodied in Laksmi, God is the fulcrum on which the whole phenomenon of existence is supported. God does not will the world, and yet the world is grounded in Him; He is transcendence, and yet the world is attached to Him; He is above matter, and yet the material occurrences are due to His dynamism.

It would not be impertinent to remark that for Madhva, as for Rāmānuja, although the ultimate constituents of Being, namely, God, the individual souls and matter, are all real, the latter two have their foundation in God and hence figure only as the attri-

[15] Ghate, V. S.: *The Vedānta*. Poona, Bhandarkar Oriental Research Institute, 1960, p. 19.

butes of Him. It is Rāmānuja's nondualism of the distinct many that is at the backbone of Madhva's dualism. And whatever the advantages he derives from his conception embodying both theism and dualism, he hardly proves to be in a stronger position than that of Rāmānuja's to surmount the problem of the relation of the Absolute and the world. With Madhva's coming on the scene, the vigorous world-denying logic of Śaṅkara that lay already disregarded in Rāmānuja's theism encounters a further deification and becomes responsive to the popular faith. Nimbārka and Vallabha help to complete this deification.

While Madhva tries his best to define *Brahman* as a principle disinterested in and independent of the process of creation, Nimbārka, a successor of Madhva, looks upon it as the absolutely super-empirical material and efficient cause of the universe. Nimbārka is a consistent Rāmānujite. He regards the individual souls or *jīvas* and the material universe or *acit* as forms of *Īśvara* or God. In one sense, therefore, the souls and the world are capacities of *Brahman* and different from it; but in the other sense they are identical with *Brahman.*[16] The perceptible universe cannot be dismissed as illusory, nor can it be regarded as God qua God. The souls and the world are *Brahman,* and yet not *Brahman.*

Nimbārka argues that what really produces the world is *Brahman*'s power or *śakti*. However, *Brahman* is not affected by its *śakti*. Being all-powerful and transcendental, *Brahman* remains free from creation. After the creation has sparked off from *śakti,* it forever stays dependent on *Brahman.* Every element of creation signifies *Brahman*'s individuation, its spreading in space and time, its self-differentiation. To Nimbārka, as to Rāmānuja, *Brahman*'s self-differentiation is its internal necessity; *Brahman* is identical with itself because it disperses itself. By the sheer *élan* of His will, and not out of any sense of unfulfilled purposes, God brings about the world and introduces an infinite number of souls in it.

If one concentrates only on the pantheistic element that one is inevitably bound to see underlying Nimbārka's metaphysics, one would judge Vallabha, Nimbārka's successor, as an appendix to

[16] *Ibid.,* pp. 31–32.

his thought. Vallabha's *suddhādvaita,* or pure nondualism, is an attempt to remove all distinction between God and the world and, further, to recognize the world as God *in toto*. Vallabha holds that *Brahman* creates the world, not through the instrumentality of *śakti* or *māyā* but out of itself. The world is the very being of *Brahman* or God, who is not outside the world but a part and parcel of it. The world is the embodiment of *Brahman* and as such cannot be separated from it. It is as eternal and as genuine as *Brahman* itself. Hence, when the world is created and destroyed, or composed and decomposed, what really happens is that the *śaktis* or powers of *Brahman* condense and rarefy.[17]

The Supreme Reality, Vallabha says, is one, eternal, absolutely intelligent, and of the nature of *sat-cit-ānanda* (Being-Intellect-Bliss). It is pure (*suddha*) and cannot be polluted by the deficiencies of the world. Its manifestation in the essence of every *jīva,* i.e. in the *ātman,* is complete. Vallabha does not entertain the doubt that if *Brahman* creates the world only by an extension of its being, then at least in theory it might be held responsible for the depravities in the latter. Moreover, his denial of the distinction between *Brahman* and *jīva,* or *Brahman* and the world, enables him to ignore easily any of the differences between the two. *Brahman* appears as the world, Vallabha argues, simply for the purpose of sport without undergoing any transformation in its being. It is like a serpent instinctively shaping itself into a coil.[18]

It is not difficult to see that the central motivation of the theism in the Vedānta of Rāmānuja, Madhva, Nimbārka and Vallabha was to reduce the noticeably stern intellectualism of Śaṅkara and to cater for the religious sentimentalism of the populace. They deified Being, the individual souls and the world with the clear intention of teaching all and sundry to accept the weary universe as a consequence of their own past deeds, and to look upon God as the perfect expression of beauty, truth, goodness, joy and peace. According to them, since the universe is the body of God, it is as real as God Himself. The unmitigated sense of antagonism these absolutists show towards the concept of *māyā,* or the illusoriness

[17] See, for a pointed reference to this idea, *Ibid.*, p. 34.
[18] Radhakrishnan, S.: *Indian Philosophy,* Vol. II, pp. 757–58.

of the spatiotemporal existence, indicates therefore their unwillingness to carry reflection to its furthest limit. By consistently subordinating reason to emotion and faith, they have left a tremendous influence over the devotion-oriented minds of the Indian masses, and helped to intensify the theological aspect of Hinduism which was already prevalent in India in the form of Vaiṣṇavism.[19]

It may be mentioned that the reconcilement of the original ātmalogy of the Upaniṣads with the theology, suitable to the tastes of the common people, has great resemblance with the theistic philosophies of Plotinus (third century A.D.), St. Augustine (fourth century A.D.) and St. Thomas Aquinas.

Plotinus taught that God is the foundation of all existence, the uncaused cause of material and mental beings, the original spiritual unity of the mundane plurality. No attribute can be applied to Him since He is above all description or predication. The values like beauty, truth and goodness follow from Him; yet He transcends them all as the uncreated spring of perfection, eternity and infinitude. For Plotinus, God is immanent in the world in the form of the all-pervasive world-soul. There is no decision or determination on the part of God to create the universe, but the world cannot endure without His guidance and power.

St. Augustine, much like Nimbārka, argues that the highest knowledge one should aspire after is the knowledge of God, who is the eternal, transcendent, omnipotent, omniscient and free substance at the basis of the creation. Indeed, the Christian leader's belief that being the fullest abode of spirit God created the universe out of nothing is nowhere to be found in the Vedānta. For to Rāmānuja, as to the other Indian theists, the emergence of the material world with all kinds of incongruities in it is the result of man's *karmas,* and as such, cannot be said to be necessarily willed by God. However, as far as the concept, most pleasing to Christians, that "God reflects His being in the individual souls

[19] It is a religious sect built around god Viṣṇu. As a mainly theistic movement against Buddhism, this sect came into prominence, according to R. G. Bhandarkar, around fifth century B.C. Gradually through a series of religious reformers, including Rāmānuja, Madhva, Nimbārka and Vallabha, the element of love or *bhakti* for God in it came to have greater and greater appeal to the popular feelings. The followers of the sect, called the Vaiṣṇavas, ascribe scores of names to Viṣṇu and believe in His having a consort called Laksmi or Rādhā.

in the form of love" is concerned, St. Augustine's thinking is extremely close to that of the popular Vedāntin reconcilers.

Undoubtedly, Plotinus's theistic notion that the universe is a revelation of God reaches its most organized culmination in the theology of St. Thomas Aquinas. For Aquinas, God is the Supreme Being manifesting His greatness through all beings and yet remaining outside them. Since He is immaterial and transcendental, He is not subject to time, space and change. Aquinas's famous "Five Ways" of demonstrating that God exists are in all their tenor closest to the arguments of Nimbārka and Vallabha. And his notable thesis that God is the necessary cause of the world, which eternally reveals His being, is a counterpart of Vallabha's idea that in all forms of existence in the universe God's will is self-evident.

However, the oscillation of Indian consciousness between the acceptance of *Brahman* or God as the highest principle worldly beings can look up to, and the abnegation of the universe as something basically nonexistent did not fail to conceal the central Indian notion that the *saṁsāra* results from the glue of the soul. To that extent, therefore, the Rāmānujites' view that all creation mirrors excellence of the divine spirit proved to be more romantic than optimistic. It is the illusory character of mundane existence, the vortex of ignorance man has fallen into, that could not help assert itself as the most primordial metaphysical disclosure the Indian temperament was prone to imbibe.

Chapter Eight

THE PHENOMENOLOGY OF MĀYĀ

THE DOUBTING DISPOSITION

It is one thing to view the emergence of the cosmos as a retribution of man's evil activity through his past lives, which are related to one another according to the logic of the Unknown, and quite another to attempt to explain every experienceable phenomenon causally and empirically from certain antecedent factors. None of the intellectual enquiries of ancient Indian thinkers were exclusively scientific or strictly confined to the empirical analysis of the man-and-the-world encounter. No doubt, on certain occasions Indians did pursue the investigation of interactions between physical phenomena with the passion of a scientist.[1] But this pursuit must not be read as a predominantly intellectual search for the empirical basis of the universe.

The attempt at any scientific approach to existence, in Indian philosophy, is always subservient to and often beclouded by the basic assumption that the empirical is a superimposition on the absolute. Indian metaphysicians have shown such an engrossment in this assumption that is it impossible to regard them at any time as dispassionate examiners of a universal world order, or as the pursuers of knowledge for its own sake. Their *Weltanschauung* was firmly determined by a sense of self-degradation, an awareness of life's uselessness for which moral and religious solutions were found to be more apt than rational description.

[1] As Will Durant remarks, religious search being the core of Hindu life, Indians first developed those sciences which had direct bearing on this search. Astronomy, grammar, philology and phonetics were thus developed, because they were instrumental in bringing about refinement, religious consciousness and religious expression. See Durant, Will; *Our Oriental Heritage*, p. 526.

It is only secondarily that the universe represents according to Indian philosophers a system, a pattern of uniform occurrences, to be cognized and explored as a self-governing organization of events. Their epistemological queries are tinged with extra-intellectual aims. They hardly leave the purely theoretical and the purely ethicoreligious issues unmixed. So feeble is the need felt for a clean intellectual investigation that even in the realism of the Nyāya-Vaiśeṣika school some of the most impressive logical and epistemological formulations are not directly intended to be a self-contained discipline. In fact, they appear as incidental achievements resulting from the disputes between the orthodox thinkers whose sole ideal was to realize the otherworldly peace and their dissenters. The dissension too, except when it arises from the Cārvāka materialists, is not as regards the ultimate meaning an intellectual quest can have for the destiny of human life; it is as regards what specific path or *mārga* one should adopt for the attainment of salvation.

The intellectual deliberations of Indians were consistently directed towards confirming the truth of their central world-negating presuppositions: that the worldliness experienced by us is a menace to our inward pursuits and that so long as this menace continues there is no salvation, no authentic transcendence.

The Indian distrust, with its accompanying lack of interest, in the objectivity of the world was voiced remarkably clearly for the first time by some of the early Upaniṣads. The *Kaṭha Upanisad* wants us not to be misguided by the apparent reality of the universe.[2] The *Śvetāśvatara Upaniṣad* advises us to free ourselves from the world of illusion (*viśva-māyā-nivṛttih*) by the help of God.[3] And according to the *Chāndogya Upaniṣad,* the untruth hides the golden treasure.[4] So whenever a reference to the uncertainty and fictitiousness of the universe is made, the Upaniṣads seem to take for granted that our consciousness of the empirical domain blocks our advance towards self-realization. It must therefore be made to dawn on one's intellect, the Upaniṣads suggest, that no element in our worldly experience manifests the authenticity of Being or

[2] Radhakrishnan, S. (Ed.) : *The Principal Upaniṣads,* p. 656.

[3] *Ibid.,* p. 715.

[4] *Ibid.,* pp. 495–96.

Brahman. However close and obvious our relationship to the phenomenal self might be, the basic inanity of it all would be evident when *Brahman,* the pure subjectivity veiled by *saṁsāra,* is thrown open to our vision.[5]

The Upaniṣads were concerned wholly with the contemplation of that absolute self-conscious reality which lies at the foundation of all worldly events. Inasmuch as this reality forms the heart of all that is, the entire array of empirical objects is a dreamlike existence. Whatever the reason, therefore, why there is an empirical existence rather than nothing at all from the beginning, our very involvement in the world according to Indian thinkers is an involvement in the illusory and the banal. In the *Bṛhad-āraṇyaka Upaniṣad,* for instance, a devotee offers prayers to God entreating Him to save him from non-Being, darkness and death, which are only the epithets for the deceptive world. The devotee craves for a union with *Brahman*—that spiritual experience with which an immediate and everlasting solution to the riddle of worldliness can be gained.[6]

Although man is born in the world and normally can never cease to be aware of his being bound by the fact of worldliness, he can direct his consciousness to its own innermost meaning. Man can acknowledge, by the process of inward-seeing, the total dependence of the phenomenal world on his being present in space and time. For Upaniṣads, as for numerous Indians even in the present scientific age, the entire domain of empirical existence, or of *māyā,* whose illusoriness and superficiality snare and tempt human souls, hinder all intellects from seeing the life of absolute eternity. The world is *māyā* in the sense that it is an untrue mask *Brahman* wears for all purposes of self-concealment. To penetrate through this mask and realize the transcendental is according to

[5] According to B. G. Bhandarkar, one of the authorities on ancient Oriental thought, "The opinion expressed by some eminent scholars that the burden of the Upaniṣad teaching is the illusive character of the world and the reality of one soul only, is manifestly wrong, . . . and is indicative of an uncritical judgment." See Bhandarkar, B. G.: *Vaiṣṇavism, Śaivism and Minor Religious Systems*. Poona, Bhandarkar Oriental Research Institute, 1929, p. 2. However, he does not elucidate what one should make out of the concept of *māyā* in the Upaniṣads.

[6] Rānade, R. D.: *A Constructive Survey of Upanishadic Philosophy*. Poona, Oriental Book Agency, 1926, p. 226.

Indian philosophers the sole activity man must engage himself in. And as long as this is not done, human consciousness must be said to inhabit a sphere of naïveté, ignorance, falsity, or *avidyā*.

MĀYĀ

The notion of *māyā* is a point around which the philosophical thought in India has ever revolved. At some stage or other in his life, an Indian makes it a point to brush aside a frustrating experience, a hopelessly incurable situation, even the day-to-day fact of existence, as perishable *māyā*. With the passage of time and with the ever stable impact of the Upaniṣadic *Weltanschauung* on the Indian mind, the word has acquired so popular and persuasive a usage that most often in the Indians' life and literature both poverty and richness, sickness and health, failure and success, danger and safety, death and life, are banished indiscriminately as merely diverse facets of *māyā*.

Strictly philosophically, the word *māyā* describes the spatio-temporal universe, which in relation to the self-luminous transcendence of *Brahman* or Being, is contingent and as empty as non-existence. The Vedas and the Upaniṣads show an utter lack of control on the usage of this word, so much so that, as Rānade has studiously pointed out, in some contexts in the Vedic-Upaniṣadic literature it signifies untruth (*anṛita*), in others uncertainty (*adhruva*), and in still others powers (*śakti*).[7] It is therefore reasonable to argue that at no period before Gauḍapāda's Vedānta was the theory of *māyā* set so explicitly as to vindicate the thesis that from the point of view of the transcendental domain the practical universe is a mirage.

For Śaṅkara, as for Gauḍapāda, the world is a shadow of the ontological reality; and whatever be its final destination, its emergence is a phenomenon tied to the naïve part of one's existence. Both Gauḍapāda and Śaṅkara adhere to the Upaniṣadic suggestion of the *māyā* notion in its true spirit, and unlike its fluctuating sense in the thinking of their predecessors, confer upon it a largely disciplined and unambiguous application.

[7] For an exhaustive study of different senses of the word *māyā* in the early Oriental literature, see *Ibid.*, pp. 226–29. Also see Devanandan, Paul David: *The Concept of Māyā*. London, Lutterworth Press, 1950, pp. 204–10.

The problem which the Upaniṣads posed Śaṅkara happened to see with unusual philosophic profundity. It is to explain how the world of physical phenomena is a product of man's ignorance (*avidyā*) and what exact motivation man can have for abandoning this world and for identifying himself with the reality beyond. By any evaluation, Śaṅkara exhibits tremendous acumen while pointing out that from the sphere of the highest and the most immaculate consciousness a false, but spatiotemporally perceptible, worldliness has to follow inevitably. The intensity with which he sees this question, and the ingenuity with which he leaves a totally abstract solution to it speak for his intellectual flight combined with a sense of mission.

Śaṅkara was a mystic, a determined monist and an absolutist, but not a dogmatist. His brilliance as the builder of a metaphysics out of irregular fragments of his predecessors' thoughts has remained the unique treasure in Oriental thought. He condemns the supremacy of reason, expresses a theological undertone in his argument,[8] and yet exercises logic with the poignancy of a dialectician. Although he philosophizes with a feeling of having gripped the most fundamental problem human mind can ever think of, he hardly succumbs to a sense of pride or complacence.[9] Tradition believes that he merely carried on the work of Gauḍapāda to its final point, and that his magnum opus, *The Commentary on the Brahma-Sūtra,* is an elaborate explication of the central thesis of the Upaniṣads. However, it can hardly be doubted that through Śaṅkara comes perhaps the most comprehensive metaphysical thought in India; and so far as its influence on later philosophies

[8] Ninian Smart emphasizes this point in his article on Śaṅkara, in Edwards, Paul (Ed.): *The Encyclopedia of Philosophy*. New York, Macmillan Free Press, 1967, Vol. VII, pp. 280–81. He says that the theological character of Śaṅkara's thought comprises his inevitable allusion to *śruti* or the revealed truth embodied in the utterances of the Vedic-Upaniṣadic sages. But this allusion does not in any way cripple his reasoning, for his reverence to the authority of *śruti* appears as the last and the only resort when all attempts at dialectic enquiry have failed.

[9] This was probably owing to the shockingly lonely and tragic childhood Śaṅkara spent. Although no fully reliable account of his life is available, he is said to have met with several hazards, in one of which he was almost to lose his legs to a crocodile's bite. See Chitrav, S. V.: *Bhāratvarshīya Madhyayugin Charitrkosh* (Marathi) Poona, Bhāratvarshīya Charitrkosh Mandal Ltd., 1937, p. 760.

is concerned, it cannot be equalled by any other that appeared on the Indian scene.

According to Śaṅkara, *Brahman* is the unqualified (*nirguṇa*) and unconditioned reality. In its essence it is knowable as something beyond the logical categories, or beyond the categories of empirical experience, such as space, time, causality, change, substance and relation. When in complete fusion with itself, the individual ego (*ātman, Brahman*) would acquire the experience of absolute freedom and absolute fulfilment. But because of the influence of *māyā* or the cosmic nescience, *Brahman* is manifest as God (*Īśvara*), the human souls (*jīvas*) and the phenomenal world (*jagat*), and leads to the advent of all sorts of tribulations. To belong to the world, therefore, is to remain bound by appearances and shadows. Śaṅkara describes these as constituting a *jagatprapañca* or *vyavahārikasattā* (the worldly affairs). He reiterates the value of abandoning them when we are intent on realizing transcendental consciousness (*ātman* or *Brahman*).

Although *Brahman* is originally trans-empirical and pure, it is conditioned by *māyā* in some mysterious way and made to figure, in relation to the universe, as *Īśvara*. It is to *Īśvara* that the process of the universe must be attributed. He is in complete control of the fates of individual selves (*jīvas*), which are what they are because of their body, sense organs, mind, intellect, and so on. Concealed within a *jīva* is the *ātman*—that self-shining homogeneous spirit whose apprehension implies no limitations whatsoever. The question why and how *Brahman* or *ātman* becomes *Īśvara* or *jīva* was and can be embarrassing to Śaṅkara, and for that matter, to any Vedāntin. However, while facing this question squarely, Śaṅkara does not hesitate to take clues from Gauḍapāda. Yet he approaches the whole issue in such a manner that neither *Brahman* nor *ātman* ultimately seems to retain its purity against the onslaught of *māyā*. *Māyā* in this sense has been aptly understood as *śakti* or power.

By themselves *Brahman* and *ātman* are beyond any conditioning forces, beyond names and forms (*nāma-rūpa*), beyond empirical commitments, beyond concrete representations. But once under the sway of *śakti, ātman* generates out of itself the entire panorama of world events and literally subjects the pure consciousness to contingency, untruth, illusion and error.

MĀYĀ: TWO VERSIONS

Strictly speaking, the term *"māyā"* does not describe anything real or existent. It is a hypothesis employed by Indian thinkers to account for the transition of the absolute into the empirical. Although this hypothesis does violate Ockham's Razor by creating an additional requirement for its own explanation, it has come to be valued for its profound authority on Indians' attitude towards the world. All men—victims as they are to the eternal vortex of births and deaths and rebirths—are advised to imbibe a spirit of indifference and noninvolvement towards all that they experience during their contact with the world. For all things and occurrences in the world are a false growth. To allow oneself to be permanently addicted to them, to raise hopes and ambitions about them, to be affected by them, would amount to one's surrender to falsity.

Thus for all practical purposes *māyā* is this world and every past or possible world. It is a domain of antithetical situations, subject-object distinctions, paradoxes and antinomies. Indeed, such a domain might not have sprung from the principle of absolute delight, absolute perfection, absolute truth, absolute transcendence and absolute freedom. The fact that it has come about all the same must lead us to believe that *Brahman* or *ātman* must have veiled itself by means of the world. Why has it veiled itself? Because, the Vedāntins state, it has just happened to influence itself by the power of nonexistence, unreality, *abhāsa.*

There can be two equally reasonable versions of the *māyā* hypothesis. According to one which is strong and is reflected in the Mādhyamika school of Buddhism in general and in Nāgārjuna's thoughts in particular, the world results from ignorance (*saṃvṛti* or *ajñāna*) veiling human consciousness. On account of ignorance eternal Nothingness is perceived as the spatiotemporal universe. Therefore, taken in this sense, *māyā* is generated by the naïveté of the subject, bestows positivity on what is fundamentally empty and void, and produces a formidable illusion of existence. The Mādhyamika Buddhism declares that Reality is *śūnya* or cipher and that the phenomenal universe is a cruel deception.

Under the second version, which may be described as weak and prevails from the Upaniṣadic age through the Vijñānavādins, Gauḍapāda, Śaṅkara and other Vedāntins, the reality of the external world is entirely dependent on man's consciousness, i.e. it has no subsistent being. The world is as it is perceived to be only from the mundane perspective of ours; it would not be so from a transcendental perspective. While we have every reason to believe that the strong version of *māyā* would reckon the Buddhists' view regarding the world's reducibility to Nothingness, the weak version would apply to the restrained Vedānta view that the world exists but appears different from what it really is.[10]

The mixed dimensions the *māyā* hypothesis might take in practice are not controllable, although as a metaphysical conception *māyā* can be an effective foundation for humanism. It is not likely to produce any unwanted consequence if it is prescribed as a principle for fashioning one's broad-minded, generous and tolerant view towards mankind and the world. A critical observer of the history of Indian consciousness would easily find out that the *māyā* principle has frequently demonstrated remarkable power of suggesting to an entire community the virtue of sympathy and compassion towards all. Since life is basically an illusory spectacle where the victor and the vanquished, the gifted and the miserable, the high and the low are all children of the same eternal sport (*līlā, krīḍa*) [11] of *Brahman,* it could be argued that the sole objective one may live to realize is the emancipation of all.

However, not seldom has the *māyā* hypothesis been literally adhered to, with the result that even obnoxious things have been explained away as shadowy and therefore not deserving any concern from man. Coupled with the deterministic theory of *karma,*

[10] For an emphasis on the strong version of *māyā,* see Monier-Williams: *Indian Wisdom,* pp. 118–19.

[11] Several Vedāntins, including Yamunāchārya, Rāmānuja and Vallabha, refer to the playful activity of *Brahman.* According to them the spontaneity of God in creating the universe is analogous to that of a sportsman towards arranging a game.

it has sometimes left Indian masses inactive, fatalistic, chronically oblivious of the solid circumstances of life, and to unpreparedly aspire after the otherworldly bliss at the cruel cost of indispensable material necessities. And much more strangely than its original expounders might have visualized, it has taught some to justify their behavior, however antisocial or selfish, under the pretext of world's nonbeing.

Nowhere else in the world has the impact of a metaphysical theory on the attitude of the common people been so great and so varied. It has made the mendicants and the derelicts to go about singing the virtues of poverty and self-denial, the diseased and the deformed to accept suffering without a whimper, the wealthy to give away fabulous donations, squadrons of unpaid social workers to serve and die for the people. And in a rather sinister way it has made exploiters and wrong-doers to disown responsibility for their acts, the power-thirsty to vie for superiority, the regressive to adhere to communalism and casteism, the opportunists to look at good and evil with unhealthy equanimity.

One can witness at the bottom of the variegated behavior of Indians a conflict between their strong adherence to a metaphysical presupposition and their worldly temptations. The greater the capacity of the *māyā-vāda* to prevent man from an indulgence in the worldly temptations, and to trim them to suit a catholic outlook, the greater chance it will have not to be forgotten as an undesirable myth.

The *māyā* hypothesis must have originally struck the Indian mind as a tool for counteracting the tedious complexities of the day-to-day living. Psychologically considered, it has the power to heal Indians of frustrations, failures, fears, ennui, shocks, the lack of adjustment, defeats, and so on. Particularly in its strong sense, therefore, it can be and has proved to be a tranquillizing agent to people in all situations, and perennially has made them accept both life and death with a certain amount of neutrality and unconcernedness. What should be perhaps of immense curiosity to a cultural anthropologist is the influence the *māyā* idea has cast on millions and millions of souls who are taught to imbibe an attitude that nothing really exists and that, therefore, nothing really matters.

Even in India of our own times, instances of family priests, aging folks, village chiefs, popular Puraṇas (ancient mythological lores), temple singers, cinemas, theatre, literature, oft-repeated religious quotations, or mass preachers keeping the *māyā* message ever alive in the ethos of the people are not rare.[12] It appears that the doctrine of *karma* and the doctrine of *māyā* are the main elements of a massive, though unorganized, philosophical education that have exercised tremendous teaching force on Indian consciousness at all times,

Surely the Upaniṣadic thinkers were too directly concerned with the physical environment to hold that it is all a mirage. They therefore did not explicitly stretch the *māyā* concept to the point of annulling the factual experiences *in toto*. But on the other hand, they indicated the relative status of the universe against the absolute, pure and all-inclusive unity of *Brahman*. Thus, when Gauḍapāda and Śaṅkara describe the phenomenal world as *adhyāsa* (illusion), *anirvacanīya* (indescribable), *avyakta* (potential), *bhrama* (neurosis), *ajñāna* (ignorance), *vivarta* (transformation), *nāma-rūpa* (name-form)—words more or less synonymous with *māyā*—they reassert the Upaniṣadic thesis that the world is an appearance but not a total unreality. By doing this, as a matter of fact, they water down the strong version of the *māyā* hypothesis, i.e. the Shūnya-vāda, and concede some degree of existence to the world.

Gauḍapāda, the progenitor of the Advaita Vedānta, distinguishes between the mundane or empirical knowledge (*laukika jñāna*) and the supramundane or transcendental knowledge (*lokottara jñāna*).[13] What is acquired through the former, Gauḍapāda maintains, is the impression of the external world, i.e. the dreamlike and ceaselessly fluctuating domain of *māyā,* and what is acquired through the latter is the innermost qualityless domain of *Brahman* or *ātman*.

Now Śaṅkara could not have argued in consistency with Gau-

[12] As Abraham Kaplan explains, "the Indian philosopher looks out on the world as a kind of cosmic spectacle." He himself believes and teaches others to believe that the world is a cosmic sport, which can be taken as fundamentally true. The world appears as a manifestation of the "superabundance of divine energy." See Kaplan, Abraham: *The New World of Philosophy*. New York, Vintage, 1963, pp. 214–16.

[13] For a pointed treatment of this theme, see Sinha, Jadunath: *A History of Indian Philosophy,* Vol. 2, pp. 446–47.

ḍapāda so as only to establish himself as his carbon copy. What Śaṇkara imagines is a universal rational system, a theory of the structure of the Real, in which one's own ego-consciousness plays the central role. *Brahman* or *ātman* in itself is indeterminate; but on account of the influence of *māyā,* it appears as determinate. The determinate *Brahman* is the world. Epistemologically speaking, the world is posited by the *māyā*-laden soul, and has no being of its own. It is unreal, not in the sense that it is a cipher or an inanity, but in the sense that we perceive it as a result of our being under the duress of *karma* and *avidyā.* We alone are the cause of the world, just as our *ātmans* alone are the cause of our *jīvas.* And again, we cannot be at home in the world, for the world is unable to attract our firm and final intellectual loyalty. Our *ātmans* surpass our empirical consciousnesses, i.e. our *jīvas* and, eventually, our being amidst worldly things.

Had Śaṅkara cancelled the perceptible presence of the universe altogether, he would not have aspired to construct a comprehensive theory of *Brahman,* in which everything including the illusoriness of the world is sought to be included as elements within a whole. Unfortunately, he has been misunderstood by many, and pushed into the rank of nihilists.

There is probably a reason why Śaṅkara was misunderstood, and why his conception of the universe was interpreted negatively. It is comfortable for a community, brought up in a milieu pervaded by the theory of *karma,* to be taught that the phenomenal world is there, not out of any transcendental necessity, but only appears as an outcome of man's evil deeds of the previons lives. The world is an illusion, as if suspended to the original *karma*-free *ātman.* To be in this illusion or to evolve it from one's own consciousness is the price one has to pay for one's subjection to the law of *karma.* The status of the world is therefore conditional, inasmuch as the worldliness functions merely in the life of unfreed and subtranscendental souls. Thus although Śaṅkara had no conscious intention to bind the law of *karma* and the notion of *māyā* together, and consequently twist the epistemological character of the latter by the use of the ethical considerations involved in the former, his followers have found the illusion idea a consoling corollary from the *karma* doctrine. Moreover, the voidist view, spread far and wide by the Buddhists, was, psychologically speaking, more straightforward and ascetic, and as such, could not have failed to lead people's understanding of Śaṅkara's *māyā-vāda* in the direction of extreme nihilism.

THE SEAT OF *MĀYĀ*

Śaṅkara frequently condemns the emergence of the world by equating its falsity with that of optical illusions, such as mirage, silver in a shining shell, snake in a rope seen in semidarkness, the double moon perceived by the pressed pupil of the eye. But all these metaphors must be recognized as implying that even illusions are objects of experience, possessing the power of generating mental states in us. Śaṅkara's metaphors must not be taken too literally. They serve to elucidate the incomprehensible and immanent nature of the universe against the pure and transcendent nature of *Brahman*. And as a matter of course, when Śaṅkara puts forward the notable distinction between the practical or *vyāvahārika* and the philosophic or *pāramārthika* standpoints, he clearly suggests that the experience of worldliness is conjoined with our natural existence, with our individuality.[14] We are inseparable from this experience as long as we are bound by the results of *karmas* and the laws of the cosmos. It is to commonsense and to discursive intellect that the finite reality reveals itself. On the contrary, for the philosophical standpoint all the categories of empirical knowledge are a manifestation of ignorance, error and absurdity. Further, for this standpoint the entire domain of spatiotemporal and causal relations is a fanciful fabrication.

For Śaṅkara and for all orthodox tendencies in Indian thought as for the Upaniṣads, the inauthenticity of our commonsense view of the universe can be established when by means of a con-

[14] It is interesting to observe that Dowson describes *māyā* in the following terms: "Illusion personified as a female form of celestial origin, created for the purpose of beguiling some individual." (Dowson, John: *A Classical Dictionary of Hindu Mythology*. 10th ed., London, Routledge & Kegan Paul Ltd., 1961, p. 207). According to Schweitzer, from the transcendental point of view "the world of the senses is a magic play . . . staged by the Universal Soul for itself." (Schweitzer, Albert: *Indian Thought and Its Development*. Boston, Beacon Press, 1957, p. 59).

centrated and arduous endeavor, we heighten our trans-empirical approach and reach the supreme and transcendental *Brahman.* What hinders our direct access to the higher knowledge (*parā vidyā*) is our habituation to the lower knowledge (*aparā vidyā*).[15] In fact, inherently perfect individuals or *ātmans* as we are, there is no reason why we should be reduced to a state of dislocation from our essential being and be made to live in the form of *jīvas.*

Even when it is admitted that the *karma*-infected men must undergo, by the very logic of the law of *karma,* the experience of ignorance and thence the experience of the whole array of phenomena, it is not simple to understand to what category *avidyā* belongs and how it operates towards contaminating the purity and transcendence of the *ātmans.* A series of post-Śaṅkara commentators and Vedāntins seem to have reflected on this problem, and their arguments, although always hovering around Śaṅkara's principal thesis, have presented several perspectives for its solution. A treatment of all these cannot be attempted in the present book. What would be pertinent, however, is some amount of reflection on some of the most ingenious of these perspectives.

Surely the Vedāntins must have been bothered much by the question whether ignorance is the product of *Brahman* or whether it is an inherent quality of the individual souls. It is obvious that since *Brahman* has nowhere been regarded as "defilable," it can hardly be the seat of ignorance. Again, if it is held that ignorance is inborn in individual souls, they would not be accepted as the expression of and potentially as pure as *Brahman.* Where then does ignorance originate from? A number of Vedāntins are found to have faced this question squarely and evolved solutions for it. And whatever the type of the solution offered, a Vedāntin is fully conscious of the fact that his approach to the question of the source of *avidyā* or *māyā* ought to adhere to the norms of intellectual consistency.

[15] The two kinds of knowledge, namely, the higher and the lower, or the transcendental and the empirical, are spoken of by the *Muṇḍaka Upaniṣad* as *parā vidyā* and *aparā vidyā* respectively. The same are called by the Vedāntins as *pāramārtha satya* and *vyāvahārika satya* respectively.

According to Sureśvara (A.D. 800), one of the most talented of Śaṅkara's disciples, *avidyā* should be called *māyā* or a false experience because it is neither a property (*svabhāva*) of *Brahman* nor is distinct from it, neither real nor unreal, but is indefinable and indescribable (*anirvacanīya*). He says that ignorance belongs to the *jīvas* or souls, which are modes of the psychic and spatiotemporal living. It is on account of ignorance or *ajñāna* that the pure selves fall into the ordeal of births and deaths and generate the awareness of the material world with feelings, desires, hopes, and so on.[16] Although Sureśvara sees no solution to the problem of what is prior to the soul under the influence of *ajñāna,* he does argue that the soul and the *ajñāna* exist eternally, the former causing the latter and the latter conditioning the former again. Moreover, the very separation of *jīvas* from *Brahman* has been brought about by the ignorance of *jīvas* themselves.

But how do ignorant *jīvas* emerge from *Brahman?* Sureśvara's answer is that *jīvas* are internally self-contradictory entities, and perpetually under the grip of imagination (*kalpanā*). Out of this imagination they constitute the world—the *māyā.* As long as *māyā* dominates human souls there is no freedom to them; but as soon as *vidyā* or knowledge dawns on them they become freed and enlightened.

Sureśvara also maintains that the support of ignorance is *Brahman* or the pure Self itself. Those who acknowledge Sureśvara as a thinker with an independent speculative genius attribute to him the authorship of works called the *Naiṣkarmya-siddhi* and the *Bṛhadāraṇyakopaniṣad-bhāśya-vārttika.* In the *Naiṣkarmya-siddhi,* Sureśvara defines *avidyā* as the nonperception of the ultimate oneness of the Self, and freedom or enlightenment as the ultimate realization of this oneness. It is because ignorance has rested on *Brahman* that the latter has transformed itself into the subject-object relation and has generated the entire domain of world distinctions. To account for ignorance, therefore, one must say that the pure Self is ignorant in regard to itself, and eventually produces the illusion of individual persons and empirical phenomena.

[16] Dasgupta, Surendranath: *A History of Indian Philosophy,* Vol. II, p. 101.

However, with the rise of real knowledge in the self, the self's consciousness of the objective universe with all its accompanying paraphernalia vanishes. Actually, even when the self is under the duress of ignorance, its purity is only temporarily eclipsed. The essence of self is not basically disturbed by the agency of *avidyā*. For Sureśvara as for all other Vedāntins, the entire realm of empirical experience is a superimposition on pure consciousness. To reason that had there been no ignorance in us, there would have been no consciousness of the world is the same as to assert that had there been *Brahman* without any inconsistency within it, there would have been no *māyā* at all. According to Sureśvara the emancipation of the *jīvas* is ultimately an emancipation of *Brahman* from its own artificial and absurd manifestations. Thus, the total world-being is the product of nescience or false illusion masking the self.[17]

Padmapāda (A.D. 820), the author of the famous *Pañca-pādikā* and one of the direct pupils of Śaṅkara, remarks that *avidyā* is an obstruction to the pure and self-contained reality of *Brahman*. As a result of various agencies such as *karma,* the impressions of past experiences (*pūrva-prajñā-saṁskāra*) and ignorance (*avidyā*), pure consciousness appears as an individual personality and figures in different situations as a doer and a sufferer. Padmapāda does not explicitly say whether *jīvas* alone are the seats of ignorance. He holds that it is on account of ignorance exercising its control on the self-revealing nature of *Brahman* that individual consciousnesses emerge.[18]

Avidyā, being positive and somewhat of material origin, remains the cause of the world-appearance, which is itself material. The original self-luminous *ātman* or *Brahman* by coming under the activity of *avidyā* becomes a perceiver and an enjoyer of world events. And as the existential states of a person change, he as a phenomenal being is more and more immersed in empirical consciousness, more and more aware of subject-object hiatus in experience. Therefore, once they come under the shadow of *māyā,* the whole range of possibilities happens to

[17] *Ibid.*, p. 101. As Dasgupta says, Sureśvara thinks that *avidyā* seats itself on "pure intelligence itself."

[18] *Ibid.*, p. 103.

characterize *jīvas*. The only way of release from this situation is through the knowledge of the exact nature of Being. Padmapāda calls this knowledge *"arṭha-prakāsa."*

Another Vedāntin who frequently figures as an exponent of Padmapāda's thoughts is Prakāśātman (A.D. 1200). He arrives at the conclusion consistent with Padmapāda's attitude that *Brahman* is both the support (*āśraya*) and the object of ignorance. Padmapāda is well known for his recognition of the distinction between two senses of unreality or falsehood (*mithyā*): unreality as sheer negation, and unreality as something indescribable (*anirvacanīyatā*).[19] According to Padmapāda, it is in the latter sense that the word *"avidyā"* must be understood.

Prakāśātman develops Padmapāda's concept of *avidyā* further, and asserts that when ignorance enslaves the soul, the latter functions as something positive. Prakāśātman says that there can be three possible views with regard to the notion of world-appearance: (1) that *Brahman* and *māyā* are together the cause of the world, (2) that something which has *māyā* as its power produces the world, and (3) that *Brahman,* with *māyā* on its top, creates the world.[20] In all the three cases, nevertheless, *Brahman* must be regarded to be responsible for the emergence of the world. For even if the immediate cause of the world-appearance is *māyā,* the abode of *māyā* cannot be any other reality than *Brahman.*

The problem Prakāśātman, like Padmapāda, does not care to take notice of is whether from the whole argument it would not follow that the *Brahman,* which supports the deceptive *māyā* and through its instrumentality generates the world-appearance, could not be absolute, perfect and pure.

One of the most forceful condemnations of man's ignorance about the true nature of the ultimate reality comes from Sarvajñātma Muni (A.D. 900), who is said to have been Sureśvara's disciple. Sarvajñātma Muni was a contemporary of Vācaspati Miśra (A.D. 840), a very significant commentator on Śaṅkara.

In his only known work called *Saṁkṣepa-Śārīraka,* Sarvajñātma

[19] *Ibid.,* pp. 105–6.
[20] *Ibid.,* p. 106.

Muni tells us that the ultimate cause of everything is *Brahman,* and that it is *Brahman* which through the mechanism of ignorance generates illusory consequences. He like Śaṅkara, who was his master's master, argues that God (*Īśvara*), the souls (*jīvas*) and the world (*jagat*) are the threefold activity of *Brahman* under the shadow of *ajñāna.* What then is the status of *Brahman?* Is *Brahman* also as illusory as *māyā,* which is "held" by *Brahman?* Sarvajñātma suggests that we ought to draw a distinction between two facets of *Brahman,* namely, *Brahman* as the primordial ground (*adhiṣṭhāna*) of everything, and *Brahman* as the support of ignorance. The latter facet of *Brahman* is but false. Therefore, the question of the integration of the *avidyā*-supporting *Brahman* with *Brahman*-in-itself, or with *Brahman* as the ontological principle does not arise.

Sarvajñātma thinks that *ajñāna* or *avidyā* has no real existence. Although it does misguide the soul and does create in it an awareness of the world, like butter in presence of heat it melts away the moment true knowledge of *Brahman* emerges in the soul. Sarvajñātma believes that *Brahman's* transcendence and purity are not altered or contaminated by *ajñāna.*[21] The products of *ajñāna* are felt by us in all spheres of our contact with the world; but they cease to appear no sooner than we penetrate through and grasp the inner core of things, i.e. *Brahman.*

Such perspectives about the genesis and the abode of *māyā* are numerous in the history of Indian thought. There have been Vedāntins who reverentially followed their teachers and repeated almost verbatim what the previous thinkers had said. A combined feeling of piety, loyalty and imitativeness towards the spiritual superiors has been the unique feature of the attitude of Indian philosophers. The original truisms taught by the Upaniṣadic sages, therefore, that *Brahman* in all its ontological purity is ever the destination of human endeavor, and that the phenomenal world as an offshoot of nescience is an unwanted obstacle, have always been adhered to by the Vedāntins of all times. The *māyā* hypothesis, specifically in its weak version, has remained an inseparable part of the philosophical consciousness

[21] *Ibid.,* p. 113.

of the Indian people—the very essence of Indian life and thought.

As it was pointed out earlier, the concept of *māyā* represents an exclusive metaphysical height attained by the Indian mind. Its basic aim is to show the absurdity and the grotesqueness of man's life in the world, vis-à-vis the perfect and all-inclusive domain of transcendental Being. Thus whatever their variation from the *māyā* notion of the Advaita Vedānta, the post-Śaṅkara Vedānta tendencies have consistently asserted that the world is the outcome of the inherent naïveté of man, of man's confrontation with his own projected subjectivity. They have interpreted the presence of the world from the standpoint of an extreme transcendental idealist, of a phenomenologist, and under the enchantment of *Brahman,* rejected the being of that which to commonsense always remains "natural" and indubitable.[22] Their attempt has been to doubt the world, to hold it out of consciousness, to refuse to recognize it, to put out its very existence, on account of its supposed superimposition on man's pure ego-experience.

The *māyā-vādins* cannot place both *Brahman* and the universe on an equal footing. They cannot, like realists, propose a uniform valuation of the otherworldly and the worldly. They are determined to realize a region of experience, which, they are sure, is not only complete and absolutely given, but also, in contrast with the experience of worldliness, is totally positive and blissful. Even the bhedābheda-vādins, Rāmānuja and the Vedāntin triumvirate—Madhva, Nimbārka and Vallabha—can fit into *māyā-vāda* in its weak version, in spite of their disagreement with Śaṅkara. Although they show no inclination to regard the world as illusory, and, notably like so many absolutists, firmly accept and account for the reality of the phenomenal world as a part and parcel of *Brahman,* they never suggest that man's consciousness of the world is not the outcome of his intellectual and moral imperfection. They do not digress from the fundamentally ethicoreligious assumption of the Upaniṣads

[22] Since the first systematic formulation of transcendental idealism in Plato, Western philosophy has periodically doubted the objectivity of the world of objects.

and of the entire ātmalogical movement that to be in the world is to be subject to bondage.

The question whether a metaphysics free from the *māyā* hypothesis has an edge over that of the pro-Śaṅkara Vedāntins (such as, Mandana Miśra, Sureśvara, Padmapāda, Sarvajñātma Muni) is not of direct relevance in the present context. It is enough to state that so far as their approach to the incidence of *māyā* or *avidyā* is considered, the bhedābheda-vādins, Rāmānuja, Madhva, etc., have unanimously professed a kind of universal spiritualism which tries to harmonize the transcendental and the mundane within one and the same Being. The problem of the seat of *avidyā* occurs, therefore, in the pro-Śaṅkara Vedāntins; it does not and need not occur in the latter's thinking.

For instance, whatever is empirically experienced is, according to the bhedābheda-vādins, beyond any incredibility. It construes an expression of *Brahman*. In order to explain it, they thought, we would require a method that presupposes its objective presence without at any time doubting it. Bhāskara and Yādavaprakāsha condemned Śaṅkara's *māyā-vāda* and furnished a moderate solution to the riddle of the *Brahman-avidyā* connection by holding that the universe ought to be perceived as a transition of the Supreme Reality (*Brahman*) and not rejected as a dream or hallucination.

And Rāmānuja is not a softer repudiator of the *māyā* theory. When he evolves a monistic pluralism in which God (*Īśvara*), the selves (*jīvas*) and the material world are bound up together as a transformation (*pariṇāma*) of *Brahman*, his reluctance to posit the ultimately real as divorced from and independent of the world is clearly evident. It is significant, therefore, that the anti-*māyā-vāda* of these post-Śaṅkarites with its intense theological bias did disturb the transcendentalist foundation of the *Brahman*-world relation, and introduced most successfully the notion of the divine absolute in the predominantly world-negating Vedānta thought. And yet to the extent to which they like Śaṅkara looked upon the world as a sphere man is helplessly condemned to, and aspired after a way out of it, their perspective of the world remained but negative and life forsaking.

THE *MĀYĀ* FRINGE

Very much along the spirit of *māyā-vādins* in general and of Śaṅkara in particular, phenomenologists today uphold the view that the aim of the "infinite standpoint" in their method is to transcend the "narrow framework of direct empirical givenness" and to realize the "essential" basis of the finite.[23] If its strictly metaphysical implications are considered, phenomenology would come extremely close to Śaṅkara's method of the cancellation of the world of our practical (*vyāvahārika*) awareness and proceeding "behind" it to its essence, namely, *Brahman.* Both *māyā-vāda* and phenomenology are tacitly intent on evolving a kind of metaphysical subjectivism for which the phenomenal universe with the sum total of our bodily and mental impressions can be suspended, bracketed or eliminated. What is perhaps the most impressive point of meeting between the two schools of thought is their partly psychological characterization of the two fringes of human consciousness: one merging in the infinite domain of transcendence and the other merging in the finite sphere of the constellations of physical qualities.

Phenomenology, like *māyā-vāda,* initially distinguishes between our world-consciousness and transcendental consciousness. For Husserl, for example, our life in the everyday world, our natural attitude, the subject matter of sciences, etc., relate to the field of experience whose occurrence seems to be obvious. By our very nature we are conscious of a world extended in space and enduring in time. The perceptual world is its own evidence. "But, however much this evidence is prior in itself to all the other evidences of life . . . and to all the evidences of all the world sciences . . . , we soon become doubtful about the extent to which, in this capacity, it can lay claim to being apodictic." [24] That is to say, nothing that belongs to the perceptual world is wholly beyond uncertainty, erroneousness, perceptual illusoriness and invalidity. In contrast, it is the transcendental conscious-

[23] Husserl, Edmund: *Ideas.* W. R. Boyce Gibson (trans.), p. 46.

[24] Husserl, Edmund: *Cartesian Meditations.* Dorion Cairns (trans.), The Hague, Martinus Nijhoff, 1960, p. 17.

ness, being the most primitive basis of our world-consciousness, that is most authentic, pure and free from fantasies.

According to phenomenologists, therefore, what is to be strived for is the suspension of our awareness of the world, a kind of holding back of the world, and the grasp of the reality of transcendental consciousness. Husserl writes:

> The objective world, the world that exists for me, that always has and always will exist for me, the only world that ever can exist for me—this world, with all its objects—derives its whole sense and its existential status, which it has for me, from me myself, *from me as the transcendental Ego.* . . .[25]

From the level of the transcendental Ego, the empirical world, or rather the aftermath of the suspended world-consciousness is seen through and its reality determined. For Husserl, once pure subjectivity is realized, the very foundation of the total knowledge-situation would be comprehended with clarity and inner necessity.

While the principal motivation of phenomenology is a "cleansing" of the cognitive consciousness with a view to reestablishing the entire mass of primitive concepts and categories that govern mind, the *māyā-vāda* system is loaded with ethical exigencies. The *māyā-vādins*' is not an attempt to construct, as that of phenomenologists, a method of knowledge, a *mathesis universalis,* a sort of grammar of epistemological forms, which would account for the relation between consciousness and its object. Indeed, for *māyā-vāda,* as for phenomenology, consciousness cannot be held contained within the experience of the spatiotemporal world forever. Its destiny is purity, transcendence and certainty. However, while *māyā-vāda* recognizes the attainment of this destiny as liberation or salvation (*mokṣa*) of the self, and consequently stresses its ethicoreligious value, phenomenology looks at the realm of transcendental consciousness or at the trans-empirical region of Being as an abode capable of analytically and descriptively unfolding the intricacies of the experiencing self.

This is why Husserl and all phenomenologists, for that matter,

[25] *Ibid.*, p. 26.

refrain from considering the self-withdrawal from the world as a value in and for itself.[26] One of the implications of phenomenology—probably traceable back to Descartes's procedure of universal uncertainty—is that so long as consciousness is tied to the act of experiencing the world, it would find itself unable to distinguish between the real and the unreal, the authentic and the inauthentic, the pure and the impure forms of knowledge. The phenomenologists' abolition of the world from consciousness is therefore provisional; its purpose is to channel one's inward-seeing sensibility towards a domain from which one's perspective of the whole sphere of existence is reset and regenerated.

That the aim of phenomenology does not entail a permanent cancellation of our world-consciousness, but only a temporary arrest of it as a device for "purification" is clearly emphasized by Husserlians. For example, Alfred Schutz writes that by beginning one's "meditation within the natural attitude," one must undertake a leap into "the transcendental subjectivity," but "must return to the living stream of experiences of the world." "In this stream," Schutz goes on, "the experienced world is kept exactly with the contents which actually belong to it." [27] The journey to "the pure life of consciousness" is meant for the total concentration of one's attention on the genesis of consciousness itself, or on the origin of the experiencing self. A direct knowledge of this area is expected to transform one's view of the world.

According to Marvin Farber, "the phenomenological 'suspension' is an entirely peculiar operation." [28] By it the thetic world is not abandoned. The world still remains "an experience," but is kept out of any judgment. Farber says that all "natural experiences, i.e. those referring to 'nature,'" are negated, with a view to asserting the trans-natural sphere—a sphere about which "there can be no reservation," about which one can state that "that which is intended in it is absolutely given." [29] But this

[26] For a well-defined range of this withdrawal technique, see Farber, Marvin: *The Foundation of Phenomenology*. New York, Paine-Whitman, 1962, pp. 530–36.

[27] Schutz, Alfred: *Collected Papers*. Maurice Natanson (Ed.), The Hague, Martinus Nijhoff, 1962, Vol. I, pp. 122–23.

[28] Farber, Marvin: *The Foundation of Phenomenology*, p. 526.

[29] *Ibid.*, pp. 526–27.

operation has to work as a purging of consciousness. Its objective is to accomplish a new insight into the world of science.

Therefore, since phenomenology is primarily guided by the requirements of an epistemological program, its metaphysical undercurrent, despite its remarkable resemblance to the *Brahman*-directed method of the Vedānta, is ethically uncommitted. At the same time, it is significant that both the Vedānta *māyā-vāda* and the phenomenology adhere to almost identical assumptions in respect of the empirical world, and its contingent status in relation to the necessity and infinitude of the trans-empirical consciousness. At no stage do *māyā-vāda* and phenomenology put the latter in parentheses or the former beyond dubitability.

However, it is by what is known today as the existentialist phenomenology of Sören Kierkegaard and Karl Jaspers that the fringe of the empirical consciousness, like the fringe of *māyā,* is shown to break into the realm of the transcendental subjectivity. It would be worthwhile to make here a cursory reference to the concept of the "existing" [30] person, advocated by these thinkers.

Kierkegaard, the most systematic critic of Hegel's rationalism, condemns man's universal trust in the reality of the world composed of physical objects. He aims at demonstrating the supremacy of the existing individual, the primacy of the "feeling existential subject," in all matters of experience. To an existing individual, Kierkegaard states, his own "inwardness" or "subjectivity" manifests itself as the sole eternal truth.[31] Considering the most veridical certainty of one's own dynamic "existential self," one's own exclusive self-realizing passion or one's own quest for freedom, the world known through sensations, concepts and reason, that is, the theoretically proved world, the world of sciences, is ephemeral.

What Kierkegaard, like Śaṅkara, regards as obviously discernible by our metaphysical intuition is that the more deeply we are aware of the weary world, of the melancholy and despair embodied by our contact with the world, the more intense be-

[30] The existentialist notion of the "existing" person is commensurate with the ātmalogists' notion of the man stung by the desire for self-realization or *ātmalābha.*

[31] Kierkegaard, Sören: *Concluding Unscientific Postscript.* David Swenson (trans.), Princeton, 1941, p. 276.

comes our self-involvement and, further, the more uncertainty we develop with regard to knowledge founded on reason. Ultimate truth is embedded in the transcendence of the subject. So long as one has not grasped this transcendence, the immediate datum of one's life in isolation, one remains confined to the region of "solid" impressions, to the information emanating from the "inhuman" universe. Kierkegaard could penetrate through the psychical layers of his existence as successfully as the *māyā-vādins,* and, consequently, like them could achieve the spiritualization of his being.

Jaspers describes the reality of man's trans-phenomenally directed consciousness as *Existenz. Existenz* is the very self known suddenly and intensely, directly and dynamically; as the foundation of one's intellectual capacity, it is one's authentic being. The sphere of *Existenz* is beyond reflection. No rational explanation would exhaust all the potentialities contained within it. Like Kierkegaard's conception of the "existing" individual, Jaspers's *Existenz* refers to what "I myself am."[32] I, as an *Existenz,* am a movement destined towards a state of realization incomprehensible in terms of logical categories.

Jaspers holds that the *Existenz,* with its world-consciousness and recognition of subject-object duality, is a *Dasein. Dasein* denotes the worldly condition, the phenomenal descent, of the otherwise transcendentally motivated *Existenz.* Since there is no life without the world, *Existenz* or my pure self has to be *Dasein,* and in that capacity has to live amidst other *Daseins.* Man's life in the world, Jaspers says, is his condemnation to a mortal sphere —his "shipwreck." In order to liberate himself from this sphere, man must transcend his worldly being, must exist, must be an *Existenz.*

Insofar as the transcendental horizons and possibilities of *Existenz,* and the immanent and transitory features of *Dasein* are considered, *Existenz* and *Dasein* are the existentialist counterparts of *ātman* and *jīva* in Indian philosophy. Indeed, neither Kierkegaard nor Jaspers, nor any phenomenologist for that matter, has discarded the experience of the world—as *māyā-vāda* has

[32] For a full exposition of Jaspers's *Existenz* concept, see Sinari, Ramakant: *Reason in Existentialism,* pp. 70–78. Also see Wild, John: *The Challenge of Existentialism.* Bloomington & London, Indiana U. P., 1966, pp. 152–55.

done—as false, illusory or unreal. For the phenomenologists' and existentialists' philosophization has, for its starting point, the most elementary "situation" of man-in-the-world. And yet the world-consciousness signifies for them something resulting from the naive and inauthentic attitude of human self. The world, Jaspers remarks, invites love, hatred, pity, sympathy, wrath, etc., from *me,* but at the same time it is a world from which *I* have to grow out, *I* have to be *myself.*[33]

The *māyā-vāda* thesis that man's world-consciousness figures as an impediment to his quest of transcendence, therefore, finds its echo in the writings of Husserlians and existential phenomenologists with remarkable sharpness. But the most important issue on which *māyā-vādins* would disagree with the latter thinkers is the value of man's final commitment to the "natural" world. Phenomenologists are motivated by the plan of reestablishing the world-knowledge in all its entirety; and the existentialists have an urge to "feel," to "suffer," to "accept" worldliness as boring, futile, grotesque, inane and pointless. However, no commitment of any sort would logically follow from the *māyā* hypothesis. What is the point, a *māyā-vādin* may ask, in the re-setting of the world-experience, epistemologically or otherwise, once the inauthenticity of this experience is already established from the most cherished level of self-experience or *ātmanubhava?* What is the need for the metaphysically enlightened to stage a comeback in the world and develop an attachment to it?

What Jaspers remarks with regard to what he considers as Buddha's new philosophy would aptly portray the core of the Indian *cogito.* Jaspers says that Buddha is the "embodiment of a humanity which recognizes no obligations towards the world."[34] Buddha does not struggle or resist, and teaches people to look upon the whole mankind as an existence that has come into being through ignorance. What mankind can legitimately and fundamentally desire, therefore, is only revelation; and, according to Indian philosophies, even in this desire there would be no yearning, for what is desired is beyond life and death.

[33] One can compare this self-exploration tendency with the ātmalogical tendency in the Upaniṣads which says: He who "knows" *ātman* will be *ātman.*

[34] Jaspers, Karl: *The Great Philosophers.* Hannah Arendt (Ed.), Ralph Manheim (trans.), London, Harcourt, Brace & World, 1962, p. 50.

Chapter Nine

THE BREAKTHROUGH TO KNOWLEDGE

THE AIM OF LIFE

UNDERNEATH the metaphysical system of the universe the Indian mind has built up, there is a distinct message bearing upon the ultimate meaning of human life. No appropriation in the world of natural experience and intellectual endeavors can be supposed to have even a remote pertinence to the true ideal of man. While the fact of being in the world, the fetters of *karma* and *saṁsāra,* ignorance, and the deluding empirical phenomena, keep our consciousness helplessly enslaved, the disposition to an eternal release or absolute *mokṣa* sets it on a path towards total renunciation of the mundane existence. Indian sages have always thought that the domain of consciousness one attains in *mokṣa,* the delightful silence *mokṣa* generates, would constitute a cognitive state in which one absolutely transcends finitude and bondage.

Enterprises undertaken by man would have worth inasmuch as they make his progress towards *mokṣa* sure and rapid. For the intrinsic validity of this trans-phenomenal goal cannot be questioned. However absorbing the glee and the loyalty our engagements in the world may produce in us, their final significance has to be determined from the point of view of their capacity to create enduring perfection in us. To Indian thinkers nothing is so valuable, so cherishable, so everlasting as the total withdrawal of one's self from the sensible phenomena stamping themselves on it. In order to achieve the eternal calm of existence, Indian philosophies declare, one must be a *jīvanmukta* (freed from life), a *sarva-mukta* (freed from all), a perfected savant (*siddha*).

The ambivalent role of consciousness, which at once ties man to the mundane experience and propels him towards the unconditioned self-realization, is a concept peculiar to Indian philosophy. Indian metaphysicians have consistently held that at the bottom of the empirically oriented experience every human individual amasses, there is an all-comprehensive luminous principle whose intuitive "seeing" cannot but reject the appearance of the world. All phenomena, therefore, have their origin in a functioning of consciousness which, when contrasted with the innermost trans-phenomenal selfhood, would be cognized as contingent and practical. Indeed, it is not denied that man does belong to the world, that he is bound to it through the medium of his senses and mind; but the world that is perceived as indubitable *ab extra,* would retain no such status when it is looked at from the level of inwardness or subjectivity. For Indian thinkers as for idealists in general, the single prerequisite of an enlightened view of existence—a view to which the world might disclose itself even as "nothing" (*śūnyatā*)—would be a firm recognition of the ideal of *jīvanmukti,* of the eternality of the transcendental *ātman,* of the spiritual basis of everything.

The ancient Indians believed that prior to and as a preparation for the attainment of life's perfection, an individual must pass through three long and organized orders, called *āśramas.* The *Code of Manu,* one of the most valuable documents portraying laws, customs, politics and religion of old India, gives full expression to this belief.

Each of the three orders invites one's unflinching adherence to a set of duties (*dharma, vrata*). These duties have no noticeable import on the final spiritual station one is supposed to realize, but they certainly operate as a stopgap arrangement essential for one's smooth sailing as a normal member of the society.

The three *āśramas,* namely, the chaste disciplehood (*brahmacarya*), the householdership (*gṛhasthya*) and the departure to the forest (*vānaprastha*), should culminate in the highest and the most desirable stage called *vairāgya* or *saṁnyasa,* where one is completely alienated from the society and becomes a holy wanderer in search of the eternal truth. Thus in the context of the Vedic-Upaniṣadic thought, no individual action or social phenomenon would be endowed with any permanent value unless it is instrumental to one's pursuit of *vairāgya,* and through *vairāgya* to the condition of absolute freedom. And the Indian tradition recommends the fixed orders of life, for the simple reason that, by following them, a person matures for a certain psychophysical pose. On this pose depends the success of his undertaking of the transcendental journey. On the other hand, in the postrealization period a person need not be committed to any act, for his entire being reaches a level at which there is no force to warrant activity. The wandering ascetic, that is, the *saṁnyāsin,* Manu says, "having studied the Vedas in accordance with the rule, having begat sons according to the sacred law, and having offered sacrifices according to his ability, . . . may direct his mind to the attainment of final liberation." [1]

The Indian ethics also propounds the theory of four ideals of life, called *puruśārthas: arṭha* (material acquisitions), *kāma* (earthly enjoyment), *dharma* (righteousness of conduct) and *mokṣa* (freedom). The most elaborate description of this theory one finds in the *Mahābhārata*—a work known for its ethicoreligious subtleties. Now, while the first three ideals denote man's pragmatic quests, the last denotes the central motive of everything that is directly and indirectly sought. In fact, what is outwardly difficult for one to understand is the significance of the three first *puruśārthas* to the metaphysically oriented *mokṣa* ideal. In no way whatsoever do they seem to have a heightening effect on an individual's advance towards *mokṣa.*

Even if we regard, as most interpreters of the theory of *puruśārthas* do, that *arṭha, kāma* and *dharma* are merely attitudes or "aims" governing man's career through life, one cannot help suspecting that they might bind consciousness to *saṁsāra* by generating *karmas* and *obligations* in it. As Buddhists and Jainas wisely saw, the three ideals are bound to figure as a hindrance in the course of one's total abnegation of the earthly life. The *summum bonum,* characterized by the terms like *mokṣa, mukti, niḥśreyasa, apavarga, nirvāṇa,* etc., constitutes by any denomina-

[1] Radhakrishnan, S., and Moore, Charles A.: *A Source Book in Indian Philosophy,* p. 182.

tion a state radically distinct from and antagonistic to the existence of temporal vicissitudes.

Perhaps the most plausible reason why the ancient Indian social organizers advised the adoption of the scheme of *āśramas* and *purusārthas* is that they desired to guide individual life, vis-à-vis society, to a point of saturation before letting it to seek the ideal of *mokṣa*. And this initially world-admitting scheme Indian thinkers entertained mainly in order to promote the obvious requirements of man's earthly and social life. Man was to be beckoned out of the weary world; he was to be given sufficient time to belong to the world with all his "natural" attitudes; he was to be made to find out for himself that nothing in the world is able to meet his transcendental demands.

It is important to observe that *arṭha, kāma* and *dharma,* like *brahmacarya, gṛhasthya* and *vānaprastha,* imply the controlling of life in the direction of a metaphysically postulated value, i.e. the value of absolute liberation. Whatever might be, therefore, their consequences in practice, Indians have always looked upon them as provisional measures. As S. Radhakrishnan points out, it is impossible for one to think that wealth (*arṭha*) and sensuous enjoyment (*kāma*) can have a smooth and harmonious relationship with the pursuit of self-realization. The householdership (*gṛhasthya*) may create reasons for repeated involvements in family affairs. However, if a person is motivated by the final goal, he would spontaneously know what to do with wealth, or with the family affection, and how to preserve himself as unaffected by it.[2] Besides, the two fourfold theories imply that he, while journeying through life, would feel all kinds of worldly engagements until finally it dawns on him that they are all futile. From the first three ideals to the fourth, as from the first three life stages to the fourth, the individual is expected to undergo a fundamental transition of attitude.

It is possible to argue that Indian philosophers, like Plato, preached the discipline of life along with its duties (*dharma*), not to everybody in society, but only to a few intellectually motivated truth-seekers. As a matter of fact, the Vedic-Upaniṣadic

[2] Radhakrishnan, S.: *Indian Philosohpy,* Vol. I, pp. 223–25.

teachers desired to plan a two-tier functioning of the life of everyone of the intellectual *élite:* the higher tier endeavoring after perfection or *summum bonum,* and the lower one working as its promoter. And it would not be incorrect to state that the same two-tier system became the basis of the division of society into the initiates, called *Brāhmins,* and the uninitiates.

Therefore, when it is understood that it is the *saṁnyāsa* state alone that enables one to fuse one's self into the ultimate, the other three states preclude themselves as having no independence of status. Their utility does not extend beyond the realm of practical life and social adjustment. Like the three mundane *puruśārthas,* they characterize the imperfect span of living demanded by the presence of certain vegetative and animal impulses in us. The Indian ethics, somewhat like Plato's ethics, provides the code of individual behavior in which the ignoble self has some inherent rights to be responded to. And again, as Plato suggests the inauthenticity of the ignoble self to the point of advising us "to fly away from earth as quickly as we can," so the Indian philosophers, by their sole emphasis on *mokṣa,* preach the inborn futility of all that is worldly.

So, no important thinker in ancient India has attributed absolute value to any state or action or ideal belonging to man's life in the mundane world. The only real aim of life, i.e. the aim to which all actual and possible pursuits in life stay subordinate, is the cessation of all needs for the very continuance of the world-consciousness. Never have philosophies in India shifted their principal interest from the trans-phenomenal release, from the permanent detachment from worldliness, from the supreme freedom of the self.

THE WAYS AND THE GOAL

Although all shapers of Indian thought from the Vedic-Upaniṣadic times onwards have shown a distinct awareness of the urgency of attaining the trans-worldly goal, they have not adhered to one single way or method (*mārga*) of the attainment. The three eminent ways—the way of knowledge (*jñāna-mārga*), the way of devotion (*bhakti-mārga*) and the way of action (*karma-mārga*)—upheld by Indians from time to time are intended to suit persons of diverse mental dispositions. For instance, the way of knowledge is the exclusive recommendation of the Nyāya, the Sāṅkhya, the Yoga, the Advaita Vedānta, the Buddhist and the Jaina systems which are renowned for their reflective approach to the study of consciousness. On the other hand, Rāmānuja, Madhva, Nimbārka, Vallabha, Mahāprabhu Chaitanya and several others, in whom emotion is seen to subdue intellect, have professed that a wholehearted dedication and surrender to God is all that is necessary for salvation. And the Pūrva Mīmāṁsā school, the *Bhagavad-gītā,* and the spirited followers of its message such as Mahatma Gandhi and Vinoba Bhave down to our own time have stood for moral and social reformations through action.

Strictly speaking, the three ways are not rigidly compartmentalized. That is the reason why Indian philosophers are not so much in the habit of estimating the merit of any one of them as against the other. To recognize all the three ways as equally effective, as sure paths leading to the goal of absolute freedom, has ever been the temper of Indian thinkers.

The sole end that the ways are destined towards is not fully determinable by means of thought. As the apex of all human aspirations, it is always described as something staying beyond words and statements, beyond affirmations and definitions. However, as Alan W. Watts points out when it is remarked in Indian philosophies that the negative mode is the only mode to approach the ultimately real, what is suggested is that the "denial applies strictly to the ideas, the concepts, the theories, and the fixed categories of thought whereby we try to understand and grasp what we experience." [3] Besides, negativity is an intellectual category and as such does not cast any reflection on the intensity of the invitation man feels towards the transintellectual. The expressions used by Indian philosophies in order to designate the form of salvation throughout convey the implication that man's bondage in the world arises from his dislocation from the absolute, the universal and the imperishable (*aksara*) silence of per-

[3] Watts, Alan W.: The Negative Way. In Isherwood, Christopher (Ed.): *Vedanta for Modern Man.* New York, Collier, 1962, p. 37.

fection. The dislocation has aroused the sombre feelings of anxiety, despair, loneliness and ennui, and a thirst for the attainment of something durable and wholesome, something that would surpass all the achievements possible in the mundane world.

Reflective thought in ancient India is the expression of an attitude of mind that tries to articulate the boundless. Ordinarily, the thought process, the ratiocination and the linguistic expression are natural operations of a consciousness, which by its very inner propulsion leads towards its unique trans-empirical genesis. Indeed, the question regarding the nature of this genesis, of the content of the primordial basis of life-experience, did not interest Indian philosophers. But what is most prominent in their investigation is the notion of the plenitude of the metaphysical end. The *mokṣa*-directed Indians keep before their eyes the only exit to human bondage, namely, the eternally free existence of the self or *ātman*.

At this stage some specific questions can be asked: What is the structure of *mokṣa* as an experience lived through? What constitutes the state of mind of a *jīvanmukta*? Is *mokṣa* simply a deathlike blank state in which all positivity is cancelled, or is it infinite bliss comparable to the joy of the fullest accomplishment of our basic aspirations?

In Indian literature *mokṣa* is everywhere conceived as a realization of subjectivity. It comprises an awareness of one's release from the *karma,* which keeps the wheel of births and deaths perpetually moving. Although there has been no consistent attempt in Indian philosophy to study the essence of *mokṣa,* the presupposition is that it constitutes an eternal unity of one's own life with the life of the Supreme Person or *Brahman*. Thus, a *jīvanmukta,* that is, a man who has freed himself from the entire gamut of worldliness, we are told, experiences a perfect unison with himself while living, a kind of equipoise resulting from his pure consciousness, an inward security through absolute transcendence. Jainism, Buddhism, the Sāṅkhya, the Yoga and the Vedānta, like the Upaniṣads, hold that in *mokṣa* one takes a leap outside the world of bondage and stays in harmony with oneself and with the supernatural principle of Being.

Clearly, considering man's natural endeavor to pursue the

goal of absolute freedom as the highest stage his consciousness can reach, the notion of *mokṣa* has something stoical, life denying and irrational about it. Despite the fact that *mokṣa* has not seldom been defined in terms of positive values such as peace, joy, wisdom, illumination of intellect, a supreme sense of self-existence, unity with the divine and salvation, it is never suggested that through it the entire humanity could take a plunge into a set of actions that enhance its perfection in the world as such. In fact, the attainment of *jīvanmukti* is supposed to carry one further to a stage called *videhamukti* (freedom from bodily existence). While *jīvanmukti* is deliverance enjoyed during life, *videhamukti* is a postmortality deliverance when one has annihilated the very possibility of incarnation in any of its forms.

It appears, therefore, that to the Indian thinkers of almost all times, the world and the *mokṣa* form a dichotomy, the *mokṣa*-realization ultimately amounting to a cessation of all world-consciousness. What specific urge Indians in ancient times felt in aspiring after such a realization, and whether they thought that a universal acceptance of it by the entire humanity would be a desirable ethical goal are probably questions extraneous to the rationale of *mokṣa*. For when a philosophy rules out the natural desirabilities of man-in-the-world as the products of his inauthentic living, and seeks to show him a way out of it, it is not obliged to adhere to the presupposition of human welfare in this world.

To the total spiritualistic perspective of Indian metaphysicians, man's life in the world represents an occasion, a trifling incident following from his actions in the past, a fictitious emergence having for its origin and destination the otherworldly reality of *Brahman*. For this perspective, our ordinary logic regarding the single unquestionable object of existence, namely, the attainment of perfection in the present world, may not possess any a priori validity. The leap that Indian consciousness takes beyond the spatiotemporal domain, and the manner in which it recognizes the illusory nature of all that belongs to this domain have their roots in the Vedic-Upaniṣadic idea of the trans-phenomenality of the human self. It is a leap that aims at grasping something too massive and too extraworldly to be comparable to any acquisitions in the natural universe, and hence lies too much on the opposite side of positivity. The leap throws the self into the state of "worldlessness."

M. Hiriyanna has rightly stated that "the conception of *mokṣa* marks a definite advance in the search for the ideal in India."[4] He, however, adds that "there is probably something to be said against the conception of *jīvanmukti* because it is inconceivable how all details relating to the whole of reality—past and future, far and near—can be comprehended by any one in this life."[5] By conceiving an ideal whose actual achievement does not guarantee the self's continuation in the world here, Indian thinkers imagine the possibility of a consciousness after physical death. No particular constituents of this consciousness have been exactly determined. And, therefore, we find some of the Upaniṣads saying that *jīvanmukti* can be experienced as an actual situation in the present life too. The *Kaṭha Upaniṣad* explains: "When all desires that dwell within the human heart are cast away, then a mortal becomes immortal and (even) here he attaineth to *Brahman.*"[6]

Intellection and language are believed to be not only subservient but also arbitrary to the feeling of the *mokṣa*-state. As a matter of fact, mysticism in Jainism, in Buddhism and in Hinduism is admittedly an attempt to figure out the "reach" of consciousness in *jīvanmukti,* to translate into ideas, symbols and words the dissolution of the individual self in the Supreme Self, to portray in ecstatic terms man's life in "worldlessness," to catch the essence of *nirvāṇa.*[7] As R. C. Zaehner in his treatment of some of the key terms in Indian literature puts it:

[4] Hiriyanna, M.: *The Quest After Perfection.* Mysore, Kavyalaya Publishers, 1952, p. 70.

[5] *Ibid.,* p. 71.

[6] Radhakrishnan, S.: *The Principal Upaniṣads,* pp. 646–47.

[7] What Ninian Smart says so aptly about *nirvāṇa* would bring out the ambiguity of the very conception of *mokṣa.* Smart writes: "In *nirvāṇa* the series of temporal states is replaced by a permanent state. But with the vanishing of the psychophysical states there is no longer an individual to be named or referred to. Thus, the question about survival is like 'Is the king of France bald?' except that it is only a contingent fact that there is no king of France, whereas it is a metaphysical necessity that the saint does not survive after his death." See his article on *Nirvāṇa* in *The Encyclopedia of Philosophy,* Paul Edwards (Ed.), Vol. 5, p. 517.

> (*Mokṣa*) means rather an unconditioned and absolutely static condition which knows nothing of time and space and upon which death has no hold; and because it is not only pure Being, but also pure consciousness and pure bliss, it must be analogous to life. It is, then, life-in-death: it has the immobility of death but the consciousness of life.[8]

KNOWLEDGE: A REALIST STANDPOINT

In the history of Indian philosophy there has never been any systematic and critical effort to study the salvation paths (*mokṣa-mārga*) themselves. Not only their necessity but even their unfailing capacity to produce the ultimately desirable *summum bonum* were unquestioningly accepted. Thus it would be appropriate to assume that the moral impulse behind the philosophical thought in India is so overwhelming that the question of the "method" does not anywhere form the center of Indian philosophization. And this is as much true of the schools prescribing one way for salvation as of the schools prescribing another way. However, rather surprisingly it is in the Nyāya and the Yoga systems that one comes across an admirable shift in the emphasis from the end to the means, from the ideal to the journey towards it, from the final destination of life to the act of perseverance for its attainment. With this shift, indeed, a predominantly intellectual enquiry has made itself felt in the otherwise ethically oriented pursuit of Indian sages.

The Nyāya system is a notable endeavor to explore the domain of cognitive consciousness and to determine the process by which it enters into a connection with the world of physical objects. As it has been said before, the Nyāya philosophy must have developed out of a need, felt by the orthodox Indian thinkers, to invent a science of knowledge (*pramānaśāstra*) sufficiently effective to fortify their arguments against their unorthodox opponents. But what was once a need came to be later on an independent vocation; and consequently, the Naiyāyikas have gone in the history of Indian thought as highly original epistemologists and logicians. However, as Garbe has shown, the sixteen logical concepts enumerated by Gotama in his Nyāya aphorisms

[8] Zaehner, R. C.: *Hinduism*. London, Oxford U. P., 1962, p. 94.

(*circa* 150 B.C.) presuppose that "the true knowledge of their nature leads to the attainment of final emancipation, i.e. the release of the soul from the cycle of existence . . . deliverance from the misery of empirical existence. . . ."[9]

The analysis of the entire furniture of logical thought undertaken, among other Naiyāyikas, by Gotama in his *Nyāya Sūtras,* by Vātsyāyana in the *Nyāya-bhāśya,* and by Uddyotakara in the *Nyāya-varttika* has the purpose of setting the rational faculty of man in tune with his trans-empirical demands. In fact, Vātsyāyana and Uddyotakara make it clear that if the Nyāya system had concentrated only on the nature of the soul and its ultimate liberated condition, there would have been no ground on which the Nyāya system could be distinguished from the Upaniṣadic metaphysics. Generally, contributors to the orthodox Indian ideas have least minded the fact that by focussing their doctrines mainly on the question of *mokṣa* they could only repeat, at times *ad verbum,* the thesis of the *Brahman-ātman* identity, that is, the issue that justified the very act of philosophization. The Naiyāyikas, to the contrary, have shown an intense preoccupation with the investigation of the constituents of knowledge, although as we have said, they too finally refused to divorce this investigation from the *mokṣa*-ideal.

The Nyāya mentions four sources or *pramānas* of knowledge: perception (*pratyakṣa*), inference (*anumāna*), comparison (*upamāna*) and the Vedic word (*śabda*). By holding a position close to what is today known as naive realism, the Nyāya argues that the outside world is known to us through the senses and the mind. It believes in the external things as reflecting their real nature when knowledge is true, and their unreal nature when knowledge is false. Consequently, for the Naiyāyikas, knowledge is the knowledge of things, and it constitutes the expression of reality (*arthānubhava*). Whatever its type, it is a natural response to the disposition present in human mind.

Any given knowledge-situation, we are told, presupposes the knowing mind, the object known, and the contact between the two, i.e. knowledge. Even in those cases where we cast a glancing

[9] See Garbe's article on Nyāya in *Encyclopaedia of Religion and Ethics.* James Hastings (Ed.), 3rd Impression, New York, Scribner, 1953, Vol. 9, p. 423.

beam as if at the mind in the process of knowing itself, the triad is found to be undisturbed. However, there seems to occur a typical amalgamation in this triad, not only when knowledge embodies a one-to-one correspondence with reference to the world, but also when it is such that its validity is directly and instantaneously perceived. It is this amalgamation that is suggested by the Naiyāyikas by the use of the term *pramā,* which literally signifies guarantee or certainty. "The word *pramā,*" as S. S. Barlingay writes, "does not allow in the locus of its meaning the inclusion of *bhrama* or illusory experience." [10]

Now the question arises as to whether there are forms of knowledge in which *pramā* [11] is given not objectively but through an act of inward or subjective grasp. The Naiyāyikas distinguish between two kinds of perception: ordinary or *laukika* and extraordinary or *alaukika.* Whereas in the former the certainty is obtained from the fact that what the knower knows accords with what is given in the external world, in the latter the exact source of certainty is indeterminable. For instance, our knowledge of the universals (*sāmānyalakṣaṇa*), of qualities of objects amenable to one sense but perceived by means of the power of some other sense (*jñānalakṣaṇa*),[12] and the intuitive knowledge claimed by mystics and yogis (*yogaja*), contain a type of certainty which is hardly explainable externally or logically. In this sense of the self-given certainty, *pramā* as an attribute of the *alaukika* perception indicates a kind of metalogical and extraempirical evidence similar to what Descartes has called "immediate self-evident intuition."

It might be stated that students of the Nyāya system do not attach much importance to its theory of extraordinary percep-

[10] Barlingay, S. S.: *A Modern Introduction to Indian Logic.* Delhi, National Publishing House, 1965, p. 14.

[11] In Indian logic, the terms *pramāna* and *pramā* manifest interesting subtleties of meaning. *Pramāna* means the source or means of knowledge; and *pramā* suggests the constitutive and the epistemic conditions of any true knowledge-situation. See *Ibid.,* pp. 14–15.

[12] For example, when someone says "I *see* the exciting fragrance of earth after the first monsoon showers have beaten it," what he expresses is a transfer of sense powers. Such a transfer would remind one of what psychologists refer to as the synthesis of sense-data.

tion.[13] The Nyāya confidence in a realist view of perception is at no stage so weakened as to confirm transcendentalism in its fold. To the Naiyāyikas the world of "solid" existent objects is absolutely sufficient to account for all instances of true and erroneous knowledge. Unlike the Mādhyamika thesis, on the one hand, that the nonexistent universe is perceived by us as existent, and unlike the subjective idealists' contention on the other that all reality is a mental creation, they argue that whether we perceive it or not, the spatiotemporal world exists and will continue to exist in the form in which we sense it. The Nyāya theory that the validity and the invalidity of knowledge must be established by means of a reference to the external world is known as *parātaḥprāmāṇya-vāda.*

Now, although its adherence to the phenomenal world as the sole point of reference determining the truth-value of knowledge remains ever unshaken, the Nyāya system is not oblivious of a certain inexplicable fringe surrounding the empirically verifiable knowledge-situations. It is this fringe that the Naiyāyikas have now and again returned to in their notions of inner perception (*mānasa-pratyakṣa*), reflection on experience (*anuvyavasāya*), the self-existence of the Vedic word (*śabda-prāmānya*), one's "seeing" of the intuitive judgments of the past seers, the ideal of salvation, etc., etc. It seems that when knowledge is so manifest that it leaves the knower with nothing short of an unperturbed inner guarantee, and at the same time is not connected with any externally furnishable evidence, the Nyāya is compelled to grant to it an extraordinary status. Yet, since all forms of knowledge are not such that we must grant to them such a status—a sort of intrinsic self-validity—the characteristic *alaukika* is reserved by the *Nyāya* to describe a few ontological forms only. Thus, the *alaukika* knowledge is transcendental, and

[13] See Potter, Karl: *Presuppositions of Indian's Philosophies.* New Delhi, Prentice-Hall of India (Private) Ltd., 1965, pp. 56–59. Potter rightly says that "there is disagreement among the schools of Indian philosophy as to whether each or any of these non-sensory forms of experience is trustworthy, and indeed as to whether it is proper to class them as *pratyakṣa.*" One must remark, however, that the "substantial" basis of experience, resembling what phenomenologists describe as intentionality, is widely emphasized in Indian thought.

involves practically both presentative and representative matter.[14]

The realism of the *parātaḥprāmāṇya-vāda* is often contrasted with the epistemological conception in the *svatāḥprāmāṇya-vāda*[15] of the school of Pūrva Mīmāṁsā. The whole controversy between the Nyāya and the Mīmāṁsā thinkers, despite their agreement on the basic realist proposition, is very interesting. As a matter of fact, it is comparable to the controversy between naïve realism and representative realism in the West. For all dialectical purposes the Naiyāyikas hold that when knowledge refers to something outside consciousness, its validity is to be determined empirically; but when it refers to something inherent in the knowing mind, its validity is *sui generis* and apprehended nonconceptually, i.e. extraordinarily. The Mīmāṁsā system stretches the *sui generis* certainty of the cognitive mind, and makes an ambitious attempt at equating the very act of knowing with that of gaining unquestionable guarantee. Like representative realists, it says that to know and to know validly are one and the same thing.

The Mīmāṁsakas reason that since no knowledge-situation is possible without simple prerequisites, such as the object represented in it, the normalcy of the senses, and the correspondence between the senses and the sensed, it would be superfluous to give any especial emphasis on them. What is peculiar to the conduct of knowledge, states Kumārila, a seventh century A.D. Mīmāṁsaka who was reputed for being a convert from Buddhism to Hinduism, is the incidence of ascertainment (*jñāpti*). This is not conditioned by any external factors; it has its own internally emerging compulsive conditions (*prāmāṇyam svataḥ utpadyate*). And for Prabhākara, whose work *Bṛhati* is known for its remarkably tacit arguments in support of the view that all valid

[14] See Hiriyanna, M.: *Indian Philosophical Studies* I. Mysore, Kavyalaya Publishers, 1957, pp. 20–21.

[15] Literally the expression signifies the theory of the self-validity of knowledge. The Mīmāṁsakas use this theory to demonstrate that all cognitions are valid, and that when a cognition is erroneous, it is due to some defect in some one or more of the prerequisites of knowledge.

knowledge is revelation (*anubhūti*), every cognition is valid per se. In other words, as soon as knowledge arises in the mind, its validity too arises; and the two are indivisible.

What is necessary to note in these apparently antagonistic ideas in the Nyāya and the Mīmāṁsā schools is that neither of them neglects the fact that evidence or certainty in knowledge is to be sought as the fulfilment of the knowing act. Indeed, the Naiyāyikas try their best to define this fulfilment as something wholly dependent upon external predication. But in their theory of extraordinary perception, one finds them alluding to the non-empirical, the intuitive or the a priori. In the Vaiśeṣika system also, whose affinity to Nyāya is so close, the knowledge of non-existence or *abhāva* and of inherence or *samavāya* (for instance, the whole in its parts, or the universal in the particulars) is stated to be self-evident, i.e. having no reference to anything given in the external world. This knowledge, we are told, results from a direct penetration by mind into a region of immediate representations. And, by universalizing the principle of intuitive self-evidence to all forms of cognition, the Mīmāṁsakas argue that wherever knowledge arises, there arises its validity too.

The Mīmāṁsā school, like the Nyāya school, is unhesitant to admit that the physical universe is real and exists apart from the knower. The disagreement between the two schools, therefore, is largely due to their specific stress on one of the two interrelated, but properly distinguishable, aspects of knowledge performance. The Nyāya concentrates its attention on mainly the cause or source of knowledge; the Mīmāṁsakas study the logico-psychological property of knowledge, namely, the occurrence of indubitability or of apodictic certainty.

We can agree with the Mīmāṁsakas on the point that when knowledge occurs, the incident, if viewed from the subject's side, appears to be bound with his consciousness. In this sense there is in every knowing subject an inborn assurance that the knowledge is something that takes place in "my mind," that the sensations obtained are "my sensations," and that "my mind" and "my knowledge" are inseparable. When seen in this manner, the very act of knowing can be said to involve self-certainty or intuitive indubitability. It would have a noesis-noema[16] unity, a plunge of self into not-self, an acquisition of the known as the "end" of the predisposed mind. But if we look at knowledge from the objective side, as the Nyāya thinkers have done, and direct our interests to the nature of the given, then we are bound to find it to be a product of the external world impressing upon the knower. To evaluate knowledge from the objective side is to judge the empirical conditions that go to make it true or false. The indispensability of this latter approach, emphasized by the Naiyāyikas as forcefully as by neorealists, can be easily realized in the explication of error.

KNOWLEDGE: A SUBJECTIVIST STANDPOINT

Some of the most forceful critics of the epistemologists of the Nyāya and the Mīmāṁsā schools figured between the fourth and the ninth century A.D. in the Buddhist sect of Svatantra-Vijñānavāda. The most original in their search for an antirealist basis of knowledge among them are Dinnāga, Dharmakīrti, Śāntarakṣita and Kamalaśila. A brief treatment of their thought in the present section will show that they might have figured, directly or indirectly, as an immediate prelude to Śaṅkara's theory of *māyā* and even to his notion of human consciousness as self-luminosity or *svaprakāśa,* which is surely the most fundamental breakthrough to knowledge in the whole of Indian philosophy.

It was mentioned earlier that the Vijñānavādins explain the perceptive world as being "in mind," "in sensations," "in thought and other mental dispositions," and not as being "there" irrespective of the presence or absence of the knower. The Svatantra-Vijñānavāda, also known as the Logical School of Buddhism, is an impressive assertion of the Vijñānavādins' position with an extensive contribution to it of researches on perception.

The single presupposition—Buddhistic in every sense of the

16 The Mīmāṁsā doctrine of the self-certainty in perceptual knowledge is very close to Husserl's finding that although every perception has its noema, at the base of perception there is a "perceptual meaning," a kind of "intuitively" and "certainly" "meant-thing." See Husserl, Edmund: *Ideas.*. W. R. Boyce Gibson (trans.), pp. 236–41.

term—on which the Svatantra-Vijñānavādins erect their epistemology and logic is that the entire Reality, including human consciousness, is impermanent or momentary. Momentariness being the very essence of the known and the knower, the only conception of knowledge one can justifiably form, they hold, is one in which both of them are regarded as internal manifestations of the most primordial pure consciousness. Through the typical angry debates they carried on with the realist Naiyāyikas and Mīmāṁsakas, the Svatantra-Vijñānavādins have tried to prove that both knowledge by perception and knowledge by inference reflect only "moments" of existence, i.e. something eternally moving, something so fleeting that it is as if buoyed on an infinite expanse of Nothingness.

There is no rigidity or permanence in anything that forms the object of our consciousness. As a matter of fact, at no two moments it is the same object that we refer to. For the Svatantra-Vijñānavāda, objects are not independent beings; they are posited by consciousness to itself, more in terms of "flashes" than static "wholes." Dharmakīrti says that it is consciousness itself that manifests itself as an outside object, and thereby "knows" itself. To say, therefore, that we cognize the world as something externally present is merely to affirm that our senses and consciousness, at given moments of time, "possess" it as something related to them or as something which cannot be imagined to remain unrelated to them. No thing or idea can *be* and yet not-be *in* consciousness; nothing can exist and yet be not-known.

It is well-known that the Svatantra-Vijñānavādins, like Bishop Berkeley, refuse to allude to the world of sense-perception as material or objective, because of their tacit adherence to mentalism and acosmism. By looking upon the material world as a continuous flux generated by the equally fluxlike human consciousness, they assert that the knower-known duality is fundamentally due to a two-pronged flow of the same pure consciousness. Material things, therefore, are constellations of sensations, ideas, or impressions, emerging as "moments" of experience like points along the stream of some amorphous stuff. And just as things are along a flow, the consciousness that perceives them is in a flow too. Permanence, whether of the objects sensed or of the ego-sense, is an illusion, a "practically" produced make-believe of mind.

Now, if nothing in the field of our experience is really permanent or self-identical, how could we define an object? Where does an object exist? And when our sensations and perceptions direct us to the externally and independently existent world, could we say that there is such a world?

We have already noted that questions such as these would not be entertained by the Mādhyamikas, for whom the universe is basically nonexistent. However, they are of great significance to the Vijñānavādins or Yogāchāras, such as Asaṅga and Vasubandhu, and to the Svatantra-Vijñānavādins, for the simple reason that, epistemologists as these thinkers are, they are unable to underestimate the fact that the object is a "given" to the cognitive consciousness and that as such it must be accounted for as a positivity. Moreover, they emphasize that this "given" is internal to consciousness, that it is an idea in the psychic field—a kind of self-reflection the conscious stuff throws onto itself. Thus when an object is perceived or an impression is thought of, consciousness projects itself in the form of something positively "there outside."

According to Dinnāga, sensation, thought and linguistic expression do not embody the momentary and the indescribable pure awareness forming the base of all existence. Like Bergson, Dinnāga looks upon intellectual categories as mental constructions whose application would remain confined to the phenomenal alone. Thus when something is cognized as an object, it is the intellectual principle that is in operation. Intellect sets the phenomenal psyche over pure consciousness and leaves it opaque. To perceive or to know a phenomenon is to create by means of diverse intellectual operations a peculiar inner affectation, and to fling it out "there" into space and time. Consistent with the famous Vijñānavāda aphorism that "the whole world is mental" (*Sarvam buddhimayam jagat*), therefore, the Svatantra-Vijñānavāda argues that particular things in our experience spring up like flutters of some primordial indeterminable and absolutely formless (*anirbhāsa*) substance, namely, *citta, vijñāna* or *ālaya.*

It may be observed that the Svatantra-Vijñānavāda represents the intensification of Buddhists' epistemological program that began, rather amazingly, with the naive realism in the Vaibhāṣika school around second century A.D. and produced an impressive phenomenalism in the Sautrāntika school around fourth century A.D. The fact that this intensification finally reached its extreme point in the nihilism of the Mādhyamikas shows that whatever its intermediate phases the Buddhist epistemology is built up on the transcendental—and in every sense of the word, existentialist—presupposition of Buddha that human suffering is a personification of the eternal futility at the bottom of our phenomenally governed world, life and action.

As a matter of fact, the line of demarcation between the position of the Vaibhāṣika school and that of the Sautrāntika school is very thin. For both, the existence of an extramental universe, i.e. the universe of objects independent of the knowing mind, can never be legitimately doubted. The Vaibhāṣikas, who are more emphatic in their affirmation of the world-consciousness than the Sautrāntikas, clearly distinguish between the realm of ideas and the realm of objects, and regard the latter as something "given" and as enduring through all spatiotemporal changes. But the Sautrāntikas, who like Hume concentrate on the mental representation of the objective world more than on anything else, take the diversity of the "givens" in our cognitive consciousness as itself demonstrating the existence of a world outside it. As Dharmottara, in his commentary on Dharmakīrti's *Nyāya-Bindu,* puts it:

> Direct cognition of an object in the form of a perceptive judgment is possible, i.e., (the object is really) being cognized, owing to the coordination (of an image with a point of external reality and its contrast with correlative images). Indeed, as soon as our awareness (begins to present itself as) an image of something blue, only then can we judge that we have a distinct cognition of it. . . .[17]

However, the Sautrāntikas do not alter the general Buddhist thesis that momentariness is the essential nature of reality. They explain that the impression of rigidity objects in the universe cast on us is due to a peculiar placing of the sense-data. While

[17] Stcherbatsky: *Buddhist Logic,* Vol. II, p. 42.

according to the Vaibhāṣikas our perception of a tree, for instance, proves categorically that "there" is a tree, according to the Sautrāntikas the existence of a tree "there outside" is inferred from the fact of our having "tree" sense-data or a tree-idea.

The subjectivist theory of the Vijñānavāda and of the Svatantra-Vijñānavāda, therefore, that all things are mental constructions, indicates the quest for inward concentration in Buddhism. The theory uncompromisingly states that consciousness constructs the world and is deceived by the construction, that it falls into a realm of fantasy and believes it to be truly "there," that what is *svacitta* or "of one's own mind" is mistaken for being external to mind. It is a universal deception, a *māyā* (illusion). And as long as this deception keeps the consciousness in bondage, no freedom is possible.

WHITHER KNOWLEDGE?

In Indian philosophy, the question *what* knowledge should finally attain and the question *how* the constituents of a genuine knowledge-situation should be are not clearly distinguishable. The Nyāya and the Vaibhāṣika realism, the Sautrāntika phenomenalism and the Vijñānavadins' subjective idealism have been engaged in the examination of the furniture of knowledge, and hence in the second question. Evidently, they appear to be types of what is today known as "doing philosophy." But as epistemologies founded on certain partly metaphysical and partly ethical assumptions, they could not proceed without frequently running into the first question. Strictly speaking, the acumen shown by Indian logicians and epistemologists in ancient times is largely the accompaniment of their poise in serious dialectics, a contingency in response to the circumstances in discussions, a weapon for victory against their philosophical opponents. The acumen was exercised—as it is exercised in serious intellectual discussions even today—much for the pleasure of seeing the "transcendentalist" opponents puzzled and defeated in the verbal battles.

This is not to underestimate the depth and the originality of logic and epistemologies in ancient India. What cannot be ignored is that the Indian mind, even in its realist attitude exhibited in the Nyāya and the Vaibhāṣika theories, could not abandon its essentially ego-searching and salvation-seeking posture. This posture was neither questioned nor subjected to any critical examination. The infallibility of its advance towards the ultimate destination of life, namely, freedom or *mokṣa,* was accepted as a truism.

As a matter of fact, Indian thinkers present two different notions of knowledge: one emphasizing that knowledge is an emergence from man's "normal" or natural state,[18] and the other emphasizing the "supraconscious" or supernatural experience that confronts the knower's entire person. It is the latter notion of knowledge—called *jñāna* throughout Indian philosophy—that has been kept out of any analytic enquiry in the writings of Indians. *Jñāna* is always understood as an enlightenment, throwing open the innermost being of one's own self and generating a certainty that can stand no comparison with any other type of intellectual certainty. Hindus, Buddhists and Jainas, irrespective of their epistemological and logical types, point out the significance of *jñāna* for *mokṣa,* therefore, in the most unflinching manner possible.

Jainism and Buddhism consistently maintain that a leap to the knowledge of the self is a leap from here to eternity, from the finite to the infinite, from the uncertain to the absolutely certain.

In the threefold path for salvation, called *ratnatraya,* Jainism holds the pure and omniscient knowledge (*anantajñāna, kevalajñāna*) to be of greater value than the other two constituents, namely, right belief and right conduct. Such a knowledge, the Jainas say, has the power of introducing the soul into a sphere where it would achieve absolute peace, absolute freedom and absolute joy. And for Buddhists, the state of *nirvāṇa* (literally, blowing off), "which is unsurpassed and secure from all worldly yoke," generates in one an unimaginable expanse of pure awareness, pure existence and pure vacuity. Buddha's search for such a state, like the Jainas' search for a completely worldless experi-

[18] Knowledge, emerging in this natural manner, has two sources: perception or *pratyakṣa* and inference or *anumāna.* There is hardly any system of thought in Indian philosophy which does not recognize this type of knowledge. However, every system advises one to transcend it, and to hug the supraconscious.

ence, is motivated by his desire to embrace something infinite and indefinable beyond the fringe of the worldly. Regardless of the negative element we may possibly find in the two views of life, what is definitely goal oriented in them is their extreme longing for grasping the highest imaginable moral and metaphysical abstraction. Their firm repudiation of the pragmatic side of life must be regretted; but their full-hearted impulse for the joy of the beyond must be admired.

CONSCIOUSNESS AS PURE TRANSPARENCE

Undoubtedly, the most profound statement concerning the ideal of absolute-freedom-through-knowledge is embodied in the Sāṅkhya doctrine of the dissolution of the *puruṣa-prakṛti* nexus and in the Advaita Vedānta doctrine of *Brahman*-knowledge. In these doctrines, unlike any other doctrine of moral perfection in the world, some of the most extraordinary facets of human consciousness are portrayed partly psychologically and partly ontologically. The main purpose of the doctrines is to show that a total emancipation from the state of bondage in the world is possible only when through a sweeping vision of self as transparence, a dazzling self-illumination and an absolute self-evidence, man is led to "see" and identify his fundamental being as against his false and world-conscious being, his pure knowing intuition as against his intellectually governed mind, his primordial unlimited life-awareness as against his contingent worldly station. One can draw a parallel between the insights incorporated in these doctrines and the inner penetrations of outstanding phenomenologists and existentialists in our own times.

It was seen that, according to the Sāṅkhya concept of causality, *prakṛti* is the substratum, the first cause, from which the whole universe emanates as a series of heterogeneous effects. All physical and psychical phenomena are the transformation of *prakṛti*. The principle known as *puruṣa,* on the other hand, is conceived by the Sāṅkhya thinkers as immaculate consciousness, distinct from intellect (*buddhi*), the ego-sense (*ahaṁkāra*) and the internal sense or mind (*manas*), all of which are merely the evolutes of *prakṛti*. Clearly, therefore, *puruṣa* in all its essence cannot be related to anything except itself. Its presence behind *prakṛti* and its products is described as that of the seer (*draṣṭṛ*) behind the seen (*dṛṣya*), that of the experiencer (*bhokṭṛ*) behind the experienced (*bhogya*), or that of spirit (*sacetana*) behind matter (*acetana*). It is the witnessing or *sākṣin* awareness—a kind of constantly watching eye—above all that goes on in the realm of *prakṛti*.

By defining consciousness as a reality absolutely unconnected with even the act of cognition, the Sāṅkhya has endowed it with an abstract trans-empirical status and an indescribable solitude of its own. The highly introspective method the Sāṅkhya philosophers must have used in order to eliminate, one by one, different agencies of the empirical knowledge (*vṛttijñāna*) as something extraneous to the pure self-experience of *puruṣas*, culminates in reducing the individual loci of consciousness to Nothingness, to centers of some fluvial indistinguishable matter. Indeed, the Sāṅkhya does not explicitly state that the *puruṣas* are "voids" or "empties." Had they been so, they would not have functioned as consciousnesses, seers, knowers, or witnesses. However, the peculiar unspecifiable presence they are supposed to enjoy as the silent spectators of the entire psychophysical spectrum of the universe is not different from the presence of "pure I's" that are not conscious of anything.

The Sāṅkhya view of the relation between *puruṣa* and different mental states or psychic mutations (*vṛttijñāna*) is that the former is reflected in the latter and falsely identifies itself with them. Indeed, there is nothing in the evolutionary products of *prakṛti* which can keep consciousness tied to the world. Since *puruṣa* is not a thought, nor the I-principle nor the sensing self, it cannot come into contact with the knowledge of the external world. It stays separated from all intellectual functions, although these mirror it as their underlying awareness. In their essence, Vācaspati Miśra says, *buddhi*, cognition, perception, the sense of pleasure, pain and rest, reflection and other faculties of knowledge are insentient. It is the spirit alone that is sentient; and inasmuch as the spirit appears in these faculties, they are seen to exhibit sentience.[19]

[19] Jha, Gangānath (trans.): *The Tattva-Kaumudī* (Vācaspati Misra's Commentary on the Sāṅkhya-Kārikā). Poona, Oriental Book Agency, 1965, p. 21.

Now it is not difficult to see that the Sāṅkhya thinkers had never had a program of constructing an epistemology for its own sake. The analysis of the mental life they have expounded, therefore, is with a view to demonstrating that all mutations of our empirical consciousness are ultimately the mutations of matter, and that they do not in any way affect the transcendence of the self. Since the selves are not connected even to the reflective and self-identifying mental principle, their existence belongs to a typically trans-mental realm. What exact state of consciousness one would enjoy when one is stabilized in this realm, the Sāṅkhya does not care to make clear.

According to the Sāṅkhya, it is the knowledge of the fact of one's being unrelated to any mundane experience, of one's being fundamentally free from any association with I-as-a-thinking-being, of one's being unconditioned by space, time, causality, senses, etc., that paves the way for one's *mokṣa*. Once a *puruṣa* has realized full and direct comprehension of its distinctness from all those psychophysical modes with which it has come to identify itself, it becomes wholly self-possessed and immune from existential transitions. For the self there is no value that is greater than its own release. When released, it accomplishes total annihilation of suffering, boredom and despair, and lives the life of a *jīvanmukta* (freed from attachment) or *videḥamukta* (freed from body).

Whereas, despite its remarkably close affinity to the Vedic-Upaniṣadic ātmalogy, the Sāṅkhya school stays silent on the transcendental nature of the self or consciousness,[20] the Vedānta conclusively establishes that consciousness is luminosity, transparence or radiance (*svaprakāśa*). Actually, the concept of *ātman* or *Brahman* in the Upaniṣads clearly embodies the suggestion that consciousness is an entity possessing the unique disposition of manifesting itself as a full reflection of itself, as the most primordial qualityless existence, as pure experience. In its real being, therefore, consciousness identifies itself with some sort

[20] See Garbe's article on Sāṅkhya in the *Encyclopaedia of Religion and Ethics*, Vol. XI, p. 192. Garbe maintains that for the Sāṅkhya a state similar to release is "temporarily attained in deep dreamless sleep, in swoons, and in abstraction that reaches the stage of unconsciousness as in emancipation after death."

of unincarnate, self-shining and all-encompassing spirit. The Vedānta theory of consciousness not only concurs with the Upaniṣadic thesis, but also brings out its complete metaphysical and mystical implications.

According to the Upaniṣads, the knowledge of the real contains an immediately intuitible self-validity. In an identical tenor Śaṅkara holds that the individual consciousness or *ātman* differs from all other things in that it is formless, immaculate, self-manifesting and is of the nature of "spiritual wisdom." Consciousness is the actual embodiment of bliss (*ānanda*). Like Kapila, Īśvarakṛṣṇa, Vijñānabhikśu and other Sāṅkhya thinkers, he argues that thought, imagination, feeling, desire, etc., are mental mutations foreign to pure consciousness. Consciousness supports them and clings to them in the capacity of a *draṣṭṛ* or high "seeing" awareness. Anything that passes for an impression or sensation is a mental state, a *vṛtti* directed towards an object (*dṛṣya*); it does not in any fundamental way affect consciousness per se. There is therefore nothing necessary as regards the connection between consciousness and diverse states of mind. Śaṅkara is in total agreement with the Upaniṣads when he indicates that pure *ātman* is devoid of any psychic modes. Its being is self-contained, and linguistically indeterminable. Its vision of itself is perfect illumination, perfect joyous duration, perfect peace.

It needs to be emphasized that the experience of the metaphysical core of human existence, which the Vedic-Upaniṣadic thinkers were intent on achieving more than any of their contemporaries elsewhere, finds its most lucid expression in Śaṅkara's philosophy. Śaṅkara is an unparallelled representative of all that is transcendental and inward-seeing in the Upaniṣads; and as Dasgupta aptly puts it, "if he could show that his interpretation was the only interpretation that was faithful to the Upaniṣads, and that its apparent contradictions with experience could in some way be explained, he considered that he had nothing more to do." [21] No wonder, therefore, Śaṅkara attempts an exploration of the mystery of consciousness, and through that attempt embarks upon proving the contingent character of the world. Unlike any

[21] Dasgupta, Surendranath: *A History of Indian Philosophy,* Vol. I, pp. 434–35.

attempt of this kind tried in philosophy, Śaṅkara's is an endeavor not confined to the problem of the knower-known dichotomy, but to grasp its very *raison d'être*. What he aspires after is a systematic demonstration of the incompatibility of the objective existence of the world with the inwardly graspable subjectivity.

It has been shown that, according to the Advaita Vedānta, the relation of consciousness to its objects must be looked upon as the former's entanglement in *māyā*. It is a situation from which consciousness is to be withdrawn, and then channelled towards its own abode. While in the Yoga school the actual technique for the physicopsychic control necessary to the appropriate practice of these acts is set down, in the Vedānta the final outcome of this control, namely, our grasping of consciousness as pure light or *svaprakāśạtva,* is made the center of all deliberations. In the next section we shall comment upon the exact reach of the Yoga technique, and evaluate some of its most salient features aiding what one can call "lessons in equipoise." What is enough to see at this stage is that the Vedāntins were not particularly interested in the incidental paraphernalia of *yoga;* they concentrated their attention on the nature of the ultimate transcendentalization, on the attainment of the inward peace. In the fulfillment of the self's trans-empirical urge lies one's acquisition of absolute and permanent truth.

According to the Vedānta, one's own authentic being flashes on oneself as the self-luminous cause and ground of one's life and of world-consciousness. There is, as the Vedāntins see it, a necessity and self-certainty about the knowledge of this ground. The entire world of objects rises on this ground, which is its seat (*adhisthāṇa*) , genesis and meaning.

We might point out, in the light of what we have shown regarding the elements of similarity between ātmalogy and transcendental phenomenology, that what the Vedāntins suggest by the self-luminosity of *ātman* or consciousness is not unlike what phenomenologists and existentialists have described through the notion of intentionality or directedness of the human self. If not for any ethical or religious purpose, at least out of a partly psychological and partly epistemological interest, phenomenologists since Husserl have sought to describe a stratum of subjective experience at which the impression emanating from the world of objects can be held back and the fluvial point of encounter between them and the cognitive consciousness can be figured out. Indeed, hardly any phenomenologist has shown the inclination to carry the process of transcendentalization to such an extreme as to finally nullify the existence of the world or to regard it as an illusion. But, like the Advaita Vedānta, phenomenology has acknowledged a self-revealing and world-intuiting innate capacity of the self—a capacity that is the exclusive possession of human reality.

Phenomenologists and existentialists, such as Franz Brentano, Husserl, Karl Jaspers, Sartre and Maurice Merleau-Ponty, maintain that the most characteristic feature of human consciousness is its directedness towards and transcendence over the phenomenal world. While distinguishing the physical from the mental, Brentano holds that "intentionality" or "direction upon something" (*Gerichtetsein*) is the unique character of the latter. There cannot be a mental state or mental behavior, he says, which does not tend towards some content. Whatever activity we may be engaged in, our consciousness runs out of itself to clasp an object. Brentano writes: "We cannot judge anything, cannot desire anything, cannot hope for anything, or fear anything, if it is not presented." [22] Consciousness is a correlate, always having something as its subject matter.

Now, when Husserl resets the concept of the intentionality of consciousness, he like Brentano underlines the fact that the world is offered to us because of the directedness of our pure ego. For Husserl, "to be a consciousness of something" is the most natural feature of the ego; the ego directs itself towards an object, glances the object, and apprehends itself as a "glancing-towards." [23] It is not that consciousness creates the phenomenal world; however, in order that the world be perceived as being "there," there should be consciousness. Again, every experience is given meaning, is viewed as something real and namable, because of consciousness's running towards it. It is due to this "wonderful

[22] Brentano, Franz: The Distinction between Mental and Physical Phenomena. In Chisholm, Roderick M. (Ed.) : *Realism and The Background of Phenomenology.* London, George Allen & Unwin Ltd., 1960, p. 42.

[23] Husserl, Edmund: *Ideas.* W. R. Boyce Gibson (trans.) , pp. 108–9.

peculiarity" of the human essence—to tend towards an object and yet to be able to abstract itself from it—that it manifests itself as an eternal quest.

Husserl founds his entire method of the phenomenological "bracketing" (*epoché*) on a possibility of consciousness to withdraw itself from not only total empirical experience but also from its basic directedness towards objects. In his theory of the transcendental ego, he clearly points out that when through a continued technique of the suspension of experience and its constitutive principles there remains a "residuum"—a purely formal pattern of ideas devoid of any meaning—one must practice a transcendental reduction for the suspension of the residuum too. The result of this second suspension would be that one would be face to face with the pure ego or pure consciousness. Husserl remarks that "pure ego" appears to be essential in principle, that is, as that which stays absolutely self-identical in all changes of experience. It does not form a part of the empirical experience, but different layers of experience are arranged by it meaningfully.[24]

Indeed, since phenomenology is only a procedure utilized for the purpose of reconstituting all the principles and primitives of knowledge—such as meanings, categories, grammatical and logical axioms, and relations—it does not show any specific interest in the denudation of consciousness of all its modes. In other words, with a demand for a radically new perspective of the universe, phenomenologists use the method of suspension or bracketing, inasmuch as it is the only device for gaining a grip over the origin of the knower-known relation. Thus, neither Brentano nor Husserl, nor any other phenomenologist or existentialist, for that matter, would wish to dwell on the preintentional or the purely nullified ego for its own sake. It is only in the transcendentalism of Indians that inward-seeing, the withdrawal of consciousness from all that "engages" it, the reinstallation of the *ātman* as intrinsic luminousness, is looked upon as the end and the most desirable fruition of the knowledge-seeking act.

[24] See *Ibid.*, p. 156. For a pertinent treatment of Husserl's concept of pure consciousness, see Heinemann, F. H.: *Existentialism and the Modern Predicament.* New York, Harper Torchbooks, 1958, pp. 47–58.

One of the most profound treatments of the pure consciousness, and of its operation in knowledge, is found in the Advaita Vedānta. It conceives cognitive consciousness as the principle of revelation, as the *ātman* throwing its beam on the objects, or as the innermost essence of experience. Consciousness is the subtlest inward sense, the *antaḥkāraṇa,* constantly functioning through its modes (*vṛttis*) : *manas* (mind), *buddhi* (intellect), *ahaṁkāra* (the ego-sense) and *citta* (memory). When we know something, consciousness focuses its light on it and as if alienates it from the entire expanse of darkness or ignorance. Therefore, no knowledge can occur when consciousness, or its modes, have not reached the known and illumined it. To know a thing is to be aware of a form of consciousness, of a modification of *vṛtti,* of something to which the mind or the memory has stuck.

As a matter of fact, *antaḥkāraṇa,* like the intentionality of the conscious, is the very foundation of our contact with the world. For Husserl, consciousness with its directedness towards things would become *this* and *that* in "psychical experiences," and yet would preserve the self-evidence of all its experiences within itself. Its "inner perception," Husserl says, provides it with an intuition of something being actually present, of something "touching" it from outside, of something modifying it and drawing it out of itself. And in the same manner, for Śaṅkara all mental processes—thinking, imagining, willing, acting, and the like —represent the transformation of consciousness into diverse modes (*vṛttis*) internally perceived by the self-luminous consciousness itself. All knowledge in this sense is an awareness of self's tending towards itself and towards the world. My knowledge is my self-revelation, my intellectual presence to myself, my immediate and glaring feeling of experiencing myself as the seer (*draṣṭṛ*), the experiencer (*bhokṭṛ*) and the witness (*sāksin*).

With an essentially psychogenetical point of view consistent with a full stretching of the phenomenological introspection, Sartre gives expression to the inward-seeing or self-illuminating character of human consciousness. In his *The Transcendence of the Ego* and *Being and Nothingness,* Sartre, like Śaṅkara, attempts a comprehensive analysis of the act of consciousness both in its reflective and prereflective positions. Although it is not his aim to arrive at any idea of consciousness that might vitiate his purely descriptive and epistemological method, Sartre's approach to the riddle of human existence is not devoid of a presupposition that it is within the sphere of consciousness alone that life's futility in the world can be realized. It is not difficult to find an echo of the theory of the self-luminosity of *ātman* in his existentialism.

Sartre writes that the mode of existence of consciousness is to be conscious of itself. And consciousness is conscious of itself inasmuch as it is a tendency towards the trancendental. Sartre says that everything is clear and lucid in consciousness. It is the object with its characteristic "opacity" that is spread in front of consciousness; but consciousness is purely and simply consciousness of being conscious of that object. The object of awareness is outside of itself, and this is why consciousness posits and grasps the object in the same act. "Consciousness only knows itself as absolute inwardness. . . . It is entirely lightness, entirely translucence." [25]

According to both Śaṅkara and Sartre, consciousness is as if divided within itself. Śaṅkara explains that consciousness is a witness of all its modes; but since all these modes emanate from its inward sense (*antaḥkāraṇa*), mind, intellect, the ego-sense and memory, it is its own witness. This phenomenon is evident in a highly concentrated introspection. Things seem to go on round the self-shining self that is fleetingly aware of them and of itself. For an attempt at grasping it in this process, consciousness seems to posit itself as a superperson unfolding the universe from darkness to light, from obscurity to clarity, from ignorance to knowledge. Śaṅkara, therefore, emphasizes that no experience can hold the *ātman* bound to it, can alter its transcendental character. *Ātman* as a superperson is totally immersed in its own being. The *ātman*-consciousness is a qualityless substance; it would stay in its substantial status when, as a result of its inward-seeing and its withdrawal from its *vṛttis,* it attains absolute freedom or *mokṣa.*

Sartre tells us that we are constantly face to face with "a syn-

[25] Sartre, Jean-Paul: *The Transcendence of the Ego.* Forrest Williams and Robert Kirkpatrick (trans.), New York, Noonday, 1957, pp. 40–41.

thesis of two consciousnesses," one of which reflects and the other is reflected on. In our everyday activities, our consciousness is engaged in reflective operations and hence presents itself as a *cogito*. However, its functioning as a *cogito* does not exhaust consciousness. Sartre remarks that "insofar as my reflecting consciousness is consciousness of itself, it is *non-positional* consciousness"[26] (italics original). For between its being a *cogito*—that is, being positional in activities like counting, driving, reading, etc. —and its being immediately, nonreflectively and nonpositionally given to itself, consciousness has to stay at a level higher than its directedness towards objects. Sartre, like Husserl, holds that the reflecting consciousness and the consciousness reflected-on emerge in such an order that the former is the *sine qua non* of the latter. And this is precisely what Śaṅkara too suggests when he states that knowledge assumes a self-shining self, which besides being *vṛttijñāna* or besides revealing the objective universe, is fully conscious of itself.

It is not essential to stretch this line of comparison between Śaṅkara and Sartre any further. What has to be observed is that both the Vedāntins and the existentialists speak of consciousness as a vortex, thick at the center and rarefied at the edge, which mingles with the spatiotemporal being. The fact that there is behind every instance of object awareness a self-awareness, or a sort of leap down to the metaphysical void, is stressed by them not while pursuing the same objective. The Vedāntins' objective is to seek the most enduring enlightenment by means of the maximum intensification of self-awareness; that of the existentialists is to depict a psychological ambiguity at the root of our very experience of being in the world. So when Śaṅkara points out that consciousness exhibits itself through its modes or *vṛttis,* his purpose is to not only scorn this exhibition but also to invent a panacea for the severance of the former from the latter. A consciousness that does not ultimately establish itself as pure translucence, the fullest light of *Brahman,* is not for him emancipated. On the other hand, what Sartre perhaps finds extremely impor-

[26] *Ibid.*, p. 42.

tant is a swing of our attention from the outward to the inward, from "every positional consciousness of an object" to the most spontaneous "consciousness of consciousness." [27] It is the mystery of this swing, the running of consciousness to its own genesis without sticking to any stable point, that has figured as the central theme of his philosophy.

YOGA: THE ASCENT TO SILENCE

The experience of pure consciousness or transcendental subjectivity disconnected from and carried "behind" all its modes (*vṛttis*) has been aimed at in Indian philosophies as the most valuable prerequisite of *mokṣa*. Ordinarily, the act of consciousness to withdraw itself from its various dispositions towards the world is likely to be looked upon as a kind of inward discipline devised for the reading of one's fundamental existence. But the role it is made to play by philosophers in India indicates that if there was any method of knowledge that India of old times fully developed, it is the method of coiling and recoiling consciousness until it vanished into a chiaroscuro. The most systematic exposition of this method is found in the Yoga school of Patañjali (second century B.C.).

For India the only desirable plane of existence is one which is absolutely free from the mundane conditions—births and rebirths, *karma* and bondage, ignorance and suffering, and the phenomenon of worldliness which generates all these. The Yoga school represents an attempt at carrying out the operative side of transcendentalism. It is in all its essential respects a system of rules for the inward-seeing, for a transcendental reduction [28] destined towards a total elimination of mind, intellect (*buddhi*), the I-principle, memory and senses. Whatever may be the character of experience *yoga* [29] means to induce, and whether such an experience is somewhat similar to those flashes of psychic inten-

[27] Sartre, Jean-Paul: *Being and Nothingness*. Hazel E. Barnes (trans.), pp. liii–liv.

[28] *Yoga* involves a process similar to the phenomenological suspension of the entire reflective activity. See Sinari, Ramakant: The Method of Phenomenological Reduction and Yoga, *Philosophy East and West*. Vol. 15, No. 3–4, pp. 217–228.

[29] Literally, the word *yoga* means the harnessing of one's psychic powers.

sity Aldous Huxley alludes to as "visionary or mystical," [30] the fact remains that to a yogi the extinction of the world-consciousness and the creation of inner tranquillity themselves imply the attainment of *jīvanmukti* or total freedom.

The breakthrough to the knowledge of subjectivity or to *jñāna* Yoga upholds, has its own peculiar characteristics. As a procedure, *yoga* consists of an eightfold path that begins with physical regulations like suspension of respiration, erect sitting postures, behavioral purification, and ends up with the complete absorption of consciousness within itself. As the preliminary bodily discipline becomes more and more settled and, consequently, offers greater and greater stability to the nervous structure, one starts experiencing a certain lucid feeling. However, it is not advisable, according to Yoga, to restrain the eightfold path anywhere in the middle. Although the experience of lucidity and the subsequent stages of the breaking-up of psychophysical tensions are themselves attractive, the yogi has to surpass them. His aim is to arrive at the terminal point in inward-seeing.

The climax of self-realization is attained when the entire being of the yogi possesses itself *in toto* and the world is shot out of him altogether. This is the stage of joyous silence—a breath-taking experience having no parallel in anything that we might conceive while keeping the mental faculties intact. In a sense, it is the accomplishing of a conscious state where common psychic activities, like perception, thought, imagination and desire, cease to appear. The assumption in which a yogi grounds his exercise is that his complete soul-emptying act would bring him closest to the primordial source of existence.

The idea of soul-emptying is as old as the *Taitirīya Upaniṣad,* where the famous theory of the five *kośas* or sheaths of the self is comprehensively explained. According to this theory, the *ātman* or pure consciousness is cloaked by the layers of the impure stuff,

[30] See Huxley, Aldous: *The Doors of Perception and Heaven and Hell.* Middlesex, Penguin Books, 1959, p. 113. Huxley, one of the greatest admirers of Hinduism in the West, explains: "Long suspensions of breath lead to a high concentration of carbon dioxide in the lung and blood, and this increase in the concentration of CO_2 lowers the efficiency of the brain as a reducing valve and permits the entry into consciousness of experiences . . . from 'out there.'"

namely, the alimentary (*annamaya*), the respiratory (*prāṇamaya*), the mental (*manomaya*), the intellectual (*vijñānamaya*) and the blissful (*ānandamaya*), all of which are extraneous to the essence of the metaphysical and the eternal. They are the remnants of man's evolution from his original vegetative nature to the highly concentrated trans-empirical inwardness. The *Taitirīya Upaniṣad* says that while the alimentary sheath denotes our gross body, the respiratory, the mental and the intellectual sheaths constitute our subtle body (*sukṣma-śarīra*). The blissful or *ānandamaya* sheath is the last screen of the bodily stuff, which when penetrated through, would put one's consciousness in direct contact with its own light. The blissful *kośa* is not in itself the destination of the inward-directed experience; but being the nearest veil to the self, it shows consciousness round its own region.

Yoga is an aid to one's plying one's attention across the *kośas* and, ultimately, to gaining ecstatic inner silence and liberation. According to Patañjali, therefore, as long as the mind, the senses, the discriminating power, the modes of consciousness and the ego persist, a succession of the states of consciousness would be present, and one would be enslaved by or encased in all sorts of temperamental fluctuations. The goal of the yogi is to posit his consciousness in its purest form, to let his being engulf itself, to endure as a calm subjective luminosity, to experience *samādhi* or a fusion of mind within itself.

Samādhi is the most remarkable state of human consciousness. Not only has it remained the only cherishable final goal of life, but it has also constituted a kind of trans-conscious rapturous condition to Hindus, Buddhists and Jainas alike. Indeed, it stays very near to experiences like *dhāraṇā* (concentration), *dhyāna* (meditation), *ekāgratā* (pointedness of attention) and *cittavṛttinirodha* (the suppression of the modes of consciousness). However, as Eliade has recently shown, "any degree of methodological conscience will show us that we have no right to put *samādhi* among . . . countless varieties of spiritual escape." [31]

According to the Yoga school, *samādhi* can be of two types: *saṃprajñāta* or differentiated and *asaṃprajñāta* or undifferen-

[31] Eliade, Mircea: *Yoga: Immortality and Freedom*. Willard Trask (trans.), New York, Bollingen Series LVI, Pantheon, 1958, p. 99.

tiated. When the yogi catches some object with his concentrated and furrowed consciousness, the *samādhi* is called differentiated. In this type, the subject-object distinction is not dissolved, though it is blurred and mobile. But when consciousness is so controlled that it is entirely free from its subject-matter, that is, when it is nothing but an immaculate presence to itself, the *samādhi* is called undifferentiated. The basic character of this second type is that it is without any distinguishable given, and denotes the emergence of the fact of pure duration or "mindlessness" in experience. The *asaṃprajñāta samādhi* is the real end of *yoga*. It is a gate to the intuition of transcendental bliss, absolute tranquillity, or of an indistinguishable stasis of all mental functions. The Yoga system regards that the *asaṃprajñāta samādhi* is the threshold to *kaivalya,* or to total liberation of the *puruṣa* from *prakṛti*.

The difficulty that has all along presented itself in our attempt to determine the exact nature of the destination of an *ātman*-directed quest appears also when we think of the essence of the state of *kaivalya. Brahmānubhava, nirvāṇa, kevala-jñāna, mokṣa, jīvanmukti, kaivalya,* are terms that stand for an indescribable canvas of experience spread before a consciousness that has emptied itself of all world-impressions. Being no more tied to the spatiotemporal and the mental happenings, consciousness at this level of existence is without any thought or language, feeling or commitment, emotion or desire. Such an existence might be equated to absolute blankness, Nothingness, or pure and infinite presence, provided we assume that to Indians it constitutes the highest rung of the act of living to be reached by constant inward-seeing discipline. To grasp consciousness in its intensest mode of being, to recapitulate it in all its abstraction and freedom, has been the ideal of *yoga* and hence of all those philosophical and religious tendencies in India which emphasize the value of knowledge.

Chapter Ten

BHAKTI: AN ANTIDOTE TO INTELLECT

FOR A UNION WITH GOD

IN EVERY society the training of the intellect is the preoccupation of a few. Indian masses since the Vedic-Upaniṣadic times have sought to fulfil the demands of the emotional self more vigorously than they lauded the intellectual pursuits of their philosophers. That the way of devotion, love, or *bhakti* is as effective as and more spontaneous than the intellectual way for the attainment of salvation was recognized in India as early as the fifth century B.C. when besides Jainism and Buddhism, the great epic *Mahābhārata* and numerous Purāṇas[1] were proving a sway on the mind of the people. Some of the Upaniṣads themselves propound the doctrine of man's emotional union with God by using exuberant expressions. For instance, the *Muṇḍaka Upaniṣad* says, "The Self cannot be attained by instruction nor by intellectual power nor even through much hearing. He is to be attained by the one whom (the Self) chooses."[2] However, the realization that the ultimate liberation (*mokṣa*) ought to be gained by means of devotion to and revelation of God became crystallized in the *Bhagavad-gītā,* the *Bhāgavata Purāṇa,* the *Mahābhārata,* and in some of the most powerful philosophico-religious movements in later times.

There is something mysterious about the phenomenon of

[1] These are ancient lores of India. They are mythological in character and contain stories and parables to suit the intellectual level of the ordinary. There is a large number of Purāṇas, some of which, like *Vāyu, Viṣṇu, Matsya, Bhāgavata,* must have been composed around second century A.D.

[2] Radhakrishnan, S. (Ed.): *The Principal Upaniṣads,* p. 689.

bhakti. The unison that *bhakti* is supposed to build between the individual and God is the outcome of a certain type of affective sensibility in the former. There is no doubt that being endowed with such a sensibility, people in ancient India might have launched a systematic *bhakti* movement against the intellectual highbrows and often eclipsed their importance. Thus different cults of *bhakti* figure as the expression of the popular belief that the ultimate ideal of life is to vanish oneself into the universal divine Spirit or *Brahman,* to love God and to merge in Him.

Great religions of the world are full of instances of mystics and saints who represent the fusion of individual consciousness into the consciousness of God. Apart from the psychologically explainable factors such a fusion entails, what remains baffling still is the fundamental transformation human personality undergoes as a result of it. Just as *jñāna* or knowledge was and is acknowledged as the means of freedom suitable for the intellectually mature and skeptical section in any society, *bhakti* or devotion to God is universally regarded as the easier means, and hence appropriate to the intellectually less rigorous. But whether through *jñāna* or through *bhakti* the goal of the Indian mind being the same, the two *mārgas* (ways or means) have always been valued in India from the point of view of their appeal to the emotional self of the masses. The union with the universal soul achieved in *bhakti* seems to generate visible changes in one. These changes are as mysterious as the impact they cast on the followers of the *bhakta* (the devotee).

The concept of *bhakti* is consistent with what we have described earlier as the Indians' sense of the worthlessness of human life, and with the eventual necessity felt by them to surrender themselves to the incomprehensible and the otherworldly. Having realized the fact of man's bondage in the weary world, Indians were convinced that the only path for achieving the ultimate perfection is self-resignation. For the *bhakti* movement, it is specifically by seeking a unity with God that this self-resignation is eased off and accelerated. Although, therefore, *jñāna* and *bhakti* are apparently opposite modes of behavior, it is not impossible to argue that they may both coexist harmoniously in the same culture or even in the same individual. Actually, the *Bhagavad-gītā* does recognize a compatibility between them in the pursuit of *jīvanmukti*.

Nārada in the *Nārada-sūtra*[3] equates *bhakti* with intensest affection for God. In this affection lie tenderness, spontaneity of feelings, total surrender of one's finite being to the infinite being of God, and a readiness to disappear in the womb of divine grace. And these are precisely the qualities Kṛṣṇa, the incarnation of God, entreats Arjuna to imbibe when he exhibits his supreme power to Arjuna and makes him feel the insignificance of his worldly existence.[4] In *bhakti,* the individual consciousness, the I-principle, is minimized to such an extent that it just disappears in the universal spirit, like a drop in the ocean. The ordinarily felt ego-consciousness would be extinct as soon as the devotee reaches the fullness of *bhakti*. At the conclusion of devotion, therefore, the devotee and God mingle with each other.

It is always believed that our attachment to the material ends and our desire for the realization of the divine cannot go hand in hand. Thus, *nirodha,* or the suppression of all desires, is one of the first requisites of *bhakti*. The success of devotion lies in one's ability to inter the individuality of one's existence to such a depth that one would take life and the world with equanimity, and would not be gratified or frustrated at happenings around.

Now what is of outstanding merit in the doctrine of *bhakti* is a kind of indifference to the worldly events an individual manifests after he has had a vision of God. All the doubts, fears and uncertainties are believed to disappear once the devotee is shaken by the divine faith. And, therefore, the miraculous transformation in the personality of a *bhakta* is brought about by his trust in the rule of the beyond, his voluntary submission to the will of the Almighty, his trans-intellectual realization that his authentic self is an expression of God. In different religions, as a matter of fact, the value of devotion as an indispensable instrument for the blending of the devotee with God is emphasized so often that the *bhakti-mārga* does not have many original con-

[3] *Nārada-sūtra,* 84.

[4] Swami Prabhāvananda and Isherwood, Christopher (trans.): *Bhagavad-gītā,* p. 134.

tributions to make in this regard. However, what must be noted in particular is the fact that while in other faiths devotion to God forms an end in itself, in *bhakti-mārga* it is to serve as a means towards one's absolute emancipation from the world.

Sāndilya in the *Sāndilya-sūtra*[5] defines *bhakti* as the closest attachment to God (*parā anurakti*). Both Nārada and Sāndilya are of the opinion that although one's attachment to God and to objects implies the same type of psychological involvement, one is closest to one's pure self when one is involved in the being of God. This is why *bhakti* is described in Indian literature as *rāga, prema, aṃṛit, sraddhā, anurakti,* etc., all meaning an overwhelming longing for something representing one's total interests. The involvement in God causes a basic conversion in the emotional setup of the individual. Works of Indian saints and *bhaktas* are full of deep yearning, love, acute sensitivity of the heart, dedication, surrender and the joy of selflessness; they are utterances of souls, unmarred by the coarseness of intellect. With their selves dominated wholly by poetry and passion, the devotees function as pure reflections of God in the world. Their voice emit a ring of compassion and pity towards all. They embody the confidence of those who have surpassed all human limitations.

According to the *Bhāgavata Purāṇa,* devotion has nine principal characteristics: hearing the name of God, singing songs in His praise, recollecting Him, serving Him, worshipping and praying Him, respecting Him, being ready for His use, befriending Him and dedicating oneself to Him.[6] These characteristics, however, appear to be of secondary importance, for to the *Bhāgavata Purāṇa,* true devotion would really consist of a disinterested and uninterrupted pursuit of God. It is so fundamental a pursuit that it unfailingly leads one to the fullest of the universal spirit. The *Bhāgavata Purāṇa* repeatedly tells us that unless a person's word, thought and deed are fully loaded with his yearning for the Almighty, he would not be entitled to a fusion with the divine light. In fact, God has planned His own

[5] *Sāndilya-sūtra,* 8.
[6] *Bhāgavata Purāna,* X. 29. 15.

immanence in all the objects of the world with a view to facilitating man's approach to Him.

The *Bhāgavata Purāṇa* also mentions three kinds of devotion: *tamas* or dark, *rajas* or foul, and *sāttvika* or luminous. When a devotee is stimulated by some lower passions, and under this stimulation directs his attention towards God, his *bhakti* is of *tamas* or puerile character. On the other hand, devotion motivated by the desire for a material welfare is of *rajas* or practical type. The most ideal kind of devotion is *sāttvika* or authentic. It not only burns up the whole accumulation of *karmas* and releases the soul from the vicissitudes of life, but also produces in the devotee a feeling of ecstacy, a sense of amplitude and a capacity to cultivate within him the virtuosity of God. The *sāttvika* devotion divinizes man, and establishes him and God as alike (*sārūpya*).

Also Nārada, after describing several forms of *bhakti,* insists upon a personal relationship with God comprising servitude (*dāṣya*), friendship (*sakhya*), parental affection (*vātsalya*) and sweet matrimonial love (*mādhūrya*). For all propounders of the *bhakti-mārga,* the most ideal union between man and God occurs when the former manifests an absolute purity and love of heart towards the latter. Such purity and love may be accompanied by, in W. T. Stace's words, "the calm serenity of Buddha or Eckhart" or "the hyperemotionalism of St. Teresa."[7]

The emphasis of the entire movement of *bhakti* is solely on the dissolution of the state of bondage man has fallen in by the very fact of his birth. Indeed, it would be interesting to find out whether *bhakti* as a way of life aiming at the devotee's blending with God is not psychologically rooted in the low "pain-threshold" of a few supersensitive minds. William James, while analyzing the factors involved in the "sick-mindedness" of the intensely religious persons, maintains that anybody endowed with such a mental property would possess a low "pain-threshold," an easy affectability in presence of misery, or a short pitch of en-

[7] Stace, Walter T.: *The Teachings of the Mystics.* New York, New Am. Lib., 1960, p. 131.

durance.[8] He would feel depressed and experience melancholy at the slightest awareness of evil. It is convincing to say that mystics and saints like Plotinus, Buddha, Eckhart, St. Teresa of Avila, Ramakrishna, Śri Aurobindo belong to this category and exhibit a profound sense of concern at the fact of man's being in the world.

However, as it was said before, the assumption of all the three *mārgas* or paths of salvation in Indian philosophy is that to anyone who has a sense to "see" and to "feel" the condition of man in the universe, the very emergence of human consciousness is pregnant with affliction, ennui and disappointment. This is why Kṛṣṇa, in the *Bhagavad-gītā,* is not very emphatic about professing the virtues of any one path as against those of the other. His basic suggestion is that, irrespective of the path a person chooses, the spiritual perfection is necessarily the culmination of his continuous mental endeavor to realize a state beyond this world. He says that before we prepare ourselves to plunge into the domain of transcendence, or into the consciousness hereafter, we must shape our attitude against the world of our commonsense experience. ". . . you must first control your senses," advises Kṛṣṇa, "then kill this evil thing which obstructs discriminative knowledge and realization of the *ātman.*"[9]

Thus, a kind of sympathetic preparedness, a profound conviction about the finitude of human life and of the phenomenal world, or an urge towards the attainment of limitless freedom is a prelude to one's conversion into a *bhakta* personality, as the same is the very *raison d'être* of the transcendental quest of a *jñāni* or *yogi.* In the context of Indian thought, therefore, the point of distinction between the path of knowledge and that of devotion is not to be found either in their goal or in their primitive assumptions. It is to be seen in the fact that the ego of a *bhakta* is emotion-laden, passional, self-surrendering and meek, while that of a *jñāni* is inward-seeing, grave, world-negating

[8] See William James: *The Varieties of Religious Experience.* New York, Modern Lib., 1929, pp. 132–33.

[9] Swami Prabhāvananda and Isherwood, Christopher (trans.): *Bhagavad-gītā,* p. 58.

and often drawn by the seminal Nothingness of all existence. Religious sermons and suggestions, the reading and hearing of scriptures, contacts with saints, mystics or yogis, would be of no avail in regard to a mind oriented to metaphysical and introspectional rigor; on the other hand, only a spark in the emotional self produced by the elegance of a divine song would suffice for the deification of one mellowed down by faith and compassion.

DEVOTIONALISM AND NEGATIVE FAITH

The perennial difference between the institution of *bhakti* and that of *jñāna* in India originated from an apparently innocent, but widely prevalent, antithesis between the theists and the savants, or the worshippers and the reflective thinkers in the Upaniṣads. Two equally influential opinions might have prevailed in the Vedic-Upaniṣadic era: one upholding the virtue of metaphysical speculation and the other responding to the emotive requirements of the masses. The Upaniṣads are preeminently the expression of minds that were governed by an inward-seeing sensibility. But at the same time, they hide a popular temperament, however feeble, to which metaphysical thinking must have raised hurdles beyond its power to contain them.

Just as the central thesis of all philosophical tendencies in India is traceable to the Upaniṣads, or to their transcendentalist and meditative texture, almost all religious sects colorfully practiced by Indians can be linked up with certain theistic beliefs of the Vedic-Upaniṣadic times themselves. It has been established by scholars, for instance, that the god Rūdra mentioned in the *Ṛg Veda* is the prototype of Shiva, who is the center of a multitude of religious sects prevalent in different parts of India. Some of the *bhakti* cults, such as Śāktiśm, Tamil Śaivism, Lingāyata, Kashmir Śaivism and Vīraśaivism, directly derive from the worship of Shiva. Again, Shiva in some of the Upaniṣads is identified with *Brahman* and called Rūdra-Shiva.

Shiva is the symbol of faith, love and pure heart, having for his abode universal and eternal peace. This abode of peace is an everlasting attraction to his worshippers. However, it is also said that he is potentially a terror, a powerful wielder of wrath, requiring humble entreaties and sacrifices for appeasement. It is possible, as Majumdar has recently pointed out, that the image of Rūdra-Shiva is really pre-Āryan and was assimilated by Āryans because of its remarkable combination of the elements of ferocity and anger with those of love and peace. The *Śaiva Purāṇas* describe Shiva as the savior of man from mortality, the extinguisher of his sins, and his emancipator from the world of suffering and bondage.

Another set of theistic cults is woven around Viṣṇu, one of the greatest gods in the *Ṛg Veda*. Viṣṇu is the source of light, the preserver of the universe, the ultimate goal of man's spiritual quest and devotion. Although in the beginning the Viṣṇu cult was founded on sacrifice as the main instrument of propitiation, as time went by, devotion came to be regarded as a more pleasing substitute. Later on, Viṣṇu was equated with Vāsudeva, Kṛṣṇa, Nārāyana, Baladeva, Anirudha and several other deities, around whom the *Bhagavad-gītā,* the *Māhābhāśya,* the *Vāyu Purāṇa,* the *Bhāgavata Purāṇa,* the *Mahābhārata,* etc., were woven. As the whole movement of *bhakti* in Śaivism is the development of the worship of Shiva, the movement of *bhakti* in Vaiṣṇavism is the growth of the worship of Viṣṇu.

The *bhakti-mārga* flourished in the history of India as an antidote to the central current of transcendentalist metaphysics. And a casual glance at the popular acceptance of *bhakti* as a consoling way of life shows that the common people experienced a mysterious exultation of spirit through its practice. Occasionally they must have rebelled against the metaphysical pursuits, obviously monopolized by those few who were intellectually superior to them. Although no instance of such a rebellion can be concretely pointed out in philosophies and religions in India, the very fact that the otherwise atheistic movements, such as Jainism, Buddhism, Nyāya, Sāṅkhya and Yoga, did adopt some of the elements of devotionalism is an indication of the magnitude of the people's demand prevalent at the time. Anyway, the *bhakti-mārga,* to which the masses responded with utmost spontaneity and ease, could not be ignored even by those who were in every respect undevout by temperament.

Generally, devotionalism is notable for its emphasis on a personal relationship between the devotee and God. In Vaiṣṇavism, for example, anthropomorphic tales about Kṛṣṇa, originally mentioned in the *Chāndogya Upanisad* as Vāsudeva-Kṛṣṇa, abound in such a relationship. Again, the nucleus of a widely prevalent form of Vaiṣṇavism, called Bhāgavatism, is Kṛṣṇa, who is presented there as a flirt with beautiful damsels known as *gopīs*. To them he figures as a symbol of blissful and highly charitable love and liberty. The Bhāgavatis, that is, the followers of Bhāgavatism, later on call him Hari or the God of gods with whom a personal connection can be established by his worshippers. Being on a level lower than the abstract and universal soul or *Brahman*, Kṛṣṇa must have been easily accessible to, and therefore an attraction for, the religious consciousness of millions of Indians wanting to caress his complexion, to attribute imaginary romance, buoyant zeal and lust for life to him. All these possibilities with regard to God were cherished in opposition to the expansive and inane nature of the absolute and the transcendental pursued by the extraordinary few.

Bhāgavatism has no room for a metaphysical reality. It believes in the most ideal person with whom we can communicate. God is supposed to feel anxiety for the benefaction of man; he is believed to descend into the world in order to uplift man. Even the present-day Bhāgavatis subscribe to the *bhakti* cult by accepting its god Kṛṣṇa as an extremely elegant, humane, sportive, romantic and absolutely joyous character. Love songs sung by poets, mystics and saints, and signifying Kṛṣṇa's play or *līlā* show that He is a god whose grace should be harbored by the emotion-laden much more spontaneously and naturally than those few ascetically oriented who are in pursuit of the occult and esoteric *Brahmānubhava* or absolute experience.

If Vaiṣṇavism exhibits how exuberant the emotive demands of Indians vis-à-vis their most amiable god can be, Śaivism is well-known for its most feared and revered Shiva, who stands more for rigor and abstinence than comfort and affluence. The spirit of Śaivism is that by means of sacrifice, penitence and privation alone, Shiva's beneficent sense can be appealed to and the liberation from evils in the world obtained.

There are multiple varieties of the practice of Shiva worship. They have spread over hundreds of years since the times of the

Ṛg Veda. Some are distortions of such an abominable nature that they can only be explained as different inventions for the fulfilment of the unconsciously operating sadistic and masochistic instincts of their followers. While in a number of the Śaiva sects Shiva-*liṇga* (Shiva's phallus) is the center of the devotees' attention, in Soma Siddhānta and Pāśupata Śaivism lying down in ashes, imitating the animal sounds, dadaistic dancing, etc., are looked upon as sacred. In the Kālāmukha faith—perhaps the most torturous of all Śaiva sects—it is held that the attainment of aspirations regarding this world and the next is possible if one besmears one's body with the ashes of a dead body, devours ashes, eats in a skull, holds a club, keeps a pot of wine and prays god seated therein.[10] And in Tāntrism, which is intimately connected with the rise of Śaivism, a peculiar kind of self-deification is advised by the exercise of extraordinary rituals such as consumption of alcohol, meat and fish, sexual orgies, various bodily gestures, and bloody sacrifices.

But leaving these primitive elements in some of its sects which are now obsolete, Śaivism, in its most refined forms like Tamil Śaivism and Kashmir Śaivism, is a movement wedded to the purpose of annihilating the forces of evil in Nature with the help of Shiva, the God of power. Tamil Śaivism abounds in sweet spiritual songs, which possibly had remarkable influence not only on Hinduism but even on Christianity in South India. The Kashmir Śaivism is famous for its enchanting theory of Shiva-*kridā* (Shiva's play), symbolizing the emergence and the dissolution of the universe, the awakening and the restoration of the universal Self. Finally, the Vīraśaivism places an emphasis on the mysterious and indeterminate domains of *cit* (consciousness) and *acit* (matter), and somewhat like the Sāṅkhya school, regards the former as eternally free despite its involvement in the spatiotemporal world.

It need not be supposed that devotionalism had any undesirable effect on the intensity of the transcendental quest of Indian philosophers. For, insofar as the attitude of Indians towards the ultimate destiny of man-in-the-world is concerned, it remained

[10] Bhandarkar, B. G.: *Vaiṣṇavism, Śaivism and Minor Religious Systems,* p. 181.

the same both in *bhakti-mārga* and *jñāna-mārga.* This attitude has throughout been otherworldly and futility oriented for the simple reason that the assumption around which an Indian built his hopes, interests and aspirations was an extinction of world-consciousness, or rather an escape from it. An explicit sameness can be observed, in this regard, between the *bhakti* cult and Sufism in Islam.

The basic motivation of *bhakti-mārga* is that the devotee's self and God accomplish a unison in which the former is left with no individuality of its own. Sufism,[11] which regards the dispositions of the inner self as more sacred than external religious gestures, is built around the concept that God is pure Being, absolute beauty and supreme illumination, a direct communion with Whom would make one realize the fictitiousness of the feeling of one's separate existence. There is at the root of Sufi devotionalism a belief in the possible betterment of the world and man's conditions in it through a radical reformation and leadership controlled by a handful of divinely initiated minds at the top.

As a matter of history, when Mahammed, the founder of Islam, established the cult of an all-embracing and universal faith in the seventh century A.D., his aim was to uplift a society from its prolonged primitive state to a national and religious consciousness. Sufism represents the crystallization of this aim. A Sufi, like a *bhakta,* is excited by an urge to seek identity with God and consequently to deify himself, others and the world. Eminent Sufis like El Ghazzali (eleventh century A.D.), Ibn Arabi (twelfth century A.D.) and Rumi (thirteenth century A.D.) have asserted, with a spirit akin to that of the *bhakti-vādins,* that the highest goal of man should be to attain the "kingdom" of divinity, a reconciliation between faith and reason, and to extinguish all that is nondivine and evil. However, while to Sufis ecstasy in this world through the contemplation of the pure vision of the divine is all that the life of devotion aspires after, to *bhaktas* the realization of God is only a thresh-

[11] The term *Sufi* comes from the root *suf* (wool). Sufism is the essence of the Islamic *Weltanschauung.* Clad with rough wool, the Sufis rejected the life of worldly comforts and worked for the intensification of religious consciousness.

old to the transcendental state where the ordinary sense of existence is reduced to zero. In fact, as historians have shown, insofar as the mystical elements in *bhakti-mārga* and in Sufism are considered, there must have been the influence of the former on the latter and perhaps vice versa.

VAIṢṆAVA MYSTICISM

The Vaiṣṇava devotionalism emanating from the worship of god Viṣṇu and spread far and wide in India by a chain of saints like Ālvārs, Vaikhānasas, Ācharyas, the Vedāntins Yamunāchārya and Rāmānuja, Śri Chaitanya (A.D. 1485), the Vārakaris and Dhārakaris of Maharastra, Tulasidās (sixteenth century A.D.), is perhaps the most ecstasy-arousing movement among all *bhakti* sects. On the philosophical level it is Rāmānuja who set up a coordination between the stream of *bhakti* sentiment and the idea of *Brahman* or God as Unity-in-difference. That he was impelled to do this in order to counteract the influence of Śaṅkara, or Śaṅkara's insistence on the path of knowledge, is well-known. What Rāmānuja could immediately achieve is a fortification of the devotionalist message that a boundless and unrestrained love for God is sure to emancipate man from his worldly suffering and bondage. Adhering to the mission of fighting against Śaṅkara's intellectualism, he must have collected a massive following and strengthened his grip over the emotional awakening of the devout populace. It is natural that Rāmānuja, the most philosophical theist India has ever produced, stands for a kind of devotionalism that can form the ground of a comprehensive spiritualistic humanism or of a welfare theory.

Rāmānuja looks upon the world as the body of God, and holds that man's ultimate ideal should be to realize a complete identity with Him. God, he says, manifests Himself in different forms with a limitless range of known and unknown possibilities. As an *antaryāmin* or inner ruler, the transcendent person, the creator, the maintainer and the destroyer, God is directly related to the human souls, whose ultimate destination cannot be other than Him. In expounding the theory of *vyūhas,* or God's manifestations, Rāmānuja points out that the supreme object of man's devotion descends down in the world by incarnating Himself in all kinds of human and nonhuman forms. God does all this, Rāmānuja explains, wholly for the benefaction of mankind. Being under the spirit of the *Bhagavad-gītā* message, he, in his theory of *bhakti,* insists upon a continuous love and meditation (*upāsanā*) of God as the sole way for *mokṣa.*

In the same vein in which Rāmānuja preached the course of liberation, and equated the liberated with one in the form (*prakāra*) of God, Madhva propagated his concept of *mukti* or absolute freedom as a state of abode in God (*sālokya*), as closeness to God (*sāmīpya*), as accomplishing God's form (*sārūpya*) and as entry into God's body (*sāyujya*). Travelling over Indian villages with a single mission of exciting religious emotion in their people, Madhva proved to be not only a powerful reactionary to Śaṅkara's doctrine of the oneness of Being but also the most luminous mind in his time commanding a wide following. Madhva's words are cherished even today for the transparence and lucidity and poetry of the heart they embody.

There is always something aesthetically attractive and comforting about the feeling involved in devotion. At all times in the history of India, therefore, there has been a majority to whose moral and psychological aptitude the *bhakti-mārga* suited best. The tenets of devotion are independent of any creed, caste, individuality and personal status; they do not expect in the devotees any particular qualities. A *bhakta* is, in general, a person with all pride and self-esteem shed or rather shrunk to the minimum, with a high pitch of amorousness towards God, and a readiness to remain humble and downcast. The more genuine the devotion, the more infantile the sensibilities it would embody. As it is known, the only arresting factor in relation to simple and undiluted devotionalism is a skeptical and stiff reasoning activity. In every religion it is the principal characteristic of a devotee to fall in love with God instantaneously, to bestow on Him excellence which normally a lover might bestow on the beloved, to desire a total satiation of the emotional self and, consequently, to remain fused in the life of the Almighty.

Thus, when Kṛṣṇa remarks to Arjuna, in the *Bhagavad-gītā,* that he should love Him with all his heart and be saved forever,

Kṛṣṇa demands from him nothing less than total devotion.[12] Psychologically, the act of *bhakti* entails an attitude of self-surrender and servitude on the part of the *bhakta*. One may even say that the intentionality of a devotee is directed towards that Being in whom all the best virtues and ends are concentrated. The only performance of a *bhakta,* therefore, would be a passive reception of an otherworldly trance, to seek a sanctuary within a region of consciousness that seems to flow from something pervading universally and indeterminately, to immerse himself in a well of grace. One of the most revered saints to have shrouded himself with abundance of this grace is Śri Chaitanya (1485–1533).

With a striking similarity with Saint Teresa of Avila, Śri Chaitanya appeared on the Indian scene as an incarnation of pure and simple sentiment of love-to-everybody. What is unique about his Vaiṣṇava devotionalism is that it expresses, at its bottom, a heart that strangely longed for a union with Kṛṣṇa and went about pouring out deeply moving poetry that describes God's pastimes (*līlās*) and yet manifests a mood of suffering and loneliness. Chaitanya was animated by a strong inexplicable mood of existence which affected the very process of his perception. He saw that everything around him was divine, reflected fullness of being and was the extension of an absolute and eternal life-force. The extraordinary manner of adoration he introduced consists of chanting sonorously and musically the names and epithets of Kṛṣṇa with so tearful a voice that he could carry away thousands of people and make them join a *bhakti* constellation or *saṁkiṛtana.*

Chaitanya is a vivid example of what *bhakti* movement, in its most genuine and widespread circulation, is meant to produce out of the religious initiates. Abandonment of the worldly temptations and living with a sense of insignificance innate in it should characterize the attitude of the *bhakta*. Whatever the varieties of its practice, *bhakti* is ultimately antiworld, antilife, and evidently, its fulfilment entails a negative and rejecting approach

[12] Swami Prabhāvananda and Isherwood, Christopher (trans.): *Bhagavad-gītā*, pp. 104–5.

towards everything that enhances our material interests. It is said that during the last two decades of his life in a place of pilgrimage called Puri, Chaitanya used to experience intense raptures from a union with Kṛṣṇa and get exhausted to such a degree that he aspired after nothing material.

Chaitanya looked upon Kṛṣṇa as an incarnate form of *Brahman*. According to him, *sat* (being), *cit* (intelligence) and *ānanda* (joy) are embodied in the personality of Kṛṣṇa, who is a mode of *Brahman* accessible to human conscience. The sweetness, the blissfulness, the artistic passions and the flow of emotions with which Chaitanya sang his songs inspired a unity between him and God. At one time he even thought that Kṛṣṇa too has numerous manifestations pervading all actual and possible worlds and heavens, and that he himself was one of such manifestations. In creating these manifestations, Kṛṣṇa is supposed to display his *līlā* or play. Chaitanya believed, rather like an aesthete, that Kṛṣṇa's sportive display can be seen in the beautiful figures and activities of *gopīs* (young damsels), who are, as a matter of fact, his *śaktis* or energies.

With an uncommon forcefulness in his attitude, word and deed, Chaitanya tried to show that *bhakti* is the sole means of *jīvanmukti*. The peculiar conduct of *bhakti* he lauded is called *sādhanā,* a kind of discipline of inward attention as in *yoga*. God is the object of *sādhanā*. *Sādhanā* proceeds through a number of interrelated steps, such as friendship with the holy man, religious practices for mind's purification, faith in God's benevolence and in scriptures, the purging of one's self from sins, love for spiritual meditation and an ascent to the beyond. It is a state of mind and heart where intellect has totally ceased to function, and where the only ruling emotion is *rati* or *prem* (love). Chaitanya has described *sādhanā* as ripened *sneha, praṇaya, rāga, anurāga* (all meaning love).

Chaitanya died in the middle of the sixteenth century A.D. At about the same time, another form of *bhakti* cult was developing in Maharastra which was destined to spread later on in the whole of Western India and fuse with other forms of devotionalism. The most important figures who built up and propagated this are Dñānadeva, Nāmadeva, Eknāth, Tukārāma and Ramdas.

They are the exponents of a way of Vaiṣṇava devotionalism in which a peculiar undercurrent of life's futile effort to enrich itself by means of a misguided attachment to the material pursuits is invariably present. In fact, the custom is to classify them into two groups, Vārakaris and Dhārakaris, on the ground that while in the former the emotional outburst is free and full, in the latter it is restrained by reason and by practical compromise between love for God and a need for moral education. Tukārāma, ever esteemed for his eccentric simplicity and candid behavior, was a Vārakari; Ramdas, famous for his association with King Shivaji, was a Dhārakari.

It is not the aim of the present section to give a complete survey of the Vaiṣṇava mysticism. Although the activities of the saints in Karnataka, of Tulasidās in North India, of Rāmānanda, Kabir, Sūradāsa, Guru Nanak, Śivanārāyana, Narsiṁva Mehta and scores of others can claim their individual characteristics, they collectively helped to accelerate people's emotional ethos and put it on a track towards the otherworld. The range of these saints' divine experience is fluvial; therefore, there could be no rivalry among them on the question of their centers of worship. It is conceivable that a number of medieval mystics flew from one sect to another, or even from Vaiṣṇavism to Śaivism and vice versa, without any embarrassment to themselves or to their followers. The single presupposition to which their attitudes gravitated is the ultimate meaninglessness of any effort to hug things in the world.

Here a brief mention may be made of Śaiva mysticism around sixth to eighth centuries A.D. Śaivism, after its origin in the Rūdra-Shiva worship in the Vedic-Upaniṣadic times and its modification in various Śaiva schools, received unprecedented impetus at the hands of famous Ācharyas, the most influential among them being Māṇikkavācarya, Appar, Sambandha and Sundarmūrti, and a highly esoteric woman saint of Tamil, Auvai. The common characteristic of all of them is that they condemn all external ritualistic ways in religion and uphold that it is only through clean, pure and unselfish love that the *bhakta* can communicate his self to God.

Māṇikkavācarya was a great exponent of the love path for the realization of the supreme Being. He is ever remembered for the frequent trances he used to be under and for the exquisite poetry he coined as a result of their influence. Appar, who is said to have had child's humility when in worship of Shiva, borrowed much from Jainism and combined it with his idea of amorous *bhakti*.[13] And Sambandha, about whom more miracles than truths are recorded, exhibited precocity of intellect and instincts in the most unusual manner. As for Sundermūrti, he is said to have practiced spiritual adventures and wandered extensively through villages singing songs in praise of God. To Auvai, the whole universe is the expression of God's love; it was her attempt to catch through words her vision of this love.

The development of Śaivism, particularly in South India, is awfully complex. Besides, in several respects it has extended into Śāktism, an important but largely occult *bhakti* movement centered around the worship of Śakti, the consort of Shiva. Again, a saint named Tirumūlar, who is known to have reinterpreted Śaivism in the South around ninth century A.D., so diluted it that it could not stand in hostility to the basic thesis of Vaiṣṇava mysticism and hence could not stay uninfluenced by it. What is stressed, however, by all the diverse forms of Śaiva mysticism is that through the devotion of Shiva and his absolute power, one can attain a state of being where one stays freed, not only from the vicissitudes of existence but also from the nondivine and mundane plane of one's own feelings. The worship of Shiva is a gate leading us to the ecstatic domain of inner being—a domain which comprehends all that is germinal to life's spatiotemporal continuance.[14]

WHITHER *BHAKTI*?

Strictly speaking, the history of *bhakti* mysticism in India is an account of how the alienated consciousness of a few emotion-

[13] Pillai, S. Satchidanandam: The Śaiva Saints of South India. In Bhattacharya, Haridas (Ed.): *The Cultural Heritage of India*. Calcutta, The Ramakrishna Mission, 1956, Vol. 4, p. 341.

[14] To a Śaiva devotee, once this inner domain is realized, all the malignant forces in the world lie ineffective. See Bhandarkar, B. G.: *Vaiṣṇavism, Śaivism and Minor Religious Systems*, pp. 145–51.

laden persons sought a solution to their alienation by means of an unrestrained self-surrender to the will of God. Thus, the various *bhakti* sects entail the belief that the ultimate aim of human existence is to intensify its world-negating attitude and to direct itself wholly towards the transcendental and the beyond. Notwithstanding its aesthetically creative and romantic aspects which have amply descended in myths and symbols of India's art and religions, *bhakti-vāda* is not in any way less pessimistic and less life-denying than *jñāna-vāda*. What the way of devotion has more powerful about it than the way of knowledge is, however, the fact that being suitable to the sentimental and the naive temper of the ordinary, the former, unlike the latter, has a cathartic effect on this temper. This is the main reason why the sense of futility regarding man's worldly life has been inculcated in the Indian mind more easily by *bhakti-mārga* than by *jñāna-mārga*.

When one looks at the huge congregations of worshippers at religious places chanting the pathetic and life-rejecting songs from Vaiṣṇava and Śaiva saints and utterly disregarding the colossal civilization sprouting around them, one would gauge the magnitude with which the antiworld message of the Vedic-Upaniṣadic times still reverberates in the Indian air. Portraits of saints who preach that human existence is futile decorate not only temples and habitations but even school textbooks, commercial advertisements and cinemas in India. All work is done, all plans are conceived, all ideas are launched as if mechanically with a permanent underlying conviction that the world is an endless chain of mirages, whose complete dissolution is a prerequisite to salvation. The genuine *bhakta* has to give up the life of material welfare; he cannot have the fulfilment of his love for God if he anchors his interests deep in the promotion of his empirical being.

In a mind unprepared for suggesting to itself that the world is a superimposition on human consciousness, *bhakti* can have neither propriety nor aim. The end of *bhakti-mārga* is *mokṣa*, or absolute liberation from empirical consciousness. Thus it would be ambiguous when a person, sufficiently adhering to and hopeful about the affairs in the world, still adopts the *bhakti* path out of a loyalty to tradition or to some outer factor. Such a person is often suspected of hypocrisy and lack of candor.[15] While there are, therefore, in every culture people who practice devotion without accepting the beliefs that inspire them, the path of *bhakti* would possess no sense if it is dissociated from a feeling about the insignificance of the world and the truth of *mokṣa*. *Bhakti*, in this sense, is an emotional expression concealing underneath an intellectual certainty that the worldly existence is fundamentally inane.

[15] One of the most recent commentators to describe this situation sharply is A. B. Shah. Shah writes: "The real weakness of the dominant Hindu tradition . . . lies, not in its apparent hypocrisy but in the fact that its world-negating philosophy is expected to provide guidance and justification for the pursuit of secular goals. This is bound to end in frustration and often in disaster." See Shah, A. B.: Introduction. In Shah, A. B., and Rao, C. R. M. (Eds.): *Tradition and Modernity in India*. Bombay, Manaktalas, 1965, p. 12.

Chapter Eleven

ACTION AS DUTY

THE METAPHYSICAL IMPORT OF HUMAN ACTIVITY

HAVING postulated the theory that man's existence in the world is an inevitable result of his voluntary and interested commitments to things in his past lives, Indian thinkers did not bother to discuss the ethical subtleties of human conduct. An action was significant only as an instrument, a promoter, or an aid to one's emancipation from the concrete and palpable world of suffering and bondage. Since activity was to serve the single purpose of one's cessation in the world—which is explicitly a negative purpose, inasmuch as man's physical alliance with the world is concerned—Indian philosophers might not have thought it necessary to reflect on the entire geometry of volition as such. It is therefore futile to look for a work of moral philosophy in ancient India comparable to Plato's *Republic* or Aristotle's *Nicomachean Ethics*—the works that were intended to set forth a certain examination of the question of morality and value. The study of action in all its psychosocial considerations was not the concern of Indian sages.

By any denomination, the Indian view of the conative consciousness is not an essay in the criticism of conduct but an extension of the transcendentalist metaphysics. In other words, the core of Indian ethics is to reflect on man's birth in a universe that inauthenticates his essence or *ātman,* and to give an account of the procedure by which he can break loose the chain of mundane existence and finally merge in the transcendental. Consequently, the only reason why Indian thought gives no importance to the study and education of human conation is that no need was felt for the construction of an ideal, which would fall short of the ultimate state of *mokṣa.* The ethical character of human activity, that is, activity having for its goal the right and the good in the world here and now, fell outside the inquiry of Indians.

The term "action" or *karma* in the context of Indian ethics must be taken to be synonymous with the term "duty" or *kriyā.* For actions were right or good, inasmuch as they were the expression of duties set down by the Vedic-Upaniṣadic injunctions and having for their goal the attainment of salvation. Any independent reflection on the rightness or wrongness of actions or on the rightness or wrongness of duties, for that matter, could not arise because they all descended from the ancient *Dharma* (meaning, religious duty). Neither could they be judged from a nontranscendental principle, nor could their cocksureness in leading man to absolute spiritual perfection be questioned. Rather than using their talents on the intellectual analysis of individual and social values, of laws for the day-to-day welfare of man, of the ideals of humanity, Indians thus committed themselves to a career of practical indifference and metaphysical freedom. The theory of action, in Indian philosophy, is intertwined with the theory of the most cherishable otherworldly being.

THE MĪMĀṀSĀ RITUALISM

The theory that it is only by means of *karmas* or duties performed mechanically and disinterestedly in accordance with the authority of the Vedic word that the eternal release from the spatiotemporal existence is positively guaranteed to all, is highly accentuated by the school of Pūrva Mīmāṁsā. Pūrva *Mīmāṁsā,* which is also known as Karma Mīmāṁsā, is undoubtedly a system of duties and practices centering around the *Dharma* propounded by the Vedic-Upaniṣadic savants. The Mīmāṁsakas try to comprehend the total life of Indians, and recommend to them a set of rules for so conducting themselves in the world that they might eventually attain a place in heaven.[1] The ritualistic lessons that they have prescribed notably define what station an

[1] The effectiveness of activity is often believed to be less than that of knowledge. See for comments on this Edgerton, Franklin: *The Beginnings of Indian Philosophy*. London, George Allen & Unwin Ltd., 1965, pp. 35–36.

individual prior to his *mokṣa* should take up in relation to society and God. Of course as it has been already mentioned, once an individual rises to the state of freedom or transcendence, he ceases to be under any external mandate and, consequently, obeys, so to say, his own enlightened self. The Mīmāṁsā, therefore, does not much heed to the fate of the liberated.

The ethical and religious imperatives suggested by the Mīmāṁsakas, and lauded by them as something emerging from some inexpressible nonhuman authority pervading the Vedas, have the aim of shaping the sensibilities of the Hindu society. The behavior of the orthodox Hindus is governed even today by these imperatives. And it would not be wrong to say that it is to the *Mīmāṁsā Sūtra* of Jaimini (fourth century B.C.), the founder of the school, that must go the credit of emphasizing the *Dharma* as some kind of a censor *puruśārtha* controlling *artha* (material acquisitiveness) and *kāma* (earthly enjoyment) to suit the highest *puruśārtha,* namely, *mokṣa.*

Action or *karma,* as it is defined in Indian philosophy, implies a disciplined and restrained "doing," a regulated duty, an injunction ordained by the fundamental law of the universe or by *Ṛta. Karmas,* in this sense, are believed to be necessary because they throw a bridge between souls' existence in the material world and their innate and trans-empirical being. All the duties or *Dharma* embodied by the Mīmāṁsā instructions, therefore, constitute a jurisprudence for the use of all those whose perfection lies in achieving a state beyond *saṁsāra.* No duty is a performance for any material gain; no action is to bear the motive of continuing one's existence in the world. The sole purpose of an adherence to the rules of activity is to ultimately realize absolute freedom from activity itself.

It is not necessary to describe here the bulk of acts—for example, sacrifices (*yajña*), offerings in consecrated places of fire (*homa*), charity (*dāna*)—the Pūrva Mīmāṁsā literature following the Vedic texts advises one and all to practice. Most of these acts are a guide to man to purify his soul. What is entailed by them all is that they are commandments of an eternally existent suprahuman authority, and, as such, stay infallible forever. According to Jaimini, *Dharma* is the supreme duty, the most inwardly and universally impelled action. He says that the Vedas, the self-revealed Word floating in space from times immemorial, are the first pronouncer of *Dharma,* and that it is through the mouths of the sages that they have spread to man in all times in history.

Famous Mīmāṁsakas such as Śabara (first century B.C.), Kumārila and Prabhākara (both seventh century A.D.) have consistently held that actions that are to be performed regularly and those that are to be performed occasionally collectively enable one to accomplish *svarga* (heaven). Now it is not possible to see what exact state of consciousness the Mīmāṁsakas allude to when they say that the *svarga* annuls every mental mode except happiness. In any case, *svarga* and *apavarga*—the concepts frequently occurring in the Mīmāṁsā system—do not stand for any experience different from *mokṣa.*[2] Perhaps what is implied by the Mīmāṁsā is that a continuous operation of acts under injunctions (*vidhis*) would bring about in us a state of full deliverance from interestedness, committedness and belongingness, and place us in an ocean of ecstasy. The Mīmāṁsakas trust this also on account of their unflinching acceptance of the assurance contained in the Vedas. Every action, we are told, retains behind it certain potency or *apūrva* to direct the doer towards a definite fate. The greater the adherence of a doer to the Vedic injunctions, the more favorable would be the *apūrva* of his acts and, consequently, the more his advance towards heaven or *mokṣa.*

It is obvious that with its single teleological postulate that the *svarga* should be the final destiny of all souls, the Mīmāṁsā system could not entertain any theory of social reconstruction or social amelioration on earth. The ideal life the Mīmāṁsakas, like all followers of the Vedic-Upaniṣadic *Weltanschauung,* had before their sight is not worldly but otherworldly. One can suspect an attempt in their movement, therefore, to rebel, with their ethicoreligious activism, against the widely propagated

[2] For a treatment of the question of the nature of *svarga,* see Mahāmahopadhyāya Pramatha Nath Tarkabhushan: The Pūrva Mīmāṁsā, in *The Cultural Heritage of India.* Calcutta, Shri Ramakrishna Centenary Committee, Vol. 1, pp. 469–70. Also see Sharma, I. C.: *Ethical Philosophies of India.* London, George Allen & Unwin Ltd., 1965, pp. 237–38.

antiritualism and nihilism by Jaina and Buddhist teachers. The *karma-mārga,* the path of action, preached by the Mīmāṁsā, must thus be interpreted as a program, not only for the revival of the Vedic *Dharma* but also for keeping Indians functioning according to the traditional Hindu precepts. However, the fact that by this program the Mīmāṁsā could not intend to venture on an education in practical excellence need not be overemphasized.

The most important factors that must have helped the Mīmāṁsā ritualism to spread and to put itself up as a way of salvation must be sought in the social setting prevalent in India in the olden times. If the path of devotion or *bhakti* was an easier means of salvation than the path of knowledge or *jñāna,* ritualism was still easier. Apart from the fact that the whole concept of action or duty (*vidhi, karma, kriyā, Dharma*) in Indian philosophy is founded on an inward-seeing and metaphysical attitude—the attitude that the realization of pure consciousness or *ātman* is the sole aim of life—in actuality actions, particularly of religious character, could be done by anybody without any conscious commitment to such an attitude. As Russell somewhere remarks, man conforms to the customs of whatever country he inhabits. "A modern disciple," he says, "would go to church on Sundays and perform the correct genuflexions, but without any of the religious beliefs that are supposed to inspire these actions."[3] The largest bulk of Indians have obeyed and still obey Vedic injunctions without understanding and imbibing the metaphysical attitude behind them.

Inflexible ethicoreligious ritualism is invariably a force that hinders the forward movement of society. The Mīmāṁsā conception of duties sounds so rigid that it cannot have been, even when it had a following, a very meritorious contribution to the theory of social welfare. On the contrary, the first aphorism of Jaimini that the study and the acceptance of the Vedas is obligatory for the upper classes anticipates a structure of society in which different classes can be identified in terms of their fixed duties. And Manu, the greatest theoretician of the laws of the Hindus, by strictly complying with the Vedic *Dharma* portrays

[3] Russell, Bertrand: *A History of Western Philosophy.* New York, S. and S., 1965, p. 233.

a social setup in which duties of every class are absolutely determined.[4] Not only does he regard this *Dharma* as sacrosanct, but he even holds that those who disregard it deserve no lesser a punishment than excommunication. No interchange of duties would be permissible. And if such an interchange takes place, it would amount to one's performing *nisiḍha karmas* or prohibited actions.

Positive and purposive activity suitable to exigencies of the perpetually changing worldly situations would cease to have any sense in a philosophy of life shrouded in an all-comprehensive ritualism. While confidence in the power of free action has always been the core of civilization in the West, it has remained foreign to the logic of *karma-mārga* in India. Activity without a freely and consciously chosen goal is of no ethical significance. Even when Indians have acted with a certain apparent urgency or plan or lust for victory, they have not shed their Vedic-Upaniṣadic tradition that no action falling outside the pursuit of *mokṣa* is of any basic value. All that is desirable according to the Indian view of life, therefore is that one should act according to the authority of the Veda *vākya* or sentence, that one's action be the doing of a duty prescribed by the Vedic word, that one surrender to a voice of wisdom that transcends both human and divine sanction. This wisdom has defined to man his station in this world, and has thrown precepts for him, by knowing and following which he would attain the world beyond.

MEANING OF THE WISDOM BEYOND

Perhaps the most controversial character of the philosophical thought in India is that its fundamentals are grounded on a set of eternally existent truths embodied by the Vedas, whose origin

[4] The Indian tradition since the times described by the Vedas has upheld a fourfold classification of the Indian society. The four classes, namely, *Brāhmins* (priests), *Kṣatriyas* (nobles), *Vaiśyas* (merchants and agriculturalists) and *Śūdras* (manual workers), have been supposed to be rigid, and organized by agencies beyond the control of man. The most authentic exposition of this classification is found in the *Manu Smṛti* (*Lawbook of Manu*). Tradition also maintains that one's birth in a particular class is determined by the type of deeds one has accumulated in one's past lives. Orthodox Hindus are as firm about the sanctity of preserving the fourfold classification as Plato, for instance, was about preserving the threefold classification of the Greek community in his days.

is believed to be suprahuman and supradivine. All orthodox systems of Indian philosophy have anchored themselves firmly in these truths, and whenever they have encountered unsurmountable problems, they have resorted to the authority of these truths. The function of the Vedic word (*śabda*) and sentence (*vākya*) is supposed to be to transmit eternal truths for the benefaction and ultimate liberation of man. Thus the *śabda-pramāna* or word-testimony is the center around which almost all arguments and theories in Indian philosophy hover.

The Vedic word-testimony is most leaned on by the Mīmāṁsā ritualists when they say that the *Dharma* is originless and infallible and was first transmitted to the *ṛṣis,* the authors of the Vedas. The words or sentences of the Vedas, the Mīmāṁsakas hold, are therefore mere devices for the deliverance of eternal and indubitable metalinguistic messages. According to the Mīmāṁsā system, the wisdom of the Vedas is neither of *ṛṣis* nor of God; it is prior to them both and is the very *raison d'être* of their functioning. It is believed that the Vedic wisdom transcends everything. Consequently, the Vedic *ṛṣis* or seers are some sort of careers of the trans-Vedic wisdom to the people in the bondage of the world. This wisdom is as eternal as *Brahman,* and hence should be called *Brahman-śabda* or *Brahman-vākya.*

In fact, the theory of the revealed truths is as abstruse, though impressive in some of its subtleties, as the Pythagorean theory that numbers or figures are the primodial basis of all Reality and, as such, radiate to human minds through celestial music. Apart from the variations in Indians' views regarding the exact source of the Vedic words, what is central to all of them is the belief that the certitude of the Vedic words is to be intuited and not discussed. It is the Nyāya and the Mīmāṁsā thinkers more than others who focused their attention on this belief and extensively analyzed the relation between meaning and word. The Vedic expressions, the Nyāya and the Mīmāṁsā hold, have an intrinsic and supersensible authority.

It is interesting to note that some of the Nyāya stalwarts could not accept the view that the Vedic words are originless and eternally self-subsistent, although they did admit that they have a reference to the imperceptible or *adṛṣtārtha.* The Nyāya points out that every sound has a beginning, that is, is produced by some source. Now the sounds which the Vedic words have recorded have a convention, however incomprehensible it may be. This convention, the Naiyāyikas hold, is their source. Therefore, the Vedic words cannot be eternal, and they did not certainly exist before they were perceived by the seers (*ṛṣis*). The Nyāya does not hesitate to say that the Vedic wisdom is the wisdom of God. Thus the whole theory that the Vedas embody sounds which have neither human nor divine source is *prima facie* rejected by the Nyāya. God, who is omniscient, the Naiyāyikas argue, is the authority behind the Vedas. And since He is perfectly knowledgeable, whatever the Vedas contain is absolutely trustworthy.

Some of the later Nyāya grammarians allude to a semitranscendent foundation of the meaning of the Vedic words for their theory of what is called the "sound-essence" or *sphoṭa* of words. This theory, in brief, is that the sound-essence is the very soul of a meaningful word. It is something that the word reveals or communicates to mind through its meaning. So perhaps what is eternal and self-subsistent is not the sound or the word, but the sound-essence. It can be imagined as something buoying in space (*akāsa*) like Pythagoras's numbers or Plato's Ideas, and descending onto human minds, which only incorporate them in words.

The sound-essence of a wisdom, eternal or divine, is thus believed to be the sanction behind the code of duties recommended by the Vedic tradition. For the Mīmāṁsakas in particular and for all orthodox thinkers in general, behavior according to the unfailing norms established by the superhuman agencies is sure to take man to *mokṣa*—the only desirable goal for man on earth. The sound of the eternal wisdom is the counsel for salvation.

ONLY A COG ON THE COSMIC WHEEL

In respect of its representation of the doctrine that all action must be done as duties, and its profound sway over India's ethical life and even political thinking, the *Bhagavad-gītā* has come to occupy the most remarkable place in the history of Indians. Being one of the three fundamental texts [5] that have shaped In-

[5] These texts are the *Upaniṣads*, the *Brahma Sūtra* and the *Bhagavad-gītā*. They are regarded as *prasthāna-traya* or the basic trio of Indian philosophy.

dian consciousness over centuries, it is not only in full consistency with the other two texts of the trio but also eminent for its specific emphasis on what, following Kant, can be called "practical reason" (*praktische Vernunft*). And the persuasiveness with which it preaches absolutism, pantheism and a strange mingling of activism and determinism hardly has any parallel in Indian literature. With highly condensed seven hundred verses of its text, which Hindus more often mechanically recite than understand, the *Bhagavad-gītā* advises that since *Brahman* or God is the ultimate knower and controller of the results of all actions, man's supreme duty is just to act without any attachment to or passionate involvement in the end of the action.

Thus here is a heavily deterministic view of human activity recorded by ancient Indian moralists who presumably had to their lot more of frustrations than victories, freaks from the unknown than outcome anticipated. Anyone who attempts at getting to the essential intent of this work cannot help remarking that it is a tale of the insignificance of man's status within cosmic reality, his trifling instrumental agency in relation to the process of the universe, the hollowness of his endeavor against the independent course of *Brahman* or Being.

The *Bhagavad-gītā* is fundamentally a dialogue between Kṛṣṇa, the incarnation of the Absolute, and combatant Arjuna, whose feelings and truth-seeking interrogations have something genuinely human and edifying about them. Just at the moment when Arjuna is about to launch an attack on the enemies on the battlefield,[6] he is moved by the pacifist and humane thought that

[6] The *Bhagavad-gītā* (The Song of the Blessed One) must have been composed sometime between the fifth and the second centuries before Christ. It forms a part of the great epic *Mahābhārata,* whose authorship is ascribed to Vyāsa. The central philosophy of the *Bhagavad-gītā* is stated against the background story of an enmity between Pāndavas—the sons of one Pandu—and Kauravas, who were known for their stupidity and lack of character. The enmity develops into a belicose state, and the huge armies of the two sides meet for a war on the battlefield of Kurukśetra, a place near modern Delhi. Kṛṣṇa, believed to be the incarnation of God, is shown, in the *Bhagavad-gītā,* as the charioteer of Arjuna, one of the five Pāndava heroes. The Pāndavas were known for their valor and humaneness. It happens that when the war is about to start, Arjuna is suddenly filled with sorrow and horror at the prospective death of his enemies by killing. He throws away his weapons, and asks Kṛṣṇa: "What can we hope from this killing . . . ?"

he would not kill even for "the throne of the three worlds" but rather be killed himself. This unmilitary sentimentalism sparks off Kṛṣṇa's versatile arguments in which the absolutist metaphysics of the Upaniṣads is so beautifully set that finally Arjuna changes his mind and decides to fight.

Kṛṣṇa says that all that Arjuna is supposed to do is to go on doing his *Kṣatriya* duties, like a cog on the wheel of creation, and the fruits—good or bad—would come by themselves irrespective of what Arjuna anticipated them to be. Arjuna, the unfortunate representative of the gross naive humanity, had no independent power to decide for or against, but was, as Kṛṣṇa tells him, only an occasion.[7] He had no reason to feel like a criminal, for it is not he that was going to kill the Kauravas. They, the embodiment of felony and ill-will, would have been annihilated anyhow, says Kṛṣṇa, and Arjuna need feel nothing more than being an instrument operator in the whole business. So ultimately a realization dawns on Arjuna that since it is the Absolute that bears complete ownership of his (Arjuna's) act, he ought to resign to the requirements of the situation, rather than remain a dissenter.

In almost all studies of the *Bhagavad-gītā* written so far, what is consistently overlooked is the fact that nowhere in his attempts at Arjuna's pacification does Kṛṣṇa deviate from his thesis that an individual's being and freedom are insignificant. Again and again he suggests to Arjuna that the latter's concern for his guilt, in case he fought and destroyed Kauravas, would result from his naiveté and delusion. No wonder, Kṛṣṇa says, it is a universal naiveté from which only the illumined are free. For Kṛṣṇa, Arjuna is like an innocent child who is given to a false sense of makership, or who is in the habit of feeling now and then that he is the source of many a change in the given scheme of things in the world.

Whether Kṛṣṇa's and, for that matter, man's awareness that in certain selected situations he can make or unmake things is a delusion or not is certainly debatable. But the difficulty is that

[7] Swami Prabhāvananda, and Isherwood, Christopher (trans.): *Bhagavad-gītā*, p. 123.

Kṛṣṇa gives no convincing criterion with which we can judge that Arjuna's eventual resolution to put through the fight without any attachment to its consequences, as instructed by Kṛṣṇa, is in any moral sense superior to his originally conscientious—and therefore intrinsically free—urge to lay down arms. It is obvious that had Arjuna pacifically given up the war in favor of his sense of abhorrence of killing, Kṛṣṇa, as the absolute creator and destroyer of lives, would still have brought about the ruin of Kauravas. For instance, he would have employed some other device—his choice in the unfolding of history—to realize the same end. And every other device, like Arjuna, would have been devoid of any decision-making ability. Any one device would have had to work and indeed would have worked as effectively as any other. In any case, his being a sheer pawn, to be operated as and when the Absolute wishes it, reduces Arjuna to a replaceable function.

Arjuna's liberty finds its undiluted expression in his searching questions. He asks Kṛṣṇa pointblank: How can we be happy if we kill our own people? [8] Why dost thou urge me to do this savage deed? [9] What is it that makes a man do evil, even against his own will, under compulsion as it were? [10] Kṛṣṇa actually avoids the questions, and instead indulges in a philosophical harangue which evidently bewilders rather than satisfies Arjuna's intelligence. It is difficult for one to carry an impression that after the end of this harangue, which indeed contains sparks of Vyāsa's inquiring genius but much of which must have gone over tense and impatient Arjuna's head, Kṛṣṇa did really succeed in convincing the Pāndava hero that he *ought* to kill the foes. And as Kosambi has recently suspected, the quickest possible delivery of the seven hundred verses of the *Bhagavad-gītā* would have taken, say, three hours, by which time Arjuna would have lost the whole battle.[11] So it seems that Arjuna's eventual conversion to Kṛṣṇa's point of view is like that of a person awakened to the traditional

[8] *Ibid.*, p. 35.

[9] *Ibid.*, p. 51.

[10] *Ibid.*, p. 57.

[11] Kosambi, D. D.: *The Culture and Civilisation of Ancient India in Historical Outline*. London, Routledge and Kegan Paul, 1965, p. 207.

Indian truism that every individual in this world is after all a finite paltry being totally at the mercy of forces unknown to him.

Kṛṣṇa prompts Arjuna to act according to *Dharma,* that is, to do as any other *Kṣatriya* in his situation would have done. According to Kṛṣṇa neither sentimentalism nor the pose of being a free and independent doer was befitting for the situation Arjuna was in, or, for that matter, for any situation an individual would happen to be in. Consequently, Arjuna assures Kṛṣṇa that he would fight as indicated by his advice.

Perhaps the main reason why the *Bhagavad-gītā* episode has settled, in spite of utterly unorganized media of its propagation, as the conveyor of an imperishable ethical truth in Indian consciousness is its amazingly construed blending between determinism and activism. Teachers, unpaid roving Hindu preachers and hundreds of lucidly composed expositions of the *Bhagavad-gītā* philosophy have endeavored to create throughout India a *Weltanschauung* that the essence of life consists in acting disinterestedly and humbly, i.e. in doing things not for any gain but because one's station in the world demands them. Thus the way of action (*karma-mārga, karma-yoga*), expounded by Kṛṣṇa, has gone on well with even those who notwithstanding their inveterate allegiance to fatalism have made it a vocation to work for the good of their fellowmen. Besides, its constant preoccupation being activity and not retirement, the *Bhagavad-gītā* word unhesitatingly extols those who are reluctant to flinch from their *Dharma* or duties.

As it has been shown before, the dichotomy between absolutism and individual effort for the attainment of *mokṣa,* determinism and activism, fatalism and freedom, is totally blurred in Indian philosophy. It would be futile to look for samples of reasoning in Indian systems of thought forwarding solely one or the other of these opposed tendencies. Indian thinkers, regardless of the paths of salvation to which they subscribe, represent a consensus of view in respect of the inevitability of phenomena in the universe, or more precisely, in respect of the determination of total human experiences in accordance with the law of *karma.*

In the Indian theory of human existence, almost every attempt at justifying the fact of man's being in the world, his urgency to perform deeds, religious or otherwise, his planning for the future, etc., is grounded on the assumption that all activity is good in itself provided it is offered to *Brahman* or God. You are what you are made to be by your past deeds, you will live and act in a manner already destined for you, the author of the *Bhagavad-gītā* appears to say, and your liberty consists in recognizing this fact and going on acting as if it were not you who act but the supreme spirit or *Brahman* within you. What does this liberty amount to? It is the liberty to *know,* to pass from the state of ignorance to that of self-awareness, from the delusion of being a master to the wisdom of being an instrument. It is with this import in mind that Kṛṣṇa cautions Arjuna that the value of an act depends entirely on the agent's enlightened attitude, on the passion of dutifulness it is done with, on the trust underlying it that it is done for its own sake. In the last chapter of the *Bhagavad-gītā,* Kṛṣṇa advises Arjuna: "Mentally resign all your action to me. Regard me as your dearest loved one. Know me to be your only refuge. Be united always in heart and consciousness with me." [12]

The brand of ethics—carved in all its essentials on the Vedic-Upaniṣadic metaphysics—which the *Bhagavad-gītā* has put forward is unlike any that has appeared in the West so far.[13] Its diffusedness, its swing away from the day-to-day truth that actions can hardly be committed with complete inattention to their outcome, its stress on man's insignificant status as a doer, its defence of what can be called the "determined freedom" of the individual, represent an amazing admixture of metaphysical indifference and practical obligatoriness in the Indian mind. Here theory and practice, stern truths regarding the nature of the cosmos and

[12] Swami Prabhāvananda, and Isherwood, Christopher (trans.) : *Bhagavad-gītā,* p. 171.

[13] There have been arguments showing a resemblance between the *Bhagavad-gītā* path of "selfless action" and Kant's famous law that a course of action is "morally good" only if it is done for the sake of doing one's duty. One may also draw a parallel between it and F. H. Bradley's thesis that the main significance of man's life lies in his fulfilment of his "station" and its "duties." While such arguments do make themselves interesting, it must be noted that for both Kant and Bradley one's knowledge of one's duty is "rational," but for Kṛṣṇa it depends on one's acceptance of *Dharma* or the authority of the Vedic words.

the hope for change attainable through human agency, ultimate meaninglessness of action and the urgency for dutiful behavior are made to cohabit. It would require some kind of an existential approach to investigate whether in this unusual cohabitation the moral freedom of the individual is, in practice, safeguarded.

There is no doubt that Kṛṣṇa's message has profoundly influenced the development of the Indian mind, and has given rise to the unique attitude in it which is most humanistic or other-directed in one sense but most fatalistic in another.[14] Large numbers of Indians operate to this very time in conditions where available resources hardly suffice to keep them optimistic—with neglected ill-cared bodies, harshest reality of life with frequent failures, undernourished children and frustrated youth—as if they are devoted to their "functions," as if they have to go on operating with neither any grandiose desire nor any wholesome plan to change their world. One witnesses Indians more often "doing" than "questioning," more often obeying their *Dharma* silently than doubting its foundation. Seminars, debates and group discussions of even university graduates and of intellectuals in India on issues which affect the betterment of human life most are abruptly geared into blind alleys when someone brings in a note of resignation and says: But what can one possibly do? Whatever happens was bound to happen anyway!

Indians are not made in the image of a Moby Dick, thrusting their entire being into action with determination and singleness of purpose. They perform actions as diligently as they perform their duties, ritualistic or otherwise. They live with an innermost conviction that every action is sure to follow its own course and result. It appears that Kṛṣṇa's instructions to Arjuna perennially reverberate in the very air the Indians breathe. They seem to

[14] It is not correct to say, as Koestler in his critical work on the significance of India's transcendentalism to mankind has said, that India has no "spiritual cure" to offer for the "evils of Western civilization." (See Koestler, Arthur: *The Lotus and the Robot*. New York, Macmillan, 1960, p. 162.) What has always happened, and still happens on a large scale, is that Indians' fatalistic disposition has somehow stayed an adversary of their action-potential and put many of their plans in cold storage. Indians have the unearthly habit of shifting from dutifulness to inactivity, and of justifying the latter as effectively as the former.

say: Act, do not sit idle: act desirelessly and on His behalf; and leave the question of the result of your acts to Him alone.

As a matter of fact, when adopted as a mode of practical living, these instructions entail some of the most dangerous consequences: snobbery, unwarranted rationalization of antisocial behavior, planninglessness, diffidence in one's role in the world and paralysis of intellect. Perhaps the main reason why the weightiest contribution of India to the formation of one single metaphysical *Weltanschauung* for Man is not universally recognized is that real India cannot stand freed from the appearance of these consequences. They are, rather dialectically, a force disallowing the full stretching of her humanistic potential. However, when looked at as a pure attitude, a way of seeing mankind and its universe, there is no reason why Kṛṣṇa's instructions should not change the face of India and the world by basically transforming the whole net of interpersonal and international relations. No man is a chooser per se in the complexity of this cosmos is a truism that must cultivate in us a sense of diminutiveness, humility and insignificance.

What is necessary is to separate chaff from the corn.

FREEDOM AND COMMITMENT

Generally, any action of ethical significance has to have a project, a program, a commitment, or an intention at its basis. It is impossible to conceive of an individual as answerable to himself if he ceases to function as an intentional being. It can be easily seen, therefore, that by rejecting all decision-making independence of an individual, Kṛṣṇa has left him without any *raison d'être* of activity, except that entailed by his *Dharma,* station and the word of the Supreme Spirit. Kṛṣṇa was gratified when Arjuna agreed to act without an attachment either to the motive or the result of the action. Such a nonattachment, according to the *Bhagavad-gītā,* would logically follow from the fact that all activity is a behavior the Absolute demands of man. Since the Absolute and man are so related that the latter is in all his essence an expression of the former, a being that cannot but function as a part and parcel of the former, any act that springs up from man would be in theory determined by the Absolute itself.[15] The *Bhagavad-gītā* anticipated an absolutism of the most rigid type. It has shown not only that an individual's sense of makership is fundamentally an illusion, but also that such a sense arises because of naiveté of his world-bound state.

The most powerful representation of the doctrine of the ethical nonattachment of the enlightened is found in Vyāsa's ideas of *sthitaprajna* (the uninvolved intellect) and *niśkāma karma* (the desireless action). The *sthitaprajna* is the image of the "ontological man"[16] in his most primeval mental condition: unaffected by passions or sentiments of any kind, absolutely stable and self-possessed, a recluse in the sanctuary of his own inner domain, "undisturbed in adversity, not hankering after happiness, free from fear, free from anger, free from the things of desire."[17] The ultimate goal of a *sthitaprajna* is *jīvanmukti*,[18] i.e. the attainment of a state of perfect translucence, of a total freedom from sensual objects, of *Brahmisthiti* or the transcendental calmness. Kṛṣṇa tells Arjuna that at this level there would be no motivation whatsoever, no association with or attachment to anything whatsoever, no interest in anything in mind or senses whatsoever. In his status of a worldly and social being, a *sthitaprajna* would literally behave as a nonaligned, fully self-controlled and meditative, and active-in-will-but-passive-in-attitude agent.

[15] The profundity of the feeling of diminutiveness in an individual vis-à-vis the overwhelming immensity of the Absolute is manifest in the writings of Josiah Royce, one of the most illumined minds of our time, thus: ". . . I say: Everything finite is more or less obscure, dark, doubtful. Only the Infinite Self, the problem-solver, the complete thinker, the one who knows what we mean even when we are most confused and ignorant, the one who includes us, who has the world present to himself in unity, before whom all past and future truth, all distant and dark truth is clear in one eternal moment, to whom far and forgot is near, who thinks the whole of nature, and in whom are all things, the Logos, the world-possessor,—only his existence, I say, is perfectly sure." (See Royce, Josiah: *The Spirit of Modern Philosophy*. Boston, Houghton Mifflin, 1892, pp. 373–74.)

[16] To existentialists also, the most authentic realization of one's existence is possible only when one ontologizes oneself. For a treatment of this, see Sinari, Ramakant: *Reason in Existentialism*, pp. 213–18.

[17] Swami Prabhāvananda, and Isherwood, Christopher (trans.): *Bhagavad-gītā*, p. 47.

[18] *Ibid.*, pp. 48–50.

Thus when all incentive, internal and external, for the action is suspended, and the agent becomes as if neutralized in his general *rapprochement* with things, what would follow from him is a series of seemingly spontaneous gestures whose unfailing principle would indeed be righteousness and the benefaction of all. The *Bhagavad-gītā* suggests that a *sthitaprajna*'s behavior would always be enlightened by the virtue of the fact that it would flow from his extraordinarily pure conscience and not from any plan or purpose conceived by him. No fallibility in the decisions of such a conscience can be feared because it has reached beyond the bounds of practical intellect or contingent circumstances.

It might seem obvious that once human consciousness has realized a level at which every need for activity ceases to function, it would really be aimless, ascetic or self-abandoned. To act is to manifest a necessity for action, to be impelled by a value, to exhibit an approach to oneself and to one's being in the world. However, a *sthitaprajna*'s activity being devoid of all conceivable need is ordinarily not only unwarranted but also meaningless. Yet what is maintained by Vyāsa appears to imply that a person with "uninvolved intellect" is bound to remain active because of his pure spiritual force, that is, out of a mysterious anxiety to draw others up to his level. The goal between what one is and what one should be, or between what one does and what one should do no more prevails in a *sthitaprajna*. Hence he is the most ideal embodiment of free action —action which is not governed even by the unaccomplished goal or desire—the most genuine expression of the supreme self.

It may be pointed out here that a careful analysis of the concept of *mokṣa, kevala-jñāna, nirvāṇa,* or *Brahmānubhava,* which is the exclusive experience a *sthitaprajna* or *jīvanmukta* claims, will convince one that Indian philosophies have practically rejected the need to act in a transcendentally enlightened individual. The notion of self-realization in Indian thought is so far removed from life's pragmatic considerations—the hunger of the body and the thirst of the instincts—that it can hardly recommend any activity to the enlightened as an imperative. And, therefore, if some of the most ardent followers of Indian thought have practiced and spread the religion of universal love and work for the uplift of mankind, it is despite its metaphysical assumption that when *mokṣa*-experience dawns on one, one becomes so full and rich inwardly that one's return to the world of action is basically unnecessary.

The stimulus for any intended and purposive act would originate from a sense of nonfulfilment and noncompletion in the agent. The enlightened and the absolutely free need not act since there is nothing that he desires. As existentialists have explained, the essence of man's eternal search for transcendence or freedom must be sought in the fact that man is a "lack" within himself. Man is a craving, an ever unfilled "hole," a yearning for the infinite, an ever ungraspable awareness of being and nonbeing. It is by and through activity that he surmounts his deficiencies and climbs up the ladder of transcendental inspiration.

Nevertheless, according to Indian philosophies the sole aim of human behavior is to achieve a level of existence where the very necessity of voluntary actions is completely eradicated, the consciousness of the motive is put an end to, and all purposiveness and desirability are extinguished. Thus one of the main theses of the *Bhagavad-gītā* states that the path of action (*karma-mārga, karma-yoga*) is essentially a means towards the final state of actionlessness in *mokṣa* or *jīvanmukti* or *karma-mukti*. Just as the Jainas, the Buddhists and the followers of the Sāṅkhya, the Yoga and the Vedānta emphasize the total withdrawal of the ego as a prerequisite of *mokṣa*, Kṛṣṇa prophesies that an individual, in his *sthitaprajna* career, would do only desireless deeds (*niśkāma karma*) and thereby accomplish perfection.

To be able to act without any involvement in or desire for the result of the action is the mark of the enlightened. He belongs to a stratum of being at which he is left with no urgency to act, or at which his actions are motiveless (*niśkāma*), although as the *Bhagavad-gītā* says, it is not right for him to attach himself to inactivity.[19] What a *sthitaprajna* is, in fact, committed to is a form of life where he would cease to have any requirement to commit himself to any particular behavior any further.

It is not difficult to see that the conception of freedom Vyāsa

[19] *Ibid.*, pp. 49–50.

presents is, with all its implications, a negative and anti-individualistic conception. A free man, Vyāsa seems to emphasize, is absolutely unhindered by doubt, wholly determined by his inner voice, and never oscillating between one course of action and another. He has to plunge into one and the only path of choice or not plunge into any path at all, according to the logic of the Absolute. He must disconnect himself not only from all flexibility of decision, but also from the plausible psychological sense that it is from his choice that his actions issue forth.

Deeply ingrained in a *sthitaprajna*'s consciousness lies the feeling that he is fundamentally a mode of the Absolute and that his acts are a means of the self-fulfilment of the Supreme Spirit. However, for Vyāsa, since the state of *sthitaprajna*'s uninvolved standing has for its destination the realization of salvation, every function of his, while he lives in the world, is disinterested and motiveless as that of a man on the verge of the dissolution of the I-sense. Indeed, the *Bhagavad-gītā* lays stress on the fact that the dissolution of the I-sense demands as an antecedent measure one's journey through a period of rituals, duties or *Dharma* prescribed by one's station in the world. This is why Kṛṣṇa advises Arjuna to cultivate within him the spirit of the "ontological man": not to shun his duties, and to come to maturity by practicing the principle of uninvolvement.

An individual's commitment and answerability to his own self is far more important than his commitment and answerability to any authority outside. As existentialists often point out, the freedom of choice in a given situation is the most primordial fact an individual would value, and no matter what consequences it leads to, it bestows on his life an exclusive inward propulsion, a meaningful continuance, a dynamism. They pointedly suggest that real moral commitment would emerge in a consciousness only when it expresses itself conatively, i.e. it figures as a freely acting "existence." The criterion of a genuine moral commitment is not the cocksureness or unambiguousness an agent might experience vis-à-vis his choice. The feeling of freedom is accompanied by a peculiar sort of bewilderment, a conflict between two inner voices, so to say, a sense of being lost in the wilderness. Freedom, as Erich Fromm says, is an "ambiguous gift." Man experiences helplessness in presence of freedom; he suffers as a result of this experience.[20]

All freedom situations are ambiguous. When different alternative paths are thrown open before us, we do not know with absolute certainty which path might take us and the world to the most desirable condition. Being intricate bundles of the rational and the irrational, the conscious and the unconscious, we find ourselves utterly confused regarding the choice of the right or the good. Suppose someone with an omniscient intellect were to impress upon us the virtue of one choice as against that of the other and influence our decision. We would feel not only "crushed" under an overwhelming external authority but also deprived of the peculiar anxiety of exercising our freedom.[21] On the other hand, were we to follow our own independent judgment and choose by the force of reason or sentiment a course of action which appears to us to be most fitting to the occasion, we might still be left with a sense of frustration after we review our choice retrospectively.

In the latter case, however, we would have the satisfaction of having had our decision freely, of having owned our choice. It is this satisfaction that points to the agent's voluntariness, to his responsibility for his deed, and to his commitment to himself.

One wonders, therefore, whether by urging Arjuna to fight, or to operate according to his *Kṣatriya Dharma*, Kṛṣṇa did not deny him his self-determining individuality. The situation Arjuna was facing is of so crucial a character that it would have been apt for his divine advisor to let him commit himself to a course of action which he himself chose, and to bring upon himself the responsibility for his choice.

There is no attempt whatsoever in the *Bhagavad-gītā* to cloak

[20] Fromm, Erich: *Fear of Freedom*. London, Routledge & Kegan Paul Ltd., 1960, pp. 26–27.

[21] Arjuna's perplexity, to fight or not to fight, his acute despair, his feeling of disgust at the thought of his role as a soldier described most movingly at the beginning of the *Bhagavad-gītā*, is the expression of his anxiety of freedom. It is not impossible to argue that Vyāsa makes Arjuna question the very ethic of the *Kṣatriya Dharma*, the very sanity of man to wage a war to kill, and thereby makes him adopt an existential attitude. Arjuna is one of the most lovable pacifists in the history of mankind.

absolutism and ethical determinism. When looked at from the practical point of view, Arjuna's I-sense appears to be not only the only genuine basis of his freedom but also as an inseparable constituent of his individuality and distinctness. Who is it who questions the very wisdom of fighting? Who is it in Arjuna's person who suddenly turns compassionate, and repels the idea of killing the foe? Who is perplexed, and who doubts, in the *Kṣatriya* consciousness? It could not certainly be the Absolute or *Brahman,* for as Kṛṣṇa later tells Arjuna, it is the Absolute that had planned the fight and had chosen Arjuna to carry out the plan. Consequently, what figures as a skeptic or a dissenter in Arjuna is something human, free, unique and situational; and Kṛṣṇa ought to have heeded it as much as he heeded the logic of the Absolute.

FROM RITUALISM TO REBELLION

The most forceful supporter of the thesis that the *Bhagavad-gītā* stands for the path of action and still evolves a remarkable harmony between it and the paths of knowledge and devotion, is Bal Gangādhar Tilak (1856–1920), who is renowned for his tenacious struggle against the British rule in India. By writing an exhaustive treatise on the *Bhagavad-gītā,* Tilak has tried to establish that the real message or religion of this "vision of Paramesvara (the highest God)" is activity of every individual. Tilak thought that the *Bhagavad-gītā* was a masterpiece of the workmanship of the Supreme Lord, and that according to it imperishable truth and eternal peace could be attained by everybody by committing himself to his *Dharma* or duties. Human life is a great sacrifice (*yajña*), he says, and whoever takes it in that spirit is enlightened in the real sense of that term.

What Tilak aggrandizes, however, is that because Kṛṣṇa upholds every person's performance of his duties and suggests that even a *sthitaprajna* should act he professes a philosophy of commitment.[22] As it has been observed in the last section, the activity Kṛṣṇa preaches to Arjuna not only belittles his individuality and his decision-making ability but also ridicules his I-sense as a

[22] Tilak, Bal Gangadhar: *Srimad Bhagavadgītā Rahaṣya.* B. S. Sukthankar (trans.), Poona, Tilak Bros., 1935, Vol. 1, pp. xlix–li.

freak of his vanity. An individual's only commitment, according to Kṛṣṇa's thinking, is to his station in society, to his following the word of God, to the discipline registered by the Highest. Such a commitment is clearly devoid of individual freedom and individual involvement, and hence emptied of all moral contents.

The evolution of the individual mind from a state of religious and ethical obligatoriness to a state of uninvolvement is vindicated by the *Bhagavad-gītā* in perfect consistency with the Vedic-Upaniṣadic transcendentalist tradition. A *sthitaprajna,* i.e. a kind of uninvolved-in-attitude-*jīvanmukta*-with-total-desirelessness, is the ideal character the author of the *Bhagavad-gītā* has before his mind. This character must act not out of any interest in or motivation for the result, but out of a conviction that he is merely a representation of *Brahman*. But when is one to know for certain the validity of this conviction? Perhaps had Tilak accepted Kṛṣṇa's wisdom and made it the sole guide of his activity, he would not have conducted himself in so furious and effective manner as he actually did in his endeavor to free India from the foreign rule. Tilak was a planner, a calculating political strategist, a rebel and a reformer, who thought of his moves and of their possible consequences more like a free thinking individual than like a *sthitaprajna*.

However, this is not to underestimate Tilak's sagacious attempt to correlate his revolutionary and reformative activities with the *Bhagavad-gītā* philosophy, or to ignore the magnitude of influence the ethics of *sthitaprajna* and *niśkāma karma* has left on a host of Indian reformers and social workers to this day.[23] What is to be noted is that *sthitaprajnāvasthā,* or the state of being uninvolved, is a sort of metaphysical attitude one might adopt after one has made a choice or decided upon a way of action. When psychologically interpreted, the *sthitaprajna* intellect can be said to be uninvolved, inasmuch as it can alienate itself from the fruit of the action after the action has taken place.

[23] The ethics of *sthitaprajna* and *niśkāma karma* is only an ideal of the conduct of the masses. It presupposes a phenomenological attitude which has suspended the entire psychical and social sphere of interests and eliminated the very basis of activity. The masses being unable to actually cultivate such an attitude, they have not seldom oversimplified this ethics and equated it with a cold indifference to action.

One cannot be a *sthitaprajna* and a voluntary agent, just as one cannot act voluntarily and be unconcerned about the purpose of the action at the same time. The function of a *sthitaprajna* can be only retrospective. He must act first and then suspend from his consciousness every idea about the outcome of the action.

To act consciously is to act to produce some result. One may wonder what efficiency and punch an action would have if the agent starts with the *sthitaprajna* attitude, i.e. is neither aware of what he acts for, nor is committed to a specific plan or objective. What would be the motivation of a *sthitaprajna*'s activity? What is the *raison d'être* of one's *niśkāma karma* or desireless acts? Being enlightened, transcendentally oriented and of trans-empirical temperament, a *sthitaprajna,* like Socrates's "wise and virtuous man," cannot sever himself from the ideal of *summum bonum* before he embarks upon an action. And to the extent to which he is conscious of this ideal, he would have freely selected it and would rest involved in it.

Thus, Tilak's choice of ways and means to fight against the British in India, his frequent and programmed decisions to resist the latter, could be neither "uninvolved" nor aimless. He chose to act before he disciplined himself to remain disinterested in the result of his action. Perhaps one adopts the *sthitaprajna* view of human life when one is not certain as to what consequence a well-planned act might lead up to, or when one has experienced unfavorable fruits to acts performed with wisdom and good faith. Perhaps it is also the view of those who see the world as a bundle of absurdities, and like fatalists, lose all faith in purposeful endeavor. And when it emerges in man in some such ways, the *sthitaprajna* attitude can become the foundation of magnanimous humanistic actions. A *sthitaprajna* will have to be accepted as an "ontological man," who freely and thoughtfully takes infinitely selfless decisions; but in the event of an unexpected undesirable outcome, owns it with a calm and unruffled mind.

Unlike Mīmāṁsakas' theory of salvation-through-action where emphasis is on ritualism or religious duties, Vyāsa in the *Bhagavad-gītā* propounds a view of activity that is broad enough to include prescriptions for the conduct having social import. Despite the fact that Kṛṣṇa's message is fundamentally a message of *mokṣa,* or an everlasting emancipation from the bondage of the world, he at least indirectly gives recognition to matters related to praxis. Kṛṣṇa's message is pregnant with an array of notions about practical and transcendental life, each of which can claim horizons having bearing on changing situations and times. Amidst all that Kṛṣṇa says, his hitting upon a way of salvation in which knowledge (*jñāna*) and action (*karma*) are combined should be looked upon as the most important breakthrough to the era of praxis in India.

Chapter Twelve

THE AGE OF AWAKENING

THE FORCE OF THE CHANGING TIMES

It is true, typically with regard to India, that the history of its philosophies, religions and culture hides underneath an entire community's aspirations for a form of otherworldly and mystical calmness from which a return to the phenomenal world would amount to a return to the weary, bound, absurd and painful existence. Through nearly four thousand years of its struggle for self-preservation in the face of internal and external enemical trends, India has sustained herself as perhaps the most enduring spiritualistic tradition in the world.[1] The richness of her past triumphs in matters of the soul, the vitality of her quest for transcendental experience, her unique function as an absorbent of Islam, Christianity, Zoroastrianism and Judaism, the unrestrained renunciation of her saints and seers for the sake of trans-material ends, and her intense love for and practice of peace, speak of her spiritual excellence and valor. What the West has taken for granted in its adherence to the worldly interests and benefaction since the time of Greek Epicureans, India has essentially abnegated as regressive and pernicious.

But there is something like a spatiotemporal dimension to human existence, and much more so to the existence of a com-

[1] Jawaharlal Nehru, the first Prime Minister of India and one of the most perspicacious observers of human history in our times, writes: "Whatever the word we might use, Indian or Hindi or Hindustani, for our cultural tradition, we see in the past that some inner urge towards synthesis, derived essentially from the Indian philosophic outlook, was the dominant feature of Indian cultural and even racial development. Each incursion of foreign elements was a challenge to this culture. . . ." See Nehru, Jawaharlal: *The Discovery of India*. Bombay, Asia Publishing House, 1961, pp. 78–79.

munity, however certain that community might be of the ultimate truth of the experience of the beyond. Besides, the force of the changing times, the wind of a new civilization around, the striking achievements of other peoples in the world in respect of the domain that was given no cognizance at all over ages, and probably some vague boredom with the ascetic past of one's own might generate in a group a desire to examine and modulate its whole *Weltanschauung*. What transpired in the firmly set metaphysical tradition of India, with the augmenting influence over her of the Western law and Industrial Revolution in the seventeenth and eighteenth centuries—and what is still in process—is an examination and modulation of this kind. It struck to Indian thinkers that an evaluation of their philosophical, religious and ethical heritage in the light of the Western view of existence was imminent.

The history of the awakening of Indians from a kind of spiritual complacence to the needs of material and practical well-being would be an account full of the gradually increasing instances of the conversion of an inward-seeing sensibility into an outer-seeing one. What Herbert Marcuse,[2] for instance, significantly calls "inner freedom" or "private space" of the individual had never been challenged in the case of India at any time before the advent of the British rule on her soil. The introduction of the empiricistic way of thinking, the easy flow into the land of Western men and literature, the concept of law and liberty, the clashes between tradition and modernity sparked off by the British through their ways of educating and reforming Indians, and the new socio-politico-economic problems created by English administrators forced Indians to subject their *cogito* to a rational inquiry. It was the time for test of India's absorbent function before a culture, vastly impressive, but alien to the very spirit of her world-negating metaphysics.

It is impossible for a mass of over 450 million human beings to corner themselves when the rest of the world is marching to-

[2] Marcuse, Herbert: *One Dimensional Man*. London, Routledge & Kegan Paul Ltd., 1964, p. 10. Marcuse is interested in explaining how "technological reality" of the industrial revolution has today "invaded" and "whittled down" the "private space" of man.

wards a set of ideals comprehensive enough to include the quests of the total individual. No wonder it dawned on the most precocious minds in India towards the end of the eighteenth century that it was high time that they stopped remaining contented with the glory of the purely transcendental speculation of their Vedic-Upaniṣadic gurus. What was necessary is to take a pose of mind, to develop and spread a revised approach towards the reality of the material world, to invent a rational antidote against those elements in the tradition which were proved by time to be fossils, and to merge in the universal course of industrialization without at the same time losing the Indian ethos. What the history of India of the past two centuries exhibits is one of the most formidable endeavors of a mass of humanity to steer clear of the myths in its own tradition and the evils of Western civilization, of its own blind and primitive superstitions and the dogmas of the Western scientism, and to advance by assimilating into its existence all that the West has offered for the promotion of the dignity of man and by preserving what is of imperishable value in its own thought.

We have seen that the *bhakti* mysticism, which spread far and wide in India through its multiple ramifications and produced a devotionalistic climate among masses of all strata, is fundamentally an antiworld movement inspired by the Vedic-Upaniṣadic philosophy. *Bhakti* keeps people emotionally thrilled but often practically inactive. In terms of its capacity to excite the group consciousness, to reject the worldly and to trust the otherworldly, it is always more effective than either *jñāna* or *karma*. Moreover, as one can find out if one reads through the history of the *bhakti* movement, it makes people not only forsake the reality of life but also keep on hugging infantile innocence, indolence of reason and apathy towards the new and the progressive.

Unless, therefore, the course of India's mind was directed towards social reality, there could be no scope for the modernization of her entire functioning. Keeping this fact before them, social and moral reformers, Western-educated Hindu revivalists, revolutionaries against the British, and nationalists evolved all over India two different movements: (1) a revised devotionalism having, at least as a means, some fundamental reforms of the

Indian society, and (2) a bold and scientific attempt of educating the public conscience of Indians to accept certain ways of thinking and doing. The first may be described as *bhakti-karma* or devotion-action movement, and the second as the *jñāna-karma* or knowledge-action movement. With the beginning of India's Awakening or her entry into the New Age, and with the increasing awareness in her people of the great disparity between material conditions in the West and in the East, the shapers of the two movements could not help emphasizing the need for an improvement of man's worldly existence.

THE *BHAKTI-KARMA* MOVEMENT

Rammohun Roy (1772–1833), about whose early life nothing much is reliably known, is the first important Indian to be animated by the thought of transforming the Indian society through a "new" religion that is in continuity with the Vedānta and yet recognizes the tune of the changing times.

The situation in which India was when Roy emerged as a reformer needs no particular mention here. It was a situation of abominable illiteracy of the millions, of castes and classes and creeds at war against each other, of poverty-stricken and slothful Hindus hugging fantastic superstitions, and of blurred patriotic spirit. At the spectacle of the sadly regressing state of Indians, Roy reacted so vigorously that he was sure that the only remedy for its cure was to launch an agitation, through word and deed, by which people could be taught to live in a harmonious unity. For him, as for a number of his contemporaries, it was the comradeship of all Indians and progressively of all nations in the world that was the sole aim man could legitimately strive for.

The most significant contribution of Rammohun Roy to the beginning of Indian Renaissance is the foundation of a theistic and socially motivated Church known as the Brāhmo Samāj. Brāhmo Samāj, preaching *Brāhmo Dharma,* was initiated by Roy in accordance with his thesis stated in his *Autobiography* that the era of modernism in India should not do away with the spirit of renunciation of the material wealth. Modernism should strive to eradicate the walls of distinction between man and man and lead the entire human kind to salvation. In fact Roy had drunk so deep in the ideas of Islam and Christianity that the catholicity of his Church was wide enough to embrace the religious interests of one and all. The preamble of the Brāhmo Samāj declares: "(God) calls one and all; entrance through His gate is free; no one ever returns disappointed; the rich and the poor, the wise and the ignorant, all are equally welcome there."

The central aim of Roy's reformation movement was to bring about the spiritual integration of mankind. Holding the torch of the religion of transcendental knowledge, or *Brahmavidyā,* always bright, Roy stated that all laws for the reconstruction of society must be founded on a hope of man's inner conversion, i.e. a conversion that would produce a readiness in each to accept the rights of others with as much regard as that he would have for his own. Never before Roy was an Indian thinker concerned with the framing of a program for the moral and social uplift of his fellowmen. The eminence of the Brāhmo Samāj is evident from the fact that it proved to be a great impetus to the chain of events that started the age of national awakening in India.

The Brāhmo Samāj undoubtedly succeeded in drawing people's attention to the practical aspect of self-realization, and to the value of social stability that is needed as an indispensable part of the *summum bonum.* It was left to future reformers to see the humanistic bent of *Brāhmo Dharma* and to widen their vision of man accordingly. Roy emphasized that the humanistic message embodied in *Brāhmo Dharma* was in fact derived from the old Vedānta insight. However, his descent from the pure transcendentalism of the Vedic-Upaniṣadic heritage to a theory of social good appears to have brought in speedy radicalism in the course of Indian thought. It is this radicalism that stands prominent in the Brāhmo Samāj program, even when it ultimately gravitates towards *bhakti-mārga* or devotionalism. Like a true theistic humanist, Roy saw that the necessity of action towards a sociopolitical reform can never be ignored by a person who keeps before his eyes the ideal of total salvation.

The final objective of the Brāhmo Samāj was to take Indians to a state of consciousness that is closer to God than to the world.

The most ideal synthesis of important religions in the world Roy preached entails a kind of spiritualistic activism, a pantheistic humanism and an internationalism. And, perhaps, this is the reason why the Brāhmo Samāj religion obtained tremendous following after the death of its founder in 1833. Devendranāth Tagore, Keshub Chandra Sen, Iswar Chandra Vidyāsagar and many others advanced the movement until it became a prelude to rationalism, which India was to enter upon in the nineteenth century.

While the Brāhmo Samāj planned to fuse the basic principles of Hinduism, of Islam and of Christianity into one whole, Swami Dayananda (1824–1883), the founder of the Ārya Samāj, was drawn to the Hindu faith and the primordial Vedic *Dharma*. Swami Dayananda was an orthodox *Brāhmin,* extremely attached to the Āryan way of life and to the word of God. He succeeded in carrying activism to a point of reformation, much in the manner in which Roy was successful in carrying the Vedānta monism to a point of internationalism. Neither Roy nor Dayananda could overlook that the base of their reformation was in Hinduism. So in everything that Dayananda said and did, he sought to reassert the supremacy of the Vedic religion.

Ārya Samāj formulated the principles of social organization to suit the needs of the changing Hindu community. It suggested the abolition of casteism, the adoption of the law of brotherhood among world races, cultures and nations, and the urgency of India's material welfare. One of the objectives of the Ārya Samāj reads thus: "The primary object of this Society is to do good to the whole world, that is, to look to its physical, social and spiritual welfare."

With a missionary zeal comparable to that of the Jesuits, Dayananda tried to institutionalize the Vedic *Dharma*. He conducted the Ārya Samāj as a kind of the Church of Hinduism. His entire activity was directed towards partly a repetition and partly a restatement of the ancient Hindu beliefs. But while he ventured on all this, he did not fail to focus his attention on the improvement of the plight of the lower classes, on the improvement of the status of Indian women, and on the amelioration of the depressed castes that often fell a victim to superstitions and all kinds of blind alleys.

Although, therefore, because of his famous program of proselytizing non-Hindus into Hinduism, Dayananda inevitably came into conflict with other proselytizing religions, he is still admired for his extraordinary ambition to revive the Vedic faith and to put it up as a powerful institution against imminent foreign forces. Indeed, the depth of his insight into the reconstruction of India as a secular society may not be as impressive as that of Rammohun Roy. But the sort of pride in the tenets of Hinduism he infused into Hindus of all ranks, and even in those who had latent sympathy with that religion, left a permanent hold on the whole of India.

Another dynamic group that attempted a coordination between *bhakti* and action is the Theosophical Society, which was started in New York, in 1875, by Madame Blavatsky and then appeared in India as a vigorous defender of Hinduism. Madame Blavatsky was a Russian woman with mysterious mental energies, about whose extraordinary suggestiveness many people were convinced. After becoming her follower, Mrs. Annie Besant, an amazing admirer of Indian thought, landed in India with a view to popularizing spiritualism and theosophical studies among Indian masses. It proved to be a fertile soil that she chose for the cultivation of divinity, for her teachings were extensively received with gusto and confidence, particularly by the middle classes.

Mrs. Besant soon came to be recognized as one of the most fervent followers of the Hindu faith. Being a woman of *bhakti* temperament, she could easily catch the hearts of Indians, who despite their sociopolitical vexations were unfailingly allured into devotionalism and spiritual quests. Her teachings lay much stress on the liberation of the soul as the only real end of life. Developing a profound sense and sensibility for everything Indian, she defined liberation as *mokṣa, nirvāṇa,* a state of eternal silence, where soul is severed from the body and lives in perpetual light and bliss. She was vocal about her acceptance of the Indian notions of rebirth, reincarnation, *karma* and *jīvanmukti,* and was to a great extent responsible for making the Britishers in India respect them.

What Besant felt with utmost intensity was the universal need to realize the working of God's mind and plans. Only man's closeness to God, attainable by means of devotion and love, she said, will impress upon him how God works. No wonder she claimed that she had been a Hindu in her former life, and that God had chosen her to carry out a mission of propagating the religion of that life. Hence she looked upon Hinduism as a "womb" which is capable of giving birth to all religions in the world, and within which all of them would ultimately dissolve.

Besant also shared the Theosophist's anxiety for the freedom of all races. She argued that since all men are innately the expression of the same divine spirit, the distinctions between the low and the high, the ignorant and the learned, the barbaric and the cultured, should have no place in the ideal scheme of the universe. Her immense faith in the universal brotherhood of mankind threw her stormily into Indian politics, and made her so respectable in the nationalist movement that in 1917 she became president of the Indian National Congress.

The period of Awakening in India was full of prodigious religious currents. They were generated not only by the attacking Western highbrows, who were up and ready to ridicule Indian culture and manners, but also by a positive attitude on the part of Indians to reformulate their spiritualistic heritage. As Jawaharlal Nehru has said, the rising Indians were "politically inclined," and were not in search of a religious faith. "They wanted some cultural roots to cling on to, something that gave them assurance of their own worth, something that would reduce the sense of frustration and humiliation that foreign conquest and rule had produced."[3] In their zeal to assert their rich past, they at times went so far as to reenact the role of the founders of the Vedic *Dharma* and to be oblivious of its dead wares. This is why the Ārya Samāj and the Theosophical Society, despite their definite awareness of the pragmatic issues Indian society was facing, insisted more on devotionalism and *mokṣa-mārga* than a well-defined path of activity.

However, Besant's inspiration embodied in her Theosophical message, and her fervor and passion for the preservation of Hinduism against the onslaughts of the British remain an unforgettable contribution to the heightening of the Indian *Weltanschau-*

[3] Nehru, Jawaharlal: *The Discovery of India,* p. 361.

ung. By declaring herself to be more Indian than most of her contemporaries, she advised the Indian reformers to recognize the glory of the *bhakti* cult and to spread it everywhere through word and action. She was of the opinion that the process of the Indian Renaissance must be founded on and constantly fed by immense *bhakti* to God.

Perhaps the most forceful realization of the fact that in order to act for the betterment of the suffering souls, one must have full confidence in the goodness and mercifulness of God dawned on a simple and unostentatious Bengali boy, Gangadhar, who rose to a phenomenal height in Indian spiritualism under the name of Śri Ramakrishna (1836–1886).

Śri Ramakrishna, who was born to an orthodox *Brāhmin* couple in West Bengal, grew up in a village hopelessly sinking in the grip of poverty, frustration and disease. The only things that entertained his young eyes were the hollow blue heavens, the blossoming rice fields, musically flowing waters of springs and rivulets and sportively hovering cranes. Nature filled Ramakrishna's heart with extreme ecstasy and prayerfulness. A sudden trance at the age of nine changed his entire personality; he was from then on animated by an extraordinary psychic expanse and a vision of the beyond.

Even as a small boy, Ramakrishna, it is said, was acutely sensitive to human misery and suffering. What he enjoyed most of all were states of rapture and contemplation. As he grew up he became a worshipper of goddess Kāli, whom he called the Divine Mother. He is reported to have concentrated his mind on the goddess day in, day out, from dawn to dusk, and experienced the most unique involvement in her. So powerful was his attachment to Kāli, "the Mother of the Universe," that with a sort of divine madness in him, he began to see her "peeping from every nook and corner." The height of his transcendental inspiration was Himalayan; the grasp of his mental faculties was oceanic.

Many fabulous stories are prevalent about Ramakrishna's anguish to have constant dialogues with the goddess. However, what is significant is that, like Buddha and Eckhart, he was gifted with an unbelievable penetrating consciousness into supernatural channels. The contours of experiences he narrates can be appreciated when one notices that the only dimension along which he let his mind flow was *bhakti* towards the infinite. On the advice of his guru, it is said, Ramakrishna preferred to stay continually at the apex of the *samādhi* consciousness, rather than pay a lip service to meditation.

Now there was an extension to Ramakrishna's *bhakti* path in the social system in which he functioned. He was a thorough believer in man's salvation through a union with God. And since according to him it is in Hinduism alone that real communion with God can be achieved, he taught his disciples to spread the Hindu philosophy throughout the world, not out of any desire to establish the institutional ascendancy of the Vedic *Dharma* but out of a concern for the destiny of mankind. His greatest ambition was to spiritualize the entire world, to turn it into a vast "spiritual sea," to make it pure in heart, to sow in every individual the seeds of divine grace. By this way alone, Ramakrishna thought, he could accelerate the coming of Renaissance in India and in the peoples everywhere.

Ramakrishna was often moved to tears at the sight of the dilapidated fates of his fellowmen. He was always on his feet to help them and to reduce their sorrow. Although it is true that he instructed everybody to accept suffering as the very characteristic of existence rather than to act and remedy it, and thus did not show any marked disposition for action per se, he held a humanitarian outlook broad enough to carry out the ideal of a total benefaction for all.

With the advent of Swami Vivekānanda (1863–1902), the most perceptive follower of Śri Ramakrishna, India resolved to enter upon a mission of establishing herself internationally as a spiritual power to be reckoned with in all deliberations regarding religion, morality and universal amity. Already the Brāhmo Samāj and the Theosophical Society had come to be recognized in the West as the excitements of a country determined to revive the humanistic message of Hinduism. Perhaps now the Western world was awaiting somebody more vocal and more suggestive in his exposition of the Hindu mode of action, since the challenge of the foreign domination could not fail to release such a human force. Swami Vivekānanda emerged as a stormy messenger of Indian spiritualism.

Vivekānanda received his initiation into the path of spiritual unfoldings at the hands of Ramakrishna. There was not much resemblance, however, between the situations in which the two mystics sprang up. Born in an aristocratic family, Vivekānanda was exposed in his childhood to Western ways of life and education. Later he became a worker in the Brāhmo Samāj. But what suddenly changed his entire personality is his meeting with Ramakrishna, who, it is said, electrified his mind by the touch of his hand. The young skeptic became so attached to his guru that the family ties or the concern for his inmates did not any more count in his eyes. For some time Vivekānanda indeed faced a struggle within him between intellect and emotion, *jñāna* and *bhakti;* but he was soon allured into transcendental experience and the ecstasy of *samādhi*. From then on he began to tread in Ramakrishna's footsteps.

Vivekānanda toured extensively in India before he made himself aware of the outcome of the Hindu faith in the actual life of the people. What is interesting about his observations is that he saw that the crisis of India was due to the decline of the Vedic religion and the Indians' apathy to the spirit of Indian humanism. He was so convinced in his mind about the absolute truth of the ancient Vedic path that, more than his teacher, he reverted to the Vedic-Upaniṣadic *Weltanschauung* and made up his mind to reestablish it against all cultural currents from the West.

Vivekānanda expressed his real self abroad rather than in his own country. During his stay in the United States and Europe he made himself extremely popular as a brilliant exponent of Hinduism and of the humanistic tendencies in the Vedānta. At an international gathering of the religious heads organized by the Parliament of Religions in Chicago in 1893, he boldly expounded his thesis of the fusion of all religions, and firmly established himself, in the minds of Western critics, as an unusually electrifying personality reflecting divine light.[4] His speedy

[4] No other Western writer has been more laudatory towards Swami Vivekānanda than Romain Rolland. See Rolland, Romain: *The Life of Vivekānanda and The Universal Gospel*. Calcutta, Advaita Ashrama, 1960, pp. 47–68.

thinking and magnetic speeches invited the attention of several Western philosophers, including William James, Leo Tolstoy, Max Muller, and Paul Deussen. What must have profoundly impressed them all is Vivekānanda's care and anxiety for the condition of humanity, and his insistence on the spiritualization of the world. He arranged his lectures, debates and seminars so systematically that everything that he said, finally gravitated towards his teaching of a limitless catholicism. This catholicism, he thought, is attainable, regardless of the diversity of human temperaments and pursuits.

However, it was an irony that the "cyclonic monk of India"—as Vivekānanda was called in the West—was most attentively listened to in countries which were on their way towards material prosperity, but must have found himself to be repetitive and neglected in his own spiritually rich but materially desperate land. He could not have been ignorant of the fact that his teachings were not quite in tune with the helplessness the Indians in their peculiar socio-politico-economic situation were face to face with. Probably what disturbed him all the time was a kind of incoherence between the glorious ideas of Indian religions and the national humiliation Indians were undergoing in their actual life. Surely, it is the acceptance of this incoherence that led him to found a social service league known as the Ramakrishna Mission in 1897. It was an order of selfless monks who were wedded to the propagation of the Vedānta faith through different types of organized social work. The Mission figures even today as one of the most important welfare institutions in India.[5]

Among hundreds of the English-educated Indians who came under the influence of Ramakrishna's and Vivekānanda's mysticism[6] and spiritualistic humanism, Aurobindo Ghose rose to an unbelievable height of eminence as a yogi, a philosopher and a patriot. He is the unique instance of a thoroughly Westernized intellectual who, after journeying through the politics of na-

[5] *Ibid.*, pp. 116–20. Romain Rolland emphasizes what he regards as the "panhuman, apostolic nature of" the Mission.

[6] For understanding the essence of this mysticism, see Muller, Max: *Ramakrishna: His Life and Sayings*. London, Longmans Green & Co., 1923, pp. 12–26.

tionalism over a long time, met with a tumultuous upsurge of transcendental vision within himself and suddenly turned to meditation and *yoga*. Aurobindo (1872–1950) wrote in the vein of an academic philosopher, and much to the surprise of Western thinkers, showed that one can get in and get out of philosophical polemics without surrendering one's metaphysical commitment.

Aurobindo's childhood was spent in England. When after leaving Cambridge University, he returned to India, his mind was far remote from Indian culture and philosophy. However, on reading the Upaniṣads, the *Bhagavad-gītā* and the works of his contemporaries, it dawned on him that he should cherish an alliance with the spirit of Indian thought. It is said that he used to be guided by the voice of Swami Vivekānanda, and that even while he was in jail as a result of his participation in the nationalist activities, he was being inspired by this voice to contemplate and ascend to the infinite. After being freed from jail, Aurobindo gave up politics and took to transcendental meditation and writing.

What Aurobindo presupposes in his doctrine of reality is the self-manifesting nature of God. Everything, he writes, forms the expression of the will of God, is the realization of God's work, is His incarnation.[7] He even goes to the extent of stating that one's love for one's own country is a "religion that has come from God." It is, therefore, the Hindu faith which is the *sanātan Dharma* or eternal religion that according to Aurobindo should take up the responsibility of not only securing freedom to India but also of expanding it all over the world. He tried to argue that the tenets of Hinduism constitute the most authentic humanism on earth. In order to see the destiny of India and that of the universe, in order to comprehend the mind of God and encompass His "play" of creation, one must grasp the logic of the Hindu creed.[8]

Aurobindo's most original contribution to the modernization

[7] Aurobindo, Śri: *The Synthesis of Yoga*. New York, Śri Aurobindo Lib., 1950, pp. 258–60.

[8] Aurobindo, Śri: *Speeches*. Calcutta, Arya Publishing House, 1948, pp. 7–9. See also Aurobindo, Śri: *Yoga and Its Objects*. Calcutta, Arya Publishing House, 1921, pp. 12–14.

of the ancient Indian thought centers around the idea of the Supermind. He regards Supermind as infinite consciousness, manifesting itself in descending degrees from pure joy or *ānanda* to all forms of organic and inorganic existences. The Supermind is a self-transforming and self-individuating psychic stuff. The distinctions, such as those between body and consciousness, knowledge and devotion and action, matter and spirit, are all dissolved in it. "In the Supermind," Aurobindo writes, "personality and impersonality are not opposite principles; they are inseparable aspects of one and the same reality." [9] No part of it—however incoherent or imperfect it might appear as an individual—can really be in disharmony with the Supermind. And once, by means of the "synthetic method" of *yoga,* an individual grasps the inner stream of his being, he would come to realize that he is only "a current of the Supermind." [10]

With Śri Aurobindo began a neo-Vedānta tendency in Indian philosophy—a tendency which besides bringing academic philosophy in several universities under its influence, has settled down as the most integral transcendentalism to oppose the materialistic trends in the technologically dominated West. Aurobindo was gifted with a remarkably translucent sensibility and an equally translucent style of writing. With an idiom reminiscent of that of Bergson, Josiah Royce and Karl Jaspers, he attempted to build a metaphysical system, much more alive and comprehensive than anything that has appeared in Indian thought after Rāmānuja. Although he borrowed his fundamentals from the Upaniṣads and the *Bhagavad-gītā,* he reset and developed them in such a manner that they would form the intellectual prototype of the brotherhood of mankind on earth.

Undoubtedly, Aurobindo is the last important propounder of the *bhakti-karma* blending on the rapidly changing scene of modern India. As a matter of fact, as a way of philosophization and as a cultural renaissance consistently maintaining the ethos of the Vedic-Upaniṣadic seers, the *bhakti-karma* movement is bound to be amorphous and varied. Not seldom it has swung towards parochialism and reverted to the old form of *bhakti-*

[9] Aurobindo, Śri: *The Life Divine,* p. 881.
[10] *Ibid.,* p. 889.

mārga. Unless, therefore, the fusion of *bhakti* and *karma* is made to offer to man an indubitable ground for activity towards the welfare and unity of all, unless it is made to recognize the world of praxis as an indispensable part of human reality, it will recede to the background and be forgotten as a self-contained device for escapism. It is by keeping in mind the force of practical circumstances of the New Age that we must examine the other direction of reformation in India. This may be called the *jñāna-karma* movement.

THE *JÑANA-KARMA* MOVEMENT

While India was asserting her transcendentalist and spiritualist way of thinking, and making herself immune from the process of Westernization, a more positive attitude was shaping itself among the English-educated Indian intellectuals. This attitude was not only action oriented and pragmatic but also animated by a political aim. It had emerged from the rapidly declining freedom of the Indian: his tremendous lagging behind the West, his remoteness from the scientific and industrial epoch in the West, his excessive preoccupation with the otherworldly bliss, his habitual abnegation of the world and its problems, and his almost chronic fatalism. Although this attitude was largely due to the inflow of the Western men and literature, and also was deliberately chosen by a few who were the stronghold of patriotism, it was well directed towards the total uplift of Indians. It combined knowledge and activity, or *jñāna* and *karma,* and posited material well-being as a part and parcel of salvation, absolute freedom, *mokṣa.*

Traditionally the theory of action in Indian ethics has been negative. Not only did the ancient Indian philosophers look upon man's being in the world as a state determined by his past lives, but they also professed that one's acts should be like rituals, or like expressions of a desireless and uncommitted will if one is to attain absolute perfection. That with the rise of the nineteenth and twentieth century intellectual awakening, Indians felt the need to organize their activity in such a way that it could attain a well-defined social or political objective speaks for an unprecedented transition in their outlook. Such a transition originated, indeed, from the perceptiveness of some of the most sensitive Indian seers who were exposed to the Western views of knowledge, action and freedom, and consequently afflicted at the squalid situation the whole country had been reduced to. But the sway created by this transition on the intelligent stratum of the society had, in a sense, no roots in India's tradition. For the most immediate goal of the *jñāna-karma* movement was and still is the improvement of the worldly life of Indians, which to the traditional schools of their philosophy was not at all a value.

There are always tendencies and ideals in the life of a people, which although alien to their general conceptual pattern, constitute an impetus to their progress because they make the people move and keep pace with the rest of the world. India in the present century is in the grip of the *jñāna-karma* movement. It is not a movement aimed at the creation of a "blissful heaven" or *jīvanmukti* of the type professed by the Vedic-Upaniṣadic thinkers. The human welfare that it conceives is total: freedom from material privations and the uplift of the Psyche, the realization of knowledge and peace, the creation of amity between man and man, and the fullest experience of self-fulfilment to every individual. The success of the movement rests on its capacity to cultivate in Indian consciousness a new *Weltanschauung*, which while upholding the fundamental quest of man to transcend the world and to grasp the primordial inanity of his existence, admits worldliness at least as an unignorable extension of human reality, or of the complete human phenomenon.

Miraculous change of outlook and character in the case of a country is perhaps as possible as a new activation in the life of one single individual. Just as in a reformed personality the past may take to a new mode of functioning, be absorbed in the present state of that personality and remain its metaphysical essence, or may condition the present outlook of the personality without curbing its freedom in any way, in a nation as well its past may act as a subtle semiconscious undercurrent tilting its selections, rejections, judgments, plans, policies and its entire *joie de vivre* in a particular direction. The essentially transphenomenal *Weltanschauung* of a people cannot go interred as a fossil. Therefore, in what path Indians propelled by the *jñāna-karma* movement will steer their future, how they will bridge their inherent transcendental search and their openness to the technocratic adventures necessitated by the very logic of physical survival, and in what effective manner they will represent their spiritualistic and inward-seeing sensibility as an antidote to the scientism of the West, are questions to which future alone might have answers.

However, without any element of skepticism as regards the final good their actions and institutions would generate, the *jñāna-karma-mārga*[11] pioneers put their tremendous effort into a society-building program. The men who will be remembered for being in the forefront of this program are the following: Mahādev Govind Rānade (1841–1901), the founder of a reformist society called Prārthanā Samāj; Gopal Krishna Gokhale (1866–1915), the founder of the Servants of India Society; Rabindranath Tagore (1861–1941); Mahatma Gandhi (1869–1948), widely known as the Father of India; M. N. Roy (1887–1954), the founder of the Radical Humanist Movement; Jawaharlal Nehru (1889–1964), the first Prime Minister of India; and in the present decades, Vinoba Bhave and Jaiprakash Narayan, the saintly leaders of the Sarvodaya Movement. The single characteristic that would be found uniformly present in all these figures is their stirring determination to change India psychologically and materially, their consistent appeal to Indians to think and act as one homogeneous entity.[12]

The theory that intellect and action, or thought and moral

[11] The path of the enlightened activity, unlike *niṡkāma karma,* has something pragmatic and value-oriented about it. Without forsaking the ultimately universal and trans-empirical objective which alone is supposed to bestow absolute value on human activity, the followers of the enlightened service were fully involved in the creation of the worldly good and social welfare. The unique characteristic of the *jñāna-karma-mārga* is its recognition that it is both immanence and transcendence that are required for the constitution of the complete man.

[12] According to Nirad C. Chaudhuri, "all thinkers of modern India from Rammohun Roy to Tagore stood for what may be called the psychological approach to political questions." (See Chaudhuri, Nirad C.: *The Intellectual in India.* New Delhi, Vir Publishing House, 1967, pp. 18–19). It cannot be ignored, however, that these thinkers' preference for such an approach was governed by their partly pragmatic and partly nationalistic objectives. What Indian reformers, even today, have to bear in mind is that the main prerequisite of India's progress is a change in Indians' attitude towards things.

involvement, are inseparable constituents of any program for the social reformation in India was first propounded by Rammohun Roy and then by Mahādev Govind Rānade and Gopal Krishna Gokhale. There is so much in common between the ideas of Rānade and Gokhale that both of them can be regarded as complementary thinkers, motivated by the same concept of social welfare. Unlike the *bhakti*-oriented reformation plans formulated by the Brāhmo Samāj and the Ārya Samāj, for instance, Rānade's and Gokhale's organizations were wedded to some sort of an iconoclastic activity ripping off the shutters of illiteracy, superstitiousness, sloth and backwardness that were isolating Indians from the modern world.

True to the saying that all big reforms must start at home, Rānade and Gokhale did not leave anything unbegun for the eradication of the most chronic evils the Indian society, in contrast with the societies in the West, was suffering from. Here were, therefore, thinkers launching a kind of social activism, which India, burdened with several dead wares of her tradition, needed drastically and immediately. What Rānade and Gokhale proposed to do in their own times is to be carried through in this country for several decades, with firmness and determination, until the Indian mind is freed from the evils of its own creation.

Rānade's agitation was directed towards the purification and modernization of the Indian Psyche. He condemned the way Indians were taking shelter under the messages of the Vedas and other religious scriptures whenever they encountered times requiring independent and well thought out decisions. He was too practical to be blinded by religious faith and taboos. Without a second thought, he recognized the society around him, with all its "sacred" superstitions, unexamined traditions, communal rivalries, caste prejudices, ritualism and intellectual sluggishness, as the immediate subject of his reforms.[13] He hit with very bitter words against abominable Hindu practices like child marriage, seclusion of women, prohibition of widow marriage,

[13] See, for an account of the variety of social actions Rānade was involved in, Phatak, Narahar Raghunath: *Arvāchin Mahārastrañtil Sahā Thôr Purush* (Marathi). Bombay, Pratibha Prakashan, 1954, pp. 41–53.

observance of casteism, religious sacrifices, etc., and tried to teach his fellowmen that there were many ills which the old Hindu behavior had transmitted to the modern generation. He could not resist criticism of the doctrine of *karma,* and of the often misconstrued and too literally accepted theory that the worldly existence is an illusion. The Indian reformer according to Rānade must be stimulated by the thought of emancipating himself and his countrymen from the condensed dogmas that constantly gnaw their existence and make it miserable.

Being Rānade's closest friend and colleague, Gokhale came up to realize the necessity of invigorating the process of social amelioration. It is perhaps due to his extraordinarily suggestive writings and speeches[14] that Gokhale's thoughts sound more emphatic and cutting than Rānade's. Gokhale was a good student of mathematics and economics, and possessed the acumen of a clear-headed thinker. What irritated him most was the magnitude of ignorance and stupidity Indian masses were living in. He attributed the main cause of this situation to monstrous maladies within the Indian tradition itself. He fought against casteism and communalism, and went about speaking in condemnation of the attitude of the highbrowed higher castes towards the lower castes. That the people inheriting one culture and born in one country should erect barriers among themselves was a situation intolerable to Gokhale.

Gokhale's thinking was so action oriented that he was responsible for starting one of the most purposeful movements of social reform in India called the "Servants of India Society." Whoever joined the Society had to sign an oath which said that he would direct his efforts towards:

> creating among the people, by example and by precept, a deep and passionate love of the motherland, seeking its highest fulfilment in service and sacrifice; organizing the work of political education and agitation and strengthening the public life of the country; promoting relations of cordial goodwill and cooperation among the different

[14] See, for instance, his speeches, Discontent in India, Indian View of Indian Affairs, Self-Government for India, and The Indian Problem, in Karve, D. G., and Ambekar, D. V. (Ed.) : *Speeches and Writings of Gopal Krishna Gokhale.* Bombay, Asia Publishing House, 1966, pp. 321–25, 326–32, 350–57, 368–75.

communities; assisting educational movements, especially those for the education of women, the education of backward classes and industrial and scientific education; and the elevation of the depressed classes.[15]

However, it is ironical that without achieving any concrete success in the execution of its program the Servants of India Society is at a standstill today for lack of funds and supporters.

Amidst the rapidly spreading nationalist movement in India towards the end of the twentieth century, there appeared Rabindranath Tagore, a strange combination of poet, aesthete, educator and patriot. In Tagore India found an artistic genius of international repute, an upholder of the unity of all religions and spiritual values, a propounder of the East-West fusion under the banner of an encompassing humanism, and a quiet revivalist of what is the best in human culture. Tagore's humanistic philosophy is distinguishable from the general trend of thinking during the Age of Awakening, on the ground that it regarded aesthetic inspiration as the very *sine qua non* of action.

Tagore was a mystic and a spiritualist. He tried to propagate a peculiar combination of individualism and universalism, not founded on any particular religious faith but on the most common aspirations of mankind. Being endowed with profound aesthetic sensibilities and a rare moral perceptiveness, he argued that man's principal task is to see the ultimate reality as an embodiment of beauty and virtue and to establish an intercourse with it. Tagore's was not a religion confined to Hindu spiritualism, which had found its lucid expression in the writings of Swami Vivekānanda or Śri Aurobindo. Nor was the stimulation of his feelings the socio-politico-economic reality of India under the dominance of the Western rule. The center of Tagore's religion is love, which unites all men and converts even God into a human personality.[16]

It may be mentioned that Rabindranath Tagore had grown under two influences, one from Bankim Chandra Chatterjee, the

[15] *Constitution of the Servants of India Society.*

[16] Tagore's world-famous verses in *Gitanjali* are an expression of his religion of love. For a description of his conception of life and love, see Khanolkar, G. D.: *The Lute and the Plough: A Life of Rabindranath Tagore.* Bombay, The Book Centre Ltd., 1959, pp. 92–96.

eminent nineteeth century novelist, and the other from Brāhmo Samāj, to which his father belonged. In his early age he developed in him a strong will for the total reformation of Hinduism and Indian nationalism. The conflicting loyalties prevalent in India between those who had imbibed Western culture and those who were dedicated to the Eastern heritage were, according to him, due to a narrow-minded attachment on the part of either of the two groups to something that was only of transitional value. The regeneration of the culture of mankind, Tagore thought, required a new religion, a new pattern of aesthetic and ethical values, where what is ultimately real is looked upon as being manifest in the sum total of individuals. There is an underlying note in all his literary works that God must be cognized as nothing but Man.

The theory of perfectionism, which is the central force of Tagore's thoughts, contains as much transcendentalism as it contains pragmatism; and although he did not have any concrete scheme of social reform comparable to that of Rānade or Gokhale, he was full of an abstract picture of human welfare which presupposed that the misfortune of mankind is not due to any deficiency inherent in it but because of the obstacles that surround it. For Tagore, man's salvation lay in his ability to create a fusion of individualism and nationalism, of nationalism and internationalism, which can be ultimately bound together with the same cord of moral law. "The contemptuous spirit of separatedness," he wrote, "was perpetually hurting us and causing great damage to our own world of culture." [17]

In his particularly mystical and aesthetically oriented essays, Tagore expounded a system of values in which Indian ātmalogy and universal humanism telescope into each other. The aim of this system is to explain man as an eternally self-fulfilling spirit, reflecting divine love and beauty on earth. Human relations were the pivot of Tagore's philosophy. On the amount of love and ethical sense in these relations, he thought, depend the success of human civilization, universal comradeship, international

[17] Tagore, Rabindranath: *On Art and Aesthetics.* New Delhi, Inter-National Cultural Centre, 1961, p. 35.

amity, and understanding among races. "The races of man have poetry in their heart," he said, "and it is necessary for them to give, as far as is possible, a perfect expression to their sentiments."[18] The reach of his imaginative powers was so remarkable that he could encompass within it the ideals of the East and the West, and consequently evolve a kind of philosophy of universal interdependence.[19]

With Tagore's appearance on the Indian scene, one must say, Indian intellectualism and reformism grew richer and more idealistically inclined than before. Tagore had a disguised scorn for self-contained nationalism, and perhaps for a direct and personal involvement in any social or nationalist activities. Apart from the fact, therefore, that Tagore, Gandhi and Jawaharlal Nehru have been a triumvirate that successfully put modern India on the twentieth century map of world cultures, Tagore's role, unlike that of the other two, was strictly that of an interpreter and ambassador of the Indian *Weltanschauung* to the world.[20] But one can appreciate the importance of his place in the history of Indian Renaissance when one understands the volume of his influence on the intellectual climate of India in the first half of the present century. As Nehru says, "Tagore and Gandhi have undoubtedly been the two outstanding and dominating figures of India. . . . (They) have brought us to our present age."[21]

The acceleration that the *jñāna-karma* movement obtained,

[18] *Ibid.*, p. 37.

[19] It may be observed that the concept of organicism, put forward recently by Archie Bahm, stands very close to Tagore's theory of the complementariness of Eastern and Western cultures. Bahm works out the idea of interdependence in the domain of philosophy; Tagore preached the interdependence of cultures, surely by using the term "culture" in an indeterminate sense. (See, for Bahm's idea of interdependence, Bahm, Archie J.: Organicism: The Philosophy of Interdependence, *International Philosophical Quarterly*. Vol. 7, No. 2, pp. 252 ff., and, for Tagore's idea of the complementariness of cultures, Tagore, Rabindranath: *Nationalism*. 2nd ed., London, Macmillan & Co., Ltd., 1950, pp. 18 ff.)

[20] When this role of his is considered, Tagore appears to be a prototype of S. Radhakrishnan, the greatest living exponent of the metaphysical thought of India. Incidentally, Radhakrishnan's first major work was *The Philosophy of Rabindranath Tagore*. His view of East-West unity in culture and religion is noticeably shaped after Tagore's universal humanism.

[21] Nehru, Jawaharlal: *The Discovery of India*, pp. 360–61.

with the emergence of Mahatma Gandhi and Jawaharlal Nehru as the most revered leaders of modern India, has no parallel in the history of that movement to this day. While Gandhi figured all through his life as a formidable moral force, whose appeal to India and the world had something prophetic and superhuman about it, Nehru was a politician, an internationalist, a democratic socialist, a neutralist statesman, and, above all, a strange combination of visionary and pragmatist. The cultural internationalism that was kept as the single ideal of Indian reformation by Tagore was not allowed to subdue national interests when Gandhi and Nehru made a debut in social life. What they achieved for the Age of Awakening in India will go down in history as the contribution of two uncommon egalitarian thinkers to the new philosophy of one world and one mankind.

Gandhi was first drawn into politics during his stay in South Africa in the first decade of the twentieth century. He fought against the white racism of the South African government tooth and nail by practicing a singularly peaceful method of noncooperation or passive resistance known as *satyāgraha*. Whatever its success, it was a method which embodied Christian tolerance, Hindu love, Jaina nonviolence, and Buddhist silence, and had never been used by anyone before against a state authority. After observing that the method did work, Gandhi introduced it in India against the British and invited at the outset a mixed reaction from his co-workers. However, a patient, tenacious and consistent exercise of *satyāgraha* on a large scale by the Indian masses under his heroic leadership quickly established Gandhi as an uncontestable leader of the Indian nationalist movement.

Gandhi was a simple ascetic man of rare purposefulness, candor, and unimaginable affection for friend and foe alike. His life was an eventful saga in which the history of fifty most critical years of India has been woven. As an ethical genius, comparable to only that of the founders of the great religions of the world, Gandhi made righteousness of conduct the very essence of his life and saw reality, so to say, through activity. During his entire struggle against the British rulers in India and his simultaneous efforts to educate the conscience of Indians, he carried himself as a superb embodiment of Indian *Weltan-*

schauung—respecting all men as the reflections of *Brahman*, tolerating all individual views as mere aspects of one basic truth or reality, showering compassion and pity on the downtrodden and the profane, and always exhibiting in a subtle and ironical way his distrust in the material and sensuous world. Like all great teachers of mankind, he was intensely preoccupied with the training of human spirit, for as Schweitzer explains, he was "convinced that since all that happens in human affairs is conditioned by mind, things can only be improved by bringing about a different state of mind." [22]

Gandhi was the expression of a remarkable harmony among knowledge, devotion and activity—the three vocations which, according to the *Bhagavad-gītā*, lead to the same destination, namely, *mokṣa* or salvation. His thinking was never so knowledge bound or so devotion shrouded as to be removed from practice. At the same time, his plans and decisions, however circumscribed by the political, economic and social needs of his country, emanated from his intuitive understanding of universal well-being, from his notion of individual liberty, from his veneration to the divine spirit in man. What distressed him most was the forces of disunity between caste and caste, one religious community and another, in his own country, and between man and man in general. This explains why, at a later stage of his life, he was awfully despaired at the lack of prospect of any success to his lifelong ambition of creating a Hindu-Muslim integration and calmly voiced a sense of failure.

Gandhi's message of interpersonal understanding as the only cultured and "human" method for the solution of problems vexing mankind can be traced back to Jainism, the religion of his birth. Not being an academic philosopher, Gandhi did not articulate or theorize his own borrowing from and interpretation of the old Indian thought. It is clear, however, that his entire approach to the question of India's insistence on freedom from the foreign rule and his dedication to the path of nonviolent resistance hide underneath the metaphysical insight of

[22] Schweitzer, Albert: *Indian Thought and Its Development*, p. 230.

the Vedic-Upaniṣadic seers: regard every other individual as thyself, as real and eternally existent as thyself, for all are ultimately the same *ātman* or *Brahman*.

Two most celebrated Indian intellectuals who antagonized the traditional spiritualistic basis which neither the *bhakti-karma* movement nor the *jñāna-karma* one can do away with are Manabendra Nath Roy and Jawaharlal Nehru. The angriest and the downright Marxist phase of the development of their thought cast as great an influence on the young generations of Indians during the past fifty years as the later humanistic and internationalist standpoint of theirs, as political philosophers, determined the role free India was to play vis-à-vis other nations in the world. With Roy and Nehru on the fast changing Indian setting, Indian masses received pressing advice to cultivate a rational or scientific attitude towards things and to give up their naive and superstitious habits. Owing to their enormous confidence in the naturalistic philosophy widely reflected by thinkers in the West, and their adherence to programs that might respond to India's material needs, Roy and Nehru proved very effective in persuading their fellow-workers to rethink about their country's destiny and to concentrate on practical exigencies.

Roy's career was unbelievably eventful. It began with his nationalistic activities in Bengal at the age of fourteen, passed through a period of over a decade when he moved from country to country as a communist and became Lenin's friend, and ended in his being a peculiar combination of skeptic and humanist.[23] Roy possessed the unique honor of being an elected member of the Presidium of the Communist International for several years, and of founding the Communist Party of Mexico, the first Communist Party outside the Soviet Union. It is only after his disillusionment with communism in practice following the Second World War that there was a transition in his ideas into demo-

[23] As a matter of fact, Roy slipped out of India in 1915 to secure arms for an Indian uprise against the British rule. He returned to India in 1930—after a fifteen years' courageous term abroad as a revolutionary communist—as a new man with a "new philosophy." This "new philosophy," called by him "new humanism," is essentially a fusion of Indian transcendentalism and pragmatism.

cratic freedom and humanism. It is also said that Roy had an influence on Nehru's views in the early thirties.[24]

In the heydays of his naturalistic thought, Roy's allegiance to the philosophy of Marx was almost complete. During this period, not only did he repudiate every sort of spiritualistic interpretation of Indian philosophy but even went to the extent of saying that "India's spiritual mission" appears to be a mission with a mundane end, that is, "to salvage a social system based upon the love of lucre and lust for power." [25] And in his comments on Gandhism, which he thought was the "moralizing mysticism" grounded in Indian spiritualism, Roy held that there is little of philosophy in it. Not only did he repudiate it as a "mass of platitudes and hopeless self-contradictions," but he even summarized it as "a conception of morality based upon dogmatic faith." "The fact that even in the twentieth century India is swayed by the naive doctrines of Gandhi," Roy wrote, "speaks for the cultural backwardness of the masses of her people." [26] To Roy the elegance of the Hindu mind is not the mark of the intellectual level of the Indian people as a whole, but the creation of a "pampered intellectual elite" who rubbed shoulders with the ruling class. As a convinced materialist at the time when he reasoned in this manner, Roy prophesied that Gandhism would not have any social background and therefore would disappear soon.

However, it is the later happenings—Roy's differences with Stalin, the confounding leadership of Indian communism, the coercive nature of the Russian Government, and perhaps the rapidly declining influence of Roy on Indian politics and people —that caused a complete *volte-face* in his thinking. He stated in the *New Humanism,* published in 1947, that the Russian experiment proved that socialism or communism "could be nothing more than State Capitalism." [27] He declared further that we

[24] See Brecher, Michael: *Nehru: A Political Biography*. London, Oxford University Press, 1959, pp. 175–76.

[25] Roy, M. N.: *India's Message: Fragments of a Prisoner's Diary*. 2nd ed., Calcutta, Renaissance Publishers Ltd., 1950, Vol. 2, p. 190.

[26] *Ibid.*, pp. 209–10.

[27] Roy, M. N.: *New Humanism*. 2nd ed., Calcutta, Renaissance Publishers Ltd., 1953, p. 15.

must have faith in human ingenuity and creativeness, because these qualities are inexhaustible and basic.[28] By any denomination, it was a confession that there was something trans-empirically oriented and profoundly subjectivistic in the Indian tradition before which no materialistic philosophy would stay unrepelled. Although it is true that Roy, one of the most brilliant rationalists India has ever produced, could never appreciate the ring of the ultimate futility [29] of human existence pervading the whole of the Indian *Weltanschauung,* he, after retreating from Marxism, developed an acute regard for the inward-seeing sensibility, for the inherent trans-material essence of man, which underlies the very concept of his neohumanism. Such a humanism, Roy says, would flourish on the soil of "the fundamental democratic principle," which, further, must assume "the conduct of public affairs" in charge of "spiritually free individuals who represent their own conscience." [30]

Both Roy and Nehru displayed intense reflectiveness of mind and an awareness of practical problems India was facing along her march towards independence. Thorough analyses of these problems were needed for one to arrive at their solutions. Gandhi's approach, though emerging from his saintly and world-embracing principle of love, could not wholly satisfy the materialistically inclined Indian intellectuals. With the impact of Marxism on Indians in general and on the leaders of the Independence Movement in particular, the *jñāna-karma* movement had reached its full stretch. To allow it to stretch further would have meant to revolt violently against the British, and consequently to cancel the very spirit Indian thought and culture had stood for.

The most unique personality who kept almost no distance from the exigencies of the world of praxis and, at the same time, did not deviate very far from the idealistic and transcendental

28 *Ibid.,* p. 53.

29 G. D. Parikh, one of the closest friends of Roy, writes about him: "There was something of the universal man in him, whose company made even the most mediocre of his comrades feel that life, with all its ugly patches, was exciting and beautiful. . . ." (See Parikh, G. D.: Introduction to M. N. Roy's Memoirs, *The Radical Humanist.* Vol. 28, Nos. 3–5, p. 26.)

30 Roy, M. N.: *New Humanism,* p. 43.

foundation of the Indian ethos is Nehru. To strike a balance between what leads to a nation's material welfare and what leads to its trans-empirical elevation is as hard in politics as it is in the life of an individual. Nehru was the first Indian intellectual to reverse the courses of diehard spiritualism as it is found in the *bhakti-karma* movement, and equally diehard materialism as it was contained in the fully stretched *jñāna-karma* movement or in Marxism. If Roy, as long as he was a Marxist, is responsible for having driven the *jñāna-karma* movement to its extremity, Nehru, even while he accepted the basic tenets of Marxism, was intent on controlling it by having recourse to ideals beyond matter. Nehru confesses:

> Much in the Marxist philosophical outlook I could accept without difficulty. . . . It did not satisfy me completely, nor did it answer all the questions in my mind, and, almost unawares, a vague idealist approach would creep into my mind, something rather akin to the Vedānta approach. It was not a difference between mind and matter, but rather of something that lay beyond the mind.[31]

Nehru was an internationalist of more varied a character than Roy. Nehru's concept of a unified humanity has horizons to it far more encompassing politically and aesthetically than Roy's. As a matter of fact, in the whole history of the Indian people, there has not been a leader who understood the aspirations and interests of his nation so sympathetically, without at the same time compromising his idealism and *sui generis* trans-nationalism as Nehru did. As the Prime Minister of India for over a decade, he led India to a position that would be respected as the singular legacy of a monistic and transcendental metaphysics traceable to the Upaniṣads themselves, and yet mitigated by a modern, scientific and pragmatic sense of truth and welfare. It would not be an exaggeration to state that both as an intellectual statesman and as one of the most respected exponents of what Taya Zinkin has called "revolution by consent,"[32] Nehru largely succeeded in throwing a bridge between the old Vedic-Upaniṣadic *Weltanschauung* and the new outlook India borrowed from the

[31] Nehru, Jawaharlal: *The Discovery of India,* pp. 29–30.

[32] Zinkin, Taya: *India Changes!* New York, Oxford U. P., 1958, p. 220. According to Zinkin, the "keynotes" of Indian revolution are "consent" and "equality."

West, or rather broadly, between Eastern transcendentalism and Western empiricism.[33]

Nehru's intellectualism is shrouded by some sort of romanticism usually admired by the European and American transcendentalists of Kantian and Husserlian brand. This was undoubtedly due to his Western upbringing and Indian milieu. Science and technology could not exhaust his quests and "human" aspirations fully. His works are studded with visions and perspicacity that surpass the scientific attitude he boldly exercised while tackling problems of practical nature. He even looked at these problems, and at the irritations they obviously caused, as a passing phase in the process of India's self-unfoldment. Being an idealist to the core, Nehru could tolerate a range of diverse political opinions, inasmuch as they stood for universal peace and friendship, individual freedom, material prosperity and the ultimate goal of self-perfection. Nothing but these values could invite his fullest involvement.

It is this involvement that explains why Nehru launched the idea of India's nonalignment in international politics. He, during his Prime Ministership, was most vocal on international issues despite being nonaligned, because his commitment was a commitment to the sacredness of human existence and of human freedom. He criticized, now the U.S.A. and again the Soviet Union, now this power and again that power, and now vindicated one and again the other, with a supreme dedication to the building of universal integration and harmony. He preserved within him the neutrality of a philosopher, but not the ritualistic and dry dutifulness of an uninvolved *sthitaprajna* or *jīvanmukta*. In Nehru, the rationalist and the passionately involved existentialist, the nonaligned and the morally committed, the pragmatist and the subjectivist, were curiously combined.

REVOLUTION BY LOVE

Towards the beginning of the fifties India witnessed the rise of a nonpolitical force, unintelligible in terms of any of the so well-known theories of social change. This force put up a

[33] See Sinari, Ramakant: Some Reflections on Philosophy in India, *Philosophy and Phenomenological Research*. Vol. 26, No. 3, pp. 440–41.

promise that by means of an inner conversion of man, all problems arising out of economic and social inequality in the world might be resolved. How basic and wide-reaching a human transformation this force can bring about, and what repercussion it might have on the political course of India in the near future are questions to which prompt answers are impossible. But what is of great significance about this force is that the philosophical principle governing it is wholly Indian, and has its lineage in the doctrine of salvation-through-renunciation lauded by the Vedic-Upaniṣadic tradition.

Since Rammohun Roy, the leaders of Indian Renaissance have invariably visualized the possible conversion of the human mind by means of a revolution by love. Indian reformers, whether in support of the *bhakti-karma* unity or in that of the *jñāna-karma* unity, have always thought of some kind of moral education, or inward realization, as a prerequisite of any change in the individual or social self. Apart from the materialists and communists, for whom a violent revolution alone would sever India from her past and put her on a way towards progress, Indian thinkers, in general, do not diverge from the thesis that what the Indian society needs is a psychic transition, an inward metamorphosis, a change from within its consciousness.

The movement, called *sarvodaya* (literally, the uplift of all) and led by Vinoba Bhave, the best disciple of Gandhi, is the force with potentialities of a revolution by love. What it stands for is a comprehensive agitation directed towards the establishment of an ideal society, where socialism functions not under the pressure of law or of punishment, but by consent and willingness on the part of the haves to respond to the rights of the have-nots.

Vinoba Bhave is a *karma-yogi,* a staunch follower of the *Bhagavad-gītā* ethics, a typical admixture of the Gandhian principle of nonviolence and the Marxist motto of a classless society, a man with a Socratic conviction that nobody is knowingly wicked, and a supporter of the "withering away" of the state. He was Gandhi's most ideal practitioner of *satyāgraha* (passive resistance) against the British. But he shot up into world fame when he hit upon a solution to the most dangerous problem of poverty in Hyderabad, a place in South India, in 1951. The place was prone to a violent uprising, engineered by the Communist Party of India. It is here, while talking to the landlords and the landless, that he launched the revolution by love. He said to the few wealthy landlords: "I come to loot you with love, I am not begging. I ask for what is mine. If you give with love you will stop Communism and hate."

The revolution by love showed a tremendous working power. Bhave entreated the landlords, through his untiring marches from province to province and from village to village, to donate a part of their land to the landless, to make *bhoodān* (gift of land). It was an appeal to the conscience of the rich not to deprive their poor fellowmen of the barest means for survival. What Bhave, unlike communists, relied upon is the voice of *ātman* in man, which, he thought, would supersede his ignoble instinct of greed or possessiveness.

Next came the appeals for *sampattidān* (gift of riches), *shramdān* (gift of labor) and *jīvandān* (gift of one's life to the movement). Underlying all these appeals is the conviction which Bhave learnt from Gandhi that a society would be cohesive and friendship-bound only when relations among its members are firmly grounded in selflessness, tolerance and a feeling for others. Besides, the very assumption on which Bhave conducts the movement is the ancient Indian doctrine that nothing that belongs to man's physical being should tempt and bind his *ātman*. One need not even be proud of making a *dāna* (gift), because by giving away what does not belong to one's true self one does not really give anything. Thus, Bhave's is perhaps the most original way of grafting the tenets of socialism, or of *sarvodaya,* into the Hindu ethics of renunciation and spiritual perfection.

Gandhi had argued that the ultimate ideal of the peaceful revolution he had initiated against the British in India could not remain confined to the attainment of Independence. The revolution should have, for its true destination, the creation of a society in which the deprived and the downtrodden would be able to enjoy freedom from economic handicaps, a state of human dignity, and self-respect. Bhave selected the socialistic ideology from Gandhi's main philosophy, and extended it to reach closest to communism but with one significant distinction. To Bhave, all social, political and economic reforms must be brought about by first educating the ethical sense of the individual. He writes: ". . . I am surprised to hear that the Communists do not believe in the change of mind. This is an important point in which I differ from them. I ask them why they say that there is no room for change of heart in their philosophy. . . ."[34] In order to establish *lokniti* (the rule by the people), he says, we are required to purify the dispositions of men towards one another, to cultivate in each a sense of service and dedication for the good of the other.

It would be hasty to judge the exact width of the *sarvodaya* movement in the political setting of modern India. Although according to its most severe critics it is finally bound to be an abortive "crusade" against the chronic wrongdoers in society, there is no doubt that it has posited itself as the only democratic type of revolution suitable to a country with an eminent tradition of broad humanistic metaphysics. Further, it is not only the most desirable condition of a just and integral society but also a challenge to the oppressive and outwardly functioning Marxist revolution. Contrary to all the political theories ever put forward, the concept of *sarvodaya* has directed our attention to perhaps the most primordial truth that any permanent social change must be preceded by a change in the character of the individuals. To change the condition of the society, Bhave remarks, one must change the qualities of its individuals.[35]

The vitality of Bhave's agitation increased immensely when Jaiprakash Narayan, one of the most renowned Indian intellectuals and a socialist, abandoned active politics and became his follower. In Narayan, as in Nehru, the *jñāna-karma* movement has found its most ideal fulfilment. With no ambition to work as a member of any political party or to make an entry into the government, he is out and out a Gandhian. He holds an unshakable conviction that no message, political or otherwise, will go down the minds of Indians unless it is in continuity with their

[34] Bhave, Vinoba: Communism and Sarvodaya, *Sarvodaya*. May, 1957, p. 4.

[35] Bhave, Vinoba: *Sarvodaya-vichār ani Swarāj-sāstra* (Marathi). Wardha, Paramdhām Vidyāpeeth, 1956, pp. 124–25.

spiritual and moral heritage. One of the reasons why Narayan lost his faith in the genuineness of the political parties in India is, as he often confesses, that their activity does not inspire the Indian heart, does not have an appeal to inwardness and spirituality.[36]

Jaiprakash Narayan went to the United States at the age of twenty. After seven years' stay in different American universities, he returned to India in 1929 and entered the nationalist movement as a convinced Marxist. In the early thirties his adherence to the method and the aim of Marxism was so thorough that he wrote in 1936: ". . . today more than ever before it is possible to say that there is only one type, one type of Socialism—Marxism." [37] However, passing through an extremely active career in the Congress Socialist Party, which at one time pursued the idea of blending socialism and communism, Narayan, almost like M. N. Roy and Nehru, developed a firm revulsion to the method and to some of the assumptions of Marxism. Towards the late forties and the early fifties, he thought of some sort of nonviolent Marxism—Marxism that would cater to the goal of democracy—and chose to describe it as democratic socialism. While defining that the objective of this new socialism is to bring into being the free Indian State, or *swarāj,* he declared in *An Outline Picture of Swarāj* that it would guarantee "full individual and civil liberty and cultural and religious freedom," "would not discriminate in any manner between citizens of the nation," would maintain "equal rights" of everyone, "social justice and economic freedom," would bring "all large-scale collective production" under "collective ownership and control," and would not remain satisfied with mere material welfare.[38]

Narayan's mode of thought, at this stage, forestalls his later transition into a comprehensive humanistic ideology, not unlike that of M. N. Roy and of Nehru. But even when he was moving away from conventional Marxism to an open-minded

[36] Narayan, Jaiprakash: *Three Basic Problems of Free India*. Bombay, Asia Publishing House, 1964, pp. 19–21.

[37] Narayan, Jaiprakash: *Socialism, Sarvodaya and Democracy*. Bimla Prasad (Ed.), Bombay, Asia Publishing House, 1964, p. 3.

[38] *Ibid.,* pp. 37–39.

democratic theory, he could not give up the thesis that it is primarily through a politicoeconomic action that the desirable state of society could be achieved. Despite his admiration of Gandhi during this period, he, therefore, was not hesitant to advocate the use of arms against the British. But this way of thinking continued till a little after independence. Around 1951 Narayan's mind underwent a fundamental change, and he announced his complete loyalty to the movement of *sarvodaya.*

Narayan explains *sarvodaya* as Gandhian socialism. In the well-known essay *Socialism and Sarvodaya,* he states that the most important aspect of Gandhism that the socialist must pay great attention to is its "moral or ethical basis, its insistence on values." He writes:

> Russian or Stalinist interpretation of socialist philosophy has reduced it to a crass Machiavellian code of conduct utterly devoid of any sense of right or wrong, good or evil. . . . To the horror of this unscrupulous, amoral, political philosophy Gandhism offers a corrective that socialists would overlook only at the cost of the very substance of their creed.[39]

And in another essay called *From Socialism to Sarvodaya,* he confesses that socialism without Gandhism in it cannot lead humanity to "the sublime goals of freedom, equality, brotherhood and peace."[40] He predicts that if unaccompanied by *sarvodaya,* socialism may only leave the "taste of ashes" behind.

It is not difficult to see that Vinoba Bhave and Jaiprakash Narayan, like Nehru, have recognized the fact that for a total uplift of the Indian society, an effective handling of her socio-politico-economic problems is as important as the renaiscence of her metaphysical and humanistically predisposed attitude. Moreover, to Bhave and Narayan, much more than to Nehru, a genuine involvement in the world of praxis can result only from a disciplined involvement in fundamental ethical values. Considering the refined humanistic assumptions incorporated by it, therefore, *sarvodaya* stays essentially as an ethical movement, a kind of secular religion, trying to throw a bridge between the spiritualistic metaphysics of ancient India and the practical re-

[39] *Ibid.,* p. 94.
[40] *Ibid.,* p. 152.

quirements of a healthy material life. Strictly speaking, what *sarvodaya,* like Gandhism, entails is the conception of a society wholly wedded to the norm of respecting every individual as an end per se—as one whose otherworldly quests warrant his emancipation from every form of social injustice—and to the path of love and consent and intersubjective tolerance as the single human path towards progress.

THE ĀTMALOGICAL PARADOX

The most unique characteristic of human reality, ambiguously expressed but extraordinarily acutely experienced by Indian philosophies, is its refusal to immerse itself totally in the realm of empirical existence. The ātmalogists, like phenomenologists and existentialists, have shown intensest awareness of the fact that our consciousness is a self-surpassing process, a perpetual act of being and not-being at the same time, a ceaseless oscillation between the worldly and the otherworldly. Therefore, nothing posits itself as rigid within the reach of human life. We "fly" beyond the realized freedom, beyond the fulfilled state of being, and beyond all that we are at any given point of time. The paradox of *ātman* consists in its being anchored in the world and yet not being exhausted by it.

The history of Indian philosophy is a narrative of how the Indian *cogito* has, in different situations, translated into language and activity, and even into religious faith, the singular experience of its calculation of the affairs of the world and its withdrawal from it. Since the Vedic-Upaniṣadic times when the primordial basis of man's empirical consciousness was explained as *Brahman, ātman,* the uncharacterizable abyss or vastness, or the simplest state of *sat-cit-ānanda* (being-intelligence-consciousness), Indian thinkers have invariably looked upon worldliness as not only a bondage but also a superimposition on self's essence. The question whether the thinking consciousness has a judging authority on that which is beyond its access cannot be attempted here. The fact remains that the Indian *cogito* has functioned as an attitude encompassing its very core, that is, a reality which stretches onwards and onwards to a chiaroscuro but does not grasp any impression as static. To this attitude the world is a shadow, a slowly vanishing apparition, a spatiotemporal and solidified emptiness.

But there could come a time in the history of thought of a people when excessive preoccupation with only one aspect of existence, at the total rejection of the other, construes dogmatism. The free traffic of thought between the East and the West has today opened up two new possibilities: an increasing awareness in the Eastern mind that it must strive to improve its material milieu by means of a pragmatic way of thinking and working, and a realization in the Western mind that it has, in the course of its total concentration on the ways and means to improve man's physical existence, ignored the trans-empirical, the ātmalogical, or the otherworldly. The principal feature of the Age of Awakening in India is the continuous attempt of her thinkers and reformers to resurrect the rejected interests, to teach Indians to seek the betterment of the worldly state without, indeed, committing to it unrestrainedly, to inject in the world ethos a humanism grounded on not a positive attachment to the world but on an inevitable rapproachement with it. What this Awakening has not yet surrendered, and cannot surrender, is the ātmalogical paradox, namely, to be worldly and to be not-worldly at the same time. This paradox is the very life force of India.

INDEX